# DON JUAN

# DON JUAN

*Variations on a Theme*

J. W. SMEED

ROUTLEDGE
London and New York

First published 1990
by Routledge
11 New Fetter Lane, London EC4P 4EE

Simultaneously published in the USA and Canada
by Routledge
a division of Routledge, Chapman and Hall, Inc.
29 West 35th Street, New York, NY 10001

© 1990 J. W. Smeed

Phototypeset by Input Typesetting Ltd., London
Printed in Great Britain by T. J. Press (Padstow) Ltd.,
Padstow, Cornwall

All rights reserved. No part of this book may be reprinted or
reproduced or utilized in any form or by any electronic,
mechanical, or other means, now known or hereafter
invented, including photocopying and recording, or in any
information storage or retrieval system, without permission
in writing from the publishers.

*British Library Cataloguing in Publication Data*

Smeed, J. W. (John William, 1926–)
Don Juan: variations on a theme.
1. Legends characters   Don Juan
I. Title
398'.352
ISBN 0–415–00750–X

*Library of Congress Cataloging in Publication Data*

Smeed, J. W. (John William)
Don Juan: variations on a theme / J. W. Smeed.
p.   cm.
Includes bibliographical references.
ISBN 0–415–00750–X
1. Don Juan (Legendary character) in literature.   2. Literature,
Comparative-Themes, motives.   I. Title.
PN57.D7S48   1990
809'.93351-dc20      89–39060

# CONTENTS

List of illustrations — vii

Acknowledgements — viii

Preface — ix

1 THE BEGINNINGS — 1

2 DON GIOVANNI: — 22
THE OPERA BY DA PONTE AND MOZART AND E. T. A. HOFFMANN'S INTERPRETATION OF IT

3 BYRON — 34

4 HOFFMANN'S INFLUENCE — 45
*Germany*
*France*

5 REACTIONS AGAINST THE ROMANTICIZED DON JUAN — 64

6 LINKS WITH FAUST — 75

7 THE MAÑARA STORY; ZORRILLA; — 91
TWO CONTRASTING RUSSIAN DON JUANS

8 THE 'SPORTING' DON JUAN; — 104
THE CONQUEST OF REMORSE;
DON JUAN AND THE PHILOSOPHERS;
DON JUANISM AS A VOCATION

## CONTENTS

| | | |
|---|---|---|
| 9 | DON JUAN AS A TYPE | 116 |
| 10 | THE LEGENDARY FRAMEWORK: AN AID OR A PITFALL? | 127 |
| 11 | RICHARD STRAUSS AND DON JUAN | 138 |
| 12 | CONCLUSION | 145 |
| | Original Versions of Passages Quoted in Translation | 152 |
| | Notes | 165 |
| | Select Bibliography | 174 |
| | Index | 187 |

# LIST OF ILLUSTRATIONS

1 'Vengeance waits on my murderer': title-page of the piano score of Mozart's *Don Giovanni*, Vienna (Steiner), n.d.
2 The wooing of Zerlina (*Don Giovanni*, Act 1, no.7). Vignette by H. Ramberg.
3 'There will be ten more names on my list by tomorrow morning' – Don Giovanni at the height of his arrogance. Max Slevogt, *Das Champagnerlied*.
4 The doomed rebel. Ricketts, *The Death of Don Juan*.
5 Don Juan deified! An illustration to Byron, with all-too clear resemblances to a *pietà*. Ford Madox Brown, *Haidée and Don Juan* (Byron, *Don Juan*, Canto 2).
6 Don Juan's story as a fearful warning to sinners. Title-page of Friedrich Spieβer's *Don Juan, oder: Der steinerne Gast*.
7 Title page to Norbert Hürte's *Wahrhaftige Historie* (1854).

# ACKNOWLEDGEMENTS

The author and publishers would like to extend their grateful thanks to the following for granting permission to reproduce the pictures in the book:

The Archive of the *Gesellschaft der Muskifreunde*, Vienna for the title-page of Mozart's *Don Giovanni*. The Hulton Picture Library, London, for the vignette of the wooing of Zerlina, by H. Ramberg. The Staatsgalerie, Stuttgart for *Das Champagnerlied*, by Max Slevogt. The Tate Gallery, London, for *The Death of Don Juan*, by Ricketts. The City Museum and Art Gallery, Birmingham for *Haidée and Don Juan*, by Ford Madox Brown. The Goethe Museum, Frankfurt/Main, for the title-page of *Don Juan, oder: Der steinerne Gast* by Friedrich Spieβer. The Württembergische Landesbibliothek, Stuttgart, for the title-page of *Wahrhaftige Historie* by Norbert Hürte.

# PREFACE

There are hundreds of plays, novels, short stories and poems which deal with the character and exploits of Don Juan. The inveterate womanizer and rebel is a perennial type, so that these literary variations-on-a-theme reveal changing moral, social and philosophical attitudes and values. In addition, once Don Juan had become established as a representative figure, we find numerous theoretical attempts to analyse his character in essays and explanatory prefaces to the plays and other works devoted to him. Later, psychoanalysts sought to relate him to some basic element in the human psyche.

There are a few obvious landmarks: works which are familiar to lovers of literature and music and which are widely studied in schools and universities. One could mention the original Spanish Don Juan play, Molière's *Dom Juan ou le Festin de Pierre*, the opera by Mozart and da Ponte, Byron's *Don Juan*, Shaw's *Man and Superman* and the tone-poem *Don Juan* by Richard Strauss. More recently, the Don Juan figure has been taken up and treated wittily by Jean Anouilh and Max Frisch. There is no lack of critical material on these individual works, but no easily accessible and concise history of the legend in English. Experience has shown that many students find themselves examining one particular version without much grasp of where the legend originated and how it developed.

In view of the mass of material, it has been impossible to be exhaustive. I have tried to redress what I think has been a critical imbalance by putting more stress on German treatments of the theme as opposed to Don Juan's fortunes in Spain, France and Italy. In the case of Byron, I have confined myself to discussing how the poem re-interprets Don Juan as a character, since a detailed account of this long and complex work would go far beyond the

## PREFACE

confines of the present book. In considering how to present the material for this study, I became convinced that the key aspect was the way in which perceptions of Don Juan have veered between seeing him as a villainous libertine and a near heroic idealist. This question of changing attitudes is what I have elected to concentrate on. But this approach brings its own problems, especially at those points where the Don Juan legend becomes entangled with the story of Dr Faust. Hoffmann's influence clearly needs a chapter of its own and reactions against his idealization must logically be considered in an immediately succeeding chapter. But since the 'Hoffmannesque' Don Juans cannot be discussed without some reference to Faust, while the links between the two legends go far beyond Hoffmann in their implications, this meant a division, whereby the story of Faust's role in the Don Juan legend is told partly in chapter 4, partly in chapter 6. This seemed the lesser of two evils, in that to have treated all this material in simple chronological order would have been confusing. Chapters 4 and 6, together with the account of Alexis Tolstoi in chapter 7, therefore complement each other.

The problem of where to draw the line is always difficult when one traces the fortunes of a literary and psychological type. Some accounts of Don Juan's metamorphoses include Richardson's *Clarissa*, *Les Egarements du coeur et de l'esprit* by Crébillon *fils* and Laclos' *Les Liaisons dangereuses*. I felt that these works were not part of this story, whereas Meyr's *Der schwarze Hans* and Anouilh's *Ornifle* qualified, since they are both recognizable and deliberate versions of the Don Juan legend. I have kept the retelling of plots to a minimum, but always with the awareness that a knowledge of the basic structure of the 'Don Juan story' and of the variations that successive writers have spun out of it is essential to an understanding of the issues.

Passages from foreign works are given in translation, except where the meaning is evident from the context or where the point to be made is a stylistic one. Originals are to be found in the Appendix. The Bibliography had to be highly selective and is subdivided for convenient reference. The puppet-plays are given in order of publication, since dating is impossible. References to Don Juan works in the body of the book will often give author and date only: exact identification is easy, since section 5 of the Bibliography is in chronological order. Where no explicit reference is made to a work in the body of the book, brief comments or details are sometimes supplied in the Bibliography: entries of this kind are marked in the Index with an asterisk.

I would like here to express my gratitude to those colleagues who read the whole or parts of the typescript and made many helpful suggestions: above all to Professor Patrick Bridgwater, Dr Richard Maber, Dr E. J. Morrall and Professor Dick Watson.

# 1

# The Beginnings

*El Burlador de Sevilla*, written by a monk, Gabriel Téllez, under the pen-name of Tirso de Molina and first published in Barcelona in 1630, is the earliest complete surviving play on the subject of Don Juan Tenorio.[1] It does not appear to have had an actual person as its model, although it may well have aimed at a generalized portrait of a contemporary type, that of the rich and unscrupulous libertine. What *is* clear is the author's didactic intention: Don Juan's fate is to serve as an awful warning. To convey his message in compellingly dramatic terms, Tirso grafted his depiction of the hardened reprobate on to an old legend, transmitted in the form of popular verse-romances, in which a reckless sinner invites a dead man (or his head, or his statue) to a banquet.[2] Tirso's play is the source, direct or indirect, of virtually all subsequent works devoted to Don Juan, helping to establish both the hero's ruling characteristics and the general pattern of dramatic events.

The work begins with Don Juan's seduction of Isabela, achieved through the ruse of pretending to be her betrothed, Don Octavio. Don Juan escapes. We presently find him shipwrecked on the shores of Taragona, where he seduces a fisher-girl, Tisbea. We move to Seville, where Don Juan, again by means of impersonation, attempts the seduction of Doña Ana, whose outcry brings her father, Don Gonzalo, hurrying to the scene. The two men fight and Gonzalo is killed. After a further seduction scene, the victim this time being Aminta, a country girl, we find Don Juan and his servant, Catalinón, back in Seville. They come across the statue of Don Gonzalo, whereupon Don Juan recklessly invites his victim (or the effigy of his victim) to supper. The Statue duly appears and issues a counter-invitation which Don Juan, as a 'man of honour', accepts.

This final meeting takes place in a chapel: the table is black, the servants too are shrouded in black, scorpions and vipers are the food, the wine is bitter . . . Don Juan, having consistently refused to repent until the very last minute when it is too late, is dragged off to Hell. In a final scene, Catalinón gives an account of his master's end to the other characters.

Tirso's Don Juan is an insatiable womanizer who relies on deceit as much as on charm or persuasion. Indeed, the title of the play means 'the Trickster of Seville'. In a famous passage of self-analysis, he says: 'Seville calls me the trickster and my greatest pleasure is to deceive a woman and destroy her honour.'[3] He has some positive features: a high degree of reckless courage, a sense of honour (patchy and selective, it must be admitted) and a pride that will not allow him to do anything that would deny or besmirch his own image of himself. Thus both honour and pride make him accept the Statue's invitation. But the limits of this code of honour are very clearly shown in the episode in which he impersonates the Marquis de la Mota in order to pursue Ana. He receives a letter intended for his friend Mota and promises, as a nobleman, to deliver it faithfully. But, scenting an adventure, he reads it, deceives Mota and keeps the assignation himself. Yet later, apparently with perfect sincerity, he assures the Statue that he will keep his word and appear at supper – again, because he is a nobleman and man of honour! An aside of Catalinón's gives us the key: Don Juan may be a nobleman, but one would do well not to trust him where women are concerned (ii, 161 ff.). But it was less the inconsistency of Don Juan's conduct than his wickedness that concerned Tirso. Don Juan is blasphemous and sinful, although not an atheist (this trait will be introduced in later versions). He is that much commoner type: a loose-living and inveterate procrastinator who persuades himself that he can delay repentance in order to enjoy his libertinism for a little longer. This idea of delayed repentance runs like a *leitmotif* through the play.

What happens is this: whenever Don Juan is urged to repent or is reminded that God's wrath may one day be visited on him, he replies with his favourite remark, 'Qué largo me lo fiáis!' or a close variant of it, 'Tan largo me lo fiáis?' or 'Tan largo me lo guardáis.' The phrases mean 'How much time you are granting me!' or 'are you granting me?', as if a debtor were talking of the day on which a debt will fall due – but the creditor in this case is God and the debt Don Juan's weight of sin. We hear the phrase when Catalinón warns his master that deceit and seduction will one day be punished with death and again when Tisbea hints at the dire consequences of breaking a vow. Don Juan even uses it in a monologue to reassure himself that retribution, if it is to come, is still in the distant future. It may be added that, in the first supper scene, a chorus of spirits echoes the phrase, thus mockingly recalling Don Juan's false and impious feelings of security. The monetary image is exactly right for this calculating sinner and probably helps to give the work a much wider application than the lurid career of one sensationally debauched individual might otherwise possess.

Don Juan is accompanied on his adventures by his servant, Catalinón, who is an earthy and commonsensical character, sharing neither the vices nor the virtue (that is, the heedless courage) of his master. He prefers safety and good food and drink to hazardous escapades, is good-hearted, feels pity for Don Juan's victims and occasionally remonstrates with his master. His terror when the Statue appears at the supper-table contrasts with Don Juan's defiance. There is no doubt that the characterization of both servant and master was in part dictated by the author's didactic intentions. The figure of Don Juan shows how wickedness and the failure to heed repeated warnings are finally punished; he is a solemn reminder to sinners that they should repent betimes. In the servant we have a fundamentally decent and godfearing 'ordinary man' whose very ordinariness allows him to survive where his master's arrogance ensures downfall. Even Catalinón's fear is more sensible – if less impressive in a superficial way – than his master's bravado; for who should not show terror when Retribution walks miraculously abroad?[4]

The two main characters, then, are already established in many essentials in this first Don Juan play, although each was to undergo important developments and alterations. In the remaining decades of the seventeenth century, Don Juan would become notably more wicked, while his servant would all too often develop into a purely comic character. Important elements in the plot of Tirso's play will persist, giving work after work a recognizable shape and structure, involving the seduction or attempted seduction of a high-born lady by means of impersonation, the wooing of a fisher-girl or peasant beauty, the duel, the Statue, the call to repentance, the invitation to supper and the descent into Hell. The closing scene, in which the servant, having witnessed his master's end, gives an account of this to the other characters, thus allowing them to comment on the libertine's punishment and to reveal their own plans for the future, rounds off the play both morally and dramatically and hence appealed to numerous later authors. The use made by da Ponte of this opportunity will be commented on later.

Tirso's play, of course, not only has a double invitation (from Don Juan to the Statue and from the Statue to Don Juan); it also includes two banquets. There has been much debate as to how this came about and whether it makes for an untidy and formally unsatisfactory ending. I am inclined to agree with Daniel Rogers[5] that it makes perfect sense and produces a symmetry that is more than merely structural. For Don Juan's invitation is to an earthly repast, in keeping with his worldly and hedonistic way of life, while the second meal scene, with its alarming and gruesome emblems of death and torment, leads to that other world which Don Juan has up till now tried to ignore. But many subsequent treatments of the legend have preferred the greater economy of one supper scene only; Don Juan invites the Statue, who thereupon appears and abruptly transforms the would-be festivity into a Judgment.

In the most general terms, it is easy to see the fascination, for both authors and audiences, of the Don Juan figure and of the legend dealing with his exploits and punishment as presented by Tirso. Those who have talked dismissively of the play as a supernatural extravaganza with a 'monkish' moral told at best only half the story. In addition, the events have dramatic force, variety and rapid movement towards an inexorable conclusion. They possess a clear shape and sequence which later authors can vary and modify ad lib. As a character, Don Juan both fascinates and appals; most audiences will probably have had an ambivalent attitude towards him, enjoying his unscrupulous ruses yet finding comfort in the thought that, at the end, divine justice is meted out to him. It is very unlikely that Tirso intended any such mixed response – but equally unlikely that a character who seemed merely sinful and shocking would have fathered such progeny and created such a lasting vogue.

From Spain the Don Juan theme quickly passed to Italy. The first extant play is *Il Convitato di Pietra* by J. A. Cicognini, probably dating from the 1640s. In its action, this play is a slightly slimmed-down version of *El Burlador*, although there are important differences both of detail and characterization. The central figure, here as in subsequent Italian versions called Don Giovanni, is represented as much more wicked than his Spanish prototype, retaining that character's audacious courage but lacking the gallantry and aristocratic nobility of manner which had helped to make the Spaniard at least superficially attractive.[6] He is now both more arrogant in general and more callous towards his victims. But the most significant difference is that he shows no readiness to repent, even at the very end:

> *Statue*  Don Giovanni, give me your hand!
> *D.G.*  Here it is. Oh God, what am I grasping!
> *Statue*  Repent, Don Giovanni!
> *D.G.*  Let go, I say. Alas!
> *Statue*  Repent, Don Giovanni!
> *D.G.*  Oh! I am dying. Help!
> *Statue*  Repent, Don Giovanni!
>   Here D.G. falls headlong and is lost from view.
>
>   (Act 3 Scene 8)

Meanwhile the servant, here called Passarino, has moved much nearer to the traditional notion of the *comic* servant. He still occasionally acts as a warning voice to his master, but the contrast between them (which, as we have seen, served a serious didactic purpose in Tirso) is taken to an extreme which threatens any serious impact that the play might otherwise have, let alone any moral significance. Thus, for instance, Passarino's terror is egregious and comic to a degree which destroys the important point made in *El Burlador* about the common man's understandable and proper fear of the Statue. Nor does Passarino show any of the pity for the betrayed women that moved Catalinón. Moreover, Cicognini's play is full of comic business for this servant-clown, even in scenes of great potential dramatic seriousness.

One can go further: there are whole scenes whose only discernible *raison d'être* is to furnish Passarino with opportunities for comic dialogue and tricks (*lazzi*). Thus the basic structure has changed somewhat in the course of the move from Spain to Italy. Tirso's work is held together by the didactic contrast between the sinful daring of the master and the conventionally 'safe' attitudes of the servant: in Cicognini, in so far as one can talk of a unifying principle, this is a sort of dramatic counterpoint between the serious action

(Don Giovanni's crimes and punishment) and his servant's *lazzi*, which can often jar in their context. This radical bifurcation into melodrama and clowning will persist and become even more drastic in some later treatments of the Don Juan theme.

As far as the plot of Cicognini's play is concerned, there are a number of innovations which will add significantly to the stock of dramatic events on which later writers will be able to draw. One such is the list of Don Giovanni's conquests (some hundreds of names) kept by his servant;[7] this, of course, will lead to Leporello's famous catalogue-aria in Mozart/da Ponte. It is also in Cicognini that the Statue nods in acceptance of the invitation to supper; this too will provide a wonderful moment in Mozart's opera. Other motifs introduced by Cicognini and gratefully taken up by later writers include Passarino's fear that his outstanding wages will not be paid now that his master has gone to Hell (Act 3 Scene 9) and the Statue's lofty refusal of earthly meats when it (he?) appears at Don Giovanni's supper table ('Non ha bisogno di cibi terrini', Act 3 Scene 5: this will recur almost verbatim in da Ponte's libretto).

Of these incidents, the servant's catalogue is by far the most important. For actually to *show* Don Juan achieving conquest after conquest would be aesthetically intolerable and probably indecent, as well as being virtually unstageable from a purely practical point of view. Dramatists and librettists have had to content themselves with a handful of episodes, one of which involved the killing of the lady's father and thus helped to bring about Don Juan's sensational punishment, while at least one other incident figured a humble girl. Thus two essential points were made: Don Juan was shown as lusting after women from all ranks of society and as sowing the seeds of his own ruin even as he ruined others. But an equally essential ingredient – Don Juan as a mass seducer, as one who made a career out of philandering – could not be dramatized. The servant's catalogue provided a way out of this undoubted dilemma.

All critics of the play and all chroniclers of the Don Juan legend known to me have compared Cicognini unfavourably with Tirso. At the very least, one must say that the virtual transformation of Tirso's Catalinón into a clown created a trap for future dramatists and librettists, an obvious opportunity for easy laughs, but at the cost of true dramatic, moral and psychological tension. There were certainly other Italian Don Giovanni plays from this period which have failed to survive, including one by Giliberto. From these Italian pieces, one line of development goes via seventeenth-century French theatre into popular stage- and puppet-plays, while another line leads to Italian opera. In both cases, the improvised Italian comedy of the day, the *commedia dell'arte*, played a part.

By the middle of the seventeenth century, the Don Juan theme had been taken into the repertoire of the *commedia*. Although much in this highly popular theatrical tradition depended on improvisation within stock situations and conventions, we can gain a good general idea of what these Don Giovanni (or Don Juan) plays were like. The Don Juan comedy quickly spread to France from Italy and we are fortunate in having scenarios relating to versions played in both countries. A scenario does not, of course, furnish details of all the comic business or give the actual words spoken. The comic set-pieces (*lazzi*) would have been to some extent improvised around an agreed situation or idea; the text was not learnt and delivered word for word and certainly not written down. But from these surviving scenarios, it is clear that the *commedia* versions owe much to Tirso, either via Cicognini or through an indebtedness, the details of which can only be surmised, to one of the lost Italian plays. The general course of events is as in Tirso and always includes the second supper scene with its funereal trappings. (In one version, Don Giovanni eats a serpent.) The action is greatly swollen by comic dialogue and pieces of buffoonery, often identified in the scenario by labels which indicate clearly enough that they have been taken from stock and inserted with little or no regard for dramatic relevance. Some of the extra material has been grafted on to the plot in order to provide roles for conventional *commedia* types such as Pantaloon or the Doctor. Although the basic sequence (impersonations, seductions, duel, escapade with a fisher-girl, encounter with the Statue, descent into Hell) is clear in the scenarios, it may well be that in performance it was swamped under a mass of tricks, mime, acrobatics, puns, witticisms and often scurrilous gestures.

So the *commedia* versions will have done little more than suggest a basic plot and the barest fundamentals of Don Giovanni's character and of his relationships with women, with his servant and with the supernatural powers. The most that can have been garnered is the impression of a wicked and violent man who revelled in his domination of women, notched up seductions and disregarded repeated calls to betterment and repentance. The form in which the Don Giovanni story was presented by the actors of the *commedia* in Italy is recorded in a collection of scenarios made by Antonio Passante, now in the possession of the National Library in Naples; a version played in Paris in 1658 or earlier has survived in the form of notes made by a famous Harlequin of the day, Biancolelli.[8] The latter is the more important, since it is the version which, together with one or other of the Italian pieces already mentioned (Cicognini, Giliberto), influenced the French Don Juan plays from the late 1650s onwards. The scenario is written in the first person by Harlequin (Biancolelli) in his role of servant to Don Giovanni and it is clear to what extent clowning and vulgar witticisms have gained the upper hand at the expense of the serious action. Indeed, as Bévotte and others have pointed out, it is noticeably more vulgar and farcical than the Italian (Passante) version. Thus we have the paradoxical situation that the more serious version exercised its influence on what, at least until Mozart and da Ponte appeared on the scene, was fundamentally *opera buffa*, while the French Don Juan plays – which, as we shall see, constitute an earnest attempt to motivate Don Juan – derive at least an important part of their inspiration from a very trivial *commedia* piece.

In France, the Don Juan theme proved so popular that four versions (or five, counting Thomas Corneille's reworking of Molière) were produced within twenty years. The question of sources is not altogether clear. Evidence of any direct influence from Spain is inconclusive and sparse. The main impulse will undoubtedly have been the Italian pieces, together with the *commedia* version as performed in Paris. Many critics believe that Giliberto's lost play must have been an important source.[9] I do not want to join in this specialized discussion; it is sufficient for our present purposes to note that all the French plays broadly follow the familiar pattern: impersonations and seductions, duel, confrontation with the Statue, invitation, banquet, call to repentance, descent into Hell. What we have is fundamentally the same plot and a very similar cast of characters, combined with a new and more searching examination of Don Juan as a character and, by implication, as representative of a contemporary type which would have been recognizable to contemporary audiences.

The plays are:

| | | |
|---|---|---|
| Dorimon, | *Le Festin de Pierre ou le fils criminel* | First performed 1658; published 1659. |
| Villiers (= Claude Deschamps, Sieur de Villiers), | *Le Festin de Pierre ou le fils criminel* | First performed 1659; published 1660. |
| Molière, | *Dom Juan ou le Festin de Pierre* | First performed 1665; published 1682. |
| Rosimond, | *Le nouveau Festin de Pierre ou l'Athée foudroyé* | First performed 1669; published 1670. |
| Thomas Corneille, | *Le Festin de Pierre* | First performed 1677. |

The first of these pieces is a significant departure in that it investigates the moral and psychological roots of the central character more profoundly and in greater detail than ever before. Dorimon's Dom Jouan (*sic*!) is proud and obstinate, unfeeling and callous. Even after his way of life and his refusal to repent have caused his father to die of grief, he refuses to shed tears (Act 3 Scene 2). He justifies his womanizing by appealing to his need for variety, that is, to his character: 'I laugh at the hopes of a languishing lover and find my pleasure in change' (Act 1 Scene 3). So, he asks the Statue blasphemously, why should God expect him to act otherwise? – 'He gave me wit, soul, knowledge, strength, reason, heart, intelligence: all in order to overcome and challenge destiny and not to mortify the work of His hands' (Act 5 Scene 8). Hence his fatalism in the reference to his 'destiny' at the moment when he rejects the last chance of repentance is more apparent than real. His destiny is his character, pre-ordained from the cradle: 'Mon destin est escrit, mesme dès le berceau' (Act 5 Scene 8). His only compulsion is that inner one which forbids him to act in any way that would be untrue to himself.

But the strangest – and certainly the newest – thing about Dorimon's conception is that he shows Dom Jouan accepting the Statue's invitation not out of pride or reckless courage, as previously, but out of curiosity:

All that one can see on earth, Briguelle, I have seen: the freethinkers, the great, the sages, war ... As far as my thoughts range, only one thing is still lacking: to see, if I can, Heaven and Hell. He whom I am going to see is no longer in that material shell which often prevents the most glorious light from reaching us. He is all spirit ... Let us go then without delay ... The man who lives in a state of stupidity is a coward; one's curiosity should reach out everywhere.

(Act 5 Scene 7)

That seems an oddly 'faustian' motive, but I find it difficult to believe that the resemblance is other than fortuitous. This speech will probably have been a reflection of Dorimon's distrust of the *esprits forts* (freethinkers) of the seventeenth century, with their uncompromising and, as it was widely held, sinful intellectual curiosity. In any case, it is a significant new trait for Don Juan. It may be recalled that, in Tirso, Don Juan accepts the Statue's invitation in order to show courage and excite admiration; pride and honour are the motive forces, not curiosity.

In keeping with this analytical understanding of the central character, Dorimon treats both the supernatural events and the servant-figure with notable earnestness. There is no intrusion of crude comedy into the scenes featuring the Statue, while Dom Jouan's servant, Briguelle, for all that he takes his name from one of the stock figures of the *commedia dell'arte*, is an almost wholly serious character, horror-struck at his master's misdeeds and concerned to bring him to repentance. Like Tirso's Catalinón, he stands for (and stands up for) ordinary decent behaviour and, again like Catalinón, he is afraid of the Statue, but not – or not simply – because he is a poltroon. His confession of fear implies that this reaction is more healthy than his master's philosophy: 'Sir, I don't understand your philosophy at all, but I am afraid of spirits' (Act 4 Scene 8). This point will be taken up and expanded by Molière.

So, in Dorimon's Dom Jouan, we have a defiant and blasphemous sinner, although still not an atheist. (The subtitle *L'Athée foudroyé*, which appears in the second edition of 1665 and subsequent editions, merely shows how vaguely that term was applied in the seventeenth century.) For the first time, a Don Juan's inconstancy and hedonism are systematically justified (by him, that is) through an appeal to nature: how, made as he is, could he act otherwise?

THE BEGINNINGS

This attempt at psychological and philosophical motivation necessarily involved an equally earnest treatment of the servant and of the spirit-world. Nothing was to detract from the solemn warning.

Villiers' play of the same year is closely modelled on that of Dorimon; the main differences have the effect of making Dom Juan more villainous. There are more seductions, there is the dishonourable killing of a defenceless man, there is a greater callousness in Dom Juan's attitude towards his father. The few redeeming features in Dorimon's Dom Jouan (notably the intellectual curiosity) are lacking. Philipin, the servant, although more of a comic character than Dorimon's Briguelle, has a serious part to play, juxtaposing a juster and more virtuous attitude against that of his master; indeed, he is given a moralizing speech at the end: 'You children, who often curse your parents, consider what it is to live and act well. We beg you all not to imitate Dom Juan, for here, I assure you, is a fine and true mirror for you' (Act 5 Scene 8). Villiers' dedicatory epistle to this play acknowledges a debt to his Italian source, but claims that his work is superior. I think it likely that this claim is based on the high moral tone struck in the French piece and its rejection of obvious comic devices. It may be added that Villiers' Don Juan, like Dorimon's, dies defiant and unrepentant, but he too is not an atheist; indeed, for a fleeting moment he fears divine retribution (Act 4 Scene 7).

In Dorimon we saw a determined attempt to combine a morality play with a psychological examination of the Don Juan type. In Molière, the investigation into character and motivation is taken yet further. (Indeed, some of Molière's contemporaries felt that this process was taken to a point where the moral impact of the play was threatened.) It cannot be without significance that Molière prefers *Dom Juan ou le Festin de Pierre* as a title rather than following Dorimon and Villiers and calling his play *Le Festin de Pierre ou le fils criminel*, thus labelling his central character in advance as a simple criminal. The plot is broadly similar to that of the plays just discussed; we may therefore concentrate on the question of characterization or, as we should perhaps say, self-characterization, since Dom Juan tirelessly analyses himself, mainly in conversations with his servant, Sganarelle. He emerges as a sort of would-be Nietzschean Superman *avant la lettre*, as one who indeed behaves as if he were 'beyond good and evil'. A. Adam[10] has produced good grounds to support the contention that, in his Dom Juan, Molière was simultaneously depicting and criticizing the 'free spirits' of mid seventeenth-century Paris.

The moral debates in this play are made to appear slightly ambivalent, since the defender of conventional morality is Sganarelle, over whom Dom Juan triumphs effortlessly, even contemptuously; Sganarelle is rendered ineffectual in debate by his master, who 'speaks like a book'. When Dom Juan challenges him to give his opinion, he replies:

> I don't know what to say, for you twist things in such a way, that it seems as if you are right and yet, to speak truth, you are not. I have the finest thoughts in the world, but your talk has made me quite confused.
>
> (Act 1 Scene 2)

This is one of the things that made Molière's play seem shocking in its day: religion and morality are ineptly defended by a servant who cannot hope to succeed in argument against his subtle and voluble master. Yet, even if Sganarelle cannot always find the right words, he is far from ridiculous. Nor is he inarticulate; he can describe Dom Juan's wickedness trenchantly enough and has the courage to remonstrate with him. But, faced with the need to *out-argue* his master, he is impotent.

It can be (and has been) argued, of course, that the play ironically shows that in the end the 'clever' man turns out to have been more stupid than his less clever servant;[11] a parallel here would be to the pieces belonging to the popular Faust tradition, in which the clown-servant survives while his learned master is carried off to Hell. At one point, incensed by Dom Juan's rationalistic scepticism, Sganarelle expresses himself thus:

> For my part, Sir, I haven't studied like you, praise be to God, and nobody could boast of ever having taught me anything. But with my little bit of sense and judgement, I see things better than all your books.
>
> (Act 3 Scene 2)

It seems certain that Molière wanted to make clear some such distinction between foolish and arrogant cleverness and the goodhearted common sense of the 'ignoramus', for he represents Dom Juan as far too reprobate for the play to be a defence or glorification of him and his kind. But whenever a truly great dramatist creates a wicked or subversive character, he is in danger of making him more attractive than he intended; it is no wonder that some who saw this play in the 1660s and 1670s regarded it as immoral.

In fact, Molière's Dom Juan is a complex character. He is brave and, within arbitrary limits, honourable. He is an uncompromising rationalist, doubting the existence of God and Devil alike, believing only that 'two and two are four' (Act 3 Scene 1). He gives alms, but for 'love of humanity', not because any moral law or authority enjoins charity on him (Act 3 Scene 2). But coupled with these good, or partially good, qualities are evil ones. He wishes to possess all women, appealing to the inexhaustibility of his desires and seemingly regarding constancy as unnatural (Act 1 Scene 2). He is a hypocrite, twice feigning repentance (Act 1 Scene 3, Act 5 Scene 1), and an ingrate, since, barely rescued from drowning by Pierrot, he instantly turns his attention to winning Charlotte away from him. 'Ce n'est pas la récompense de vous avoir sauvé d'être nayé', says Pierrot in something of an understatement (Act 2 Scene 3). And, since he is fired to make an attempt on a girl's virtue because he has seen her with her betrothed and was offended and provoked by the couple's perfect happiness, he is a moral sadist (Act 1 Scene 2). Palmer justly talks of his 'connoisseurship in wickedness' (p. 309). Yet to the end, as supernatural powers gradually break down his rationalistic and anthropocentric convictions and threaten to show that twice two does not always equal four, he retains a certain obstinate nobility. He remains true to himself.

In the Preface to *Three Plays for Puritans*, George Bernard Shaw wrote that 'no man will ever write a better tragedy than *Lear*, a better comedy than *Le Festin de Pierre* (this must mean Molière's) or *Peer Gynt* or a better opera than *Don Giovanni*.' Many would agree with Shaw on the subject of the other works, but why was *Le Festin de Pierre* thus singled out? A tentative answer to this question will lead us, as well as any other route could, to the essential qualities of the play. One reason for Shaw's preference must lie in the richness of characterization as opposed to the two-dimensionality of even the best comedy of humours. Furthermore, if we recall that the most lighthearted of Shaw's plays illustrate and dramatize some important general topic, the weightiness and the far-reaching implications of Molière's work were bound to appeal. For all its surface sensationalism, it deals with rival attitudes towards moral behaviour in society, the clash of Nietzschean 'master morality' with the interests of ordinary people, also with a confrontation between an obstinately rationalistic mind and phenomena that transcend and give the lie to rationalism.

In addition there are rich layers of irony in the play, mostly arising from that central paradox that the simple man is in the end shown to be wiser than his subtle master. I say 'in the end'; much of the irony resides in the fact that Sganarelle at first appears to have lost the argument. When he tries to defend the marvels of existence against Dom Juan's rationalism, he refers to the mystery of the will, which can command the limbs to move hither and thither. In demonstrating or miming his point, he falls flat on his face, a fact that his master comments on with mocking glee: 'voilà ton raisonnement qui a le nez cassé' (Act 3 Scene 1). Yet who will ultimately be proved right, the intellectually dominating master or the, for the moment, absurd and discomforted servant? Another thoroughly double-edged and ironic situation, this time unconnected with the running battle of words between these two, occurs when Dom Juan encounters a poor hermit who begs him for alms (Act 3 Scene 2). It will be recalled that Dom Juan complies 'for love of humanity'. The way in which this departure from the orthodox and expected 'for the love of God' points the difference between an anthropocentric and a theistic view of the world has perhaps diverted attention from the ironies of the situation. For what might be a sympathetic gesture of humanitarianism in a better character is hair-raising hypocrisy in Dom Juan, whose behaviour is regularly dominated by a readiness to ride rough-shod over his fellow-humans in pursuit of his own gratification. Even this act of alms-giving has a large element of egotism and arrogance about it. And yet – another ironic touch! – this beggar is the only *mortal* who gets the better of Dom Juan, who at first regards him as an easy target, a hungry man who can be bribed with the promise of rich alms to betray his religion by blaspheming. The terms in which 'le Pauvre' refuses this bribe ('j'aime mieux mourir de faim') show him clearly as the moral victor in this clash of wills, even if the initial impression made by him had been rather abject and cringing. Such ironies – and they could be multiplied – give this play a richness and subtlety that orthodox character-comedies lack.

Some critics have rebuked Molière for careless workmanship that resulted in a lack of structural unity.[12] I find this criticism unjust.

If the play has a certain episodic character, this derives necessarily and logically from Dom Juan's lust for change ('tout le plaisir de l'amour est dans le changement'). His debates with Sganarelle and others contribute to a prolonged and detailed examination of his character and motives, while all his adventures and encounters show facets of his personality. *Le Festin de Pierre* is not a conventional 'well-made' comedy, but a play whose cluster of closely related themes dictates its form. This form basically depends on the triangle Dom Juan/Sganarelle/Statue. As we have seen, the debates between master and servant reflect the conflict between a ruthless hedonism and the morality of the common man more profoundly and with greater richness of detail and subtlety of argument than in any previous version. Similarly, the confrontation between the libertine and the agent of a supernatural world does not simply herald retribution, but also gives the lie to Dom Juan's rationalism, fearsomely demonstrating to him (and the audience) that there is a Higher Arithmetic, according to which two plus two may sometimes equal five, or nine, or any other total which makes nonsense of human calculations. It may be noted that all these things interrelate and are interdependent. Molière found a model which, for all its surface absurdities and sensationalism, offered a clear dramatic pattern, with ingredients that seemed to invite a more profound moral and psychological diagnosis than had previously been perceived or, at least, attempted. It seems needless to add that all Dom Juan's encounters with women in Molière's play illustrate different aspects of his fickleness, treachery, hypocrisy, etc.; the fact that this discussion of the work, in common with most other attempts at critical appreciation, has *not* concentrated on the details of Dom Juan's womanizing shows, if demonstration is necessary, how far the Don Juan theme, in the hands of a master, goes beyond the mere portrait of a sexual libertine who adds to the catalogue of his victims until he is struck down with his sins still unrepented.

'Voilà par sa mort un chacun satisfait', says Sganarelle at the end of the play. But, despite this 'satisfactory' ending, there were objections to the play on moral grounds. A pamphlet of 1665 saw it as offending against religion and predictably made the point that the cause of morality and religion is attacked eloquently and audaciously, but defended weakly and by a servant.[13] We certainly find a rapid movement towards a more unambiguously hostile interpretation of the Don Juan type in the next few years. The first shot in this battle was Rosimond's *Le nouveau Festin de Pierre* of 1669. There are sufficient parallels and debts to Molière to establish that Rosimond knew the earlier version, but these are coupled with a much more severe attitude towards the main character, suggesting that Rosimond was anxious to guard against any danger of romanticizing this figure and making his wicked ways and subversive views seem appealing.[14]

Rosimond's Dom Juan is, in fact, more wicked than any previous Don Juan. It is not simply that he is an unconscionable womanizer and responsible for three deaths; he is also shown as determined to commit yet greater crimes, even at the end and after repeated warnings, including one from a lost soul: 'We suffer diverse torments. The same agony will be the due reward for your crimes and your end will serve as an example to the whole world' (Act 5 Scene 6).

Thomas Corneille's versified and bowdlerized version of Molière, dating from 1677, was an attempt to make the play less 'shocking': 'I reserved the right to soften certain expressions which had offended sensitive people,' says Corneille in his 'Avis'. The scene with the poor man is cut, removing at a stroke Dom Juan's incitement to blasphemy, his alms-giving 'for the love of humanity' and his mocking comment that it is strange that a man who prays every day should yet go hungry. Equally important is the new ending, which presents Dom Juan's death as a warning to other 'scoundrels' and omits the reference to Sganarelle's unpaid wages. Indeed, this Sganarelle has resolved to become a hermit! – 'The earth has swallowed him up! I will hasten to become a hermit. All scoundrels will be filled with amazement by this warning example. Woe to him who sees it and does not profit from it!' (Act 5 Scene 6). That alteration is perhaps more significant than it might at first appear: the explicit warning was not present in Molière's closing speech, while the famous 'Mes gages! mes gages! mes gages!' had the effect of somewhat devaluing the original Sganarelle as a mouthpiece for virtue and morality.

These works by Rosimond and Thomas Corneille, although of little intrinsic value, mark an important stage in the history of Don Juan. The edifying function of the legend had seemingly become weakened and had been made ambiguous through the manner of its presentation in Molière. By relaying the moral lesson from beyond the grave or placing it in the mouth of a Sganarelle now cleansed of any vulgar mercenary considerations, these two authors return to a simpler didacticism. The notion of an appallingly wicked, treacherous and violent Don Juan, as portrayed by Rosimond, was to be taken up in many later versions. To trace the subsequent history of Don Juan as a moral monster, we must turn to the English stage and to the popular tradition of stage- and puppet-plays in German-speaking Europe.

Thomas Shadwell's play, *The Libertine* (1675), is modelled, says the author, on the Don Juan plays popular in Italy and France. In fact the main debt is demonstrably to Rosimond's *Le nouveau Festin de Pierre*, although Shadwell's Don John is conspicuously more evil than even Rosimond's Dom Juan. Talking to his depraved friends, Don John says:

> Thus far without a bound we have enjoy'd
> Our prosp'rous pleasures, which dull Fools call Sins;
> Laugh'd at old feeble Judges, and weak Laws;
> And at the fond fantastick thing, call'd Conscience,
> Which serves for nothing but to make men Cowards.
>
> (p. 25)

The philosophy which underlies this life of self-gratification is an appeal to nature: 'My appetites are all I'm sure I have from Heav'n, since they are Natural, and them I always will obey' (p. 28). A hedonistic amorality follows with logical inevitability: 'there is no right or wrong, but what conduces to, or hinders pleasure' (ibid.). According to this philosophy of nature, Don John *cannot* remain constant, for it would be against his nature which swiftly and uncontrollably moves from desire to possession, thence to satiety and aversion. This enslavement to one's own nature is rather laboriously linked to a philosophy of deterministic materialism:

> Can that blind faculty the Will be free
> When it depends upon the Understanding? . . .
> The Understanding never can be free;
> For what we understand, spite of ourselves we do:
> All objects are ready form'd and plac'd
> To our hands; and these the Senses to the Mind convey,
> And as those represent them, this must judge.[15]

I take this to mean that our decisions are formed when the 'understanding' evaluates the sense-perceptions received in the mind. But each man's understanding will proceed from his individual character, so that free will is a chimera. Whether this is entirely logical and plausible in Don John's mouth is less important than the incontrovertible fact that Shadwell has here tried to link the godless way of life to a godless philosophy.

But he takes Don John's wickedness to almost impossible extremes, showing him robbing churches, raping nuns and having his father killed because the old man withheld money and preached at his son. The treatment of the father by the son is thus even worse than in the French plays, where Dom Juan is usually represented as causing his father to die of grief. And the sensuality has a distasteful coarseness about it: when Don John and his raffish friends encounter some nymphs, Don John is asked which girl he prefers and answers: 'Tis all one, I am not in Love but in Lust, and to such a one, a Belly-full's a Belly-full' (p. 77). And so they each rape a nymph, as hungry men might snatch fruit from a tree. (These are those same nymphs who only a few moments before had been delighting us with 'Nymphs and Shepherds come away'.) Sometimes the effect produced by Don John's boastful account of his exploits is not far from involuntary comedy: 'I could meet with no willing Dame, but was fain to commit a Rape to pass away the time' (p. 32).

Yet even this infinitely depraved character possesses courage and daredevil bravura. He scorns easy pleasures ('the more danger the more delight', p. 33), scoffs at peril and is undismayed by the appearance of the Statue and the ghosts of his victims ('these things I see with wonder, but no fear', p. 91). It seems difficult to divorce Don Juan's particular brand of wickedness from an *almost* admirable courage, even if one is determined, as Shadwell unquestionably was, to present him as an abomination to all right-thinking people.

Edward Dent is severe on this play, regarding it as of no interest save for the chance fact that Purcell composed incidental music for it.[16] He is, of course, right when he talks of the melodramatic effects and the extravagances which Shadwell permits himself, but, by overlooking Shadwell's attempt, crude though it may be, at a philosophical motivation of the Don Juan type, Dent does the play less than justice. As we shall see, Don John's self-vindication by reference to his natural appetites will assume considerable importance when we come to consider Coleridge's remarks on the motivation of Don Juan and Byron's poem, *Don Juan*.

## THE BEGINNINGS

We are well placed to follow the popular Don Juan tradition in Germany and Austria in the seventeenth and eighteenth centuries, since several old stage-pieces and puppet-plays have survived. In the 1680s and 1690s German versions of Molière were played, and throughout the eighteenth century there were various more sensational Don Juan plays based either on Dorimon or Villiers, or on Italian sources. These popular German pieces nearly all contain the traditional murder of the father of a girl pursued by Don Juan, plus some kind of rustic interlude, the episode with the Statue and Don Juan's descent, unrepentant, into Hell. That is to say: the basic dramatic shape is the traditional one.

Taken over from Dorimon or Villiers is an episode in which Don Juan impersonates a hermit in order to outwit or murder the bridegroom of one of his victims. The treatment of this incident shows Don Juan steadily becoming more evil. In Dorimon he spares both the hermit and Dom Philippe; in Villiers he kills Philippe but not the hermit; in most of the German and Austrian stage-plays, he kills both – or, as he prefers to put it, his victims carelessly run against the point of his sword. There are further killings which intensify the impression of monstrous violence; in the 'Laufen' Don Juan play, Donn Joann (*sic*!) murders the proprietress of an inn because her bill is exorbitant (Act 3 Scene 7),

But it was left to the puppet-plays to provide a climax of bloodthirstiness. Don Juan's attitude towards his father can again serve as a yardstick. In Tirso, Don Juan causes him sorrow, mocks him and ignores his pleas. But that is all. The French plays show Juan behaving in a heartless, mocking, hypocritical and sometimes violent way towards his father, who dies of grief. (This happens in Dorimon, Rosimond and Villiers; Molière is an exception, of course; here, Dom Louis is outrageously and cynically treated by his son but survives him.) The only extant popular stage-play in German which figures Don Juan's father (Marinelli) has the son taunting the old man, but stopping short of violence. But in most of the puppet-plays Don Juan kills his father, either because he has refused his son money or in order to inherit the sooner.[17] In fact, several of the German puppet-plays lay more stress on Don Juan's violence and treachery than on his womanizing. But serious and systematic attempts to motivate him are lacking in the puppet-plays.[18]

Stage-plays and puppet-plays alike gave a central role to the clown (Hans Wurst, Kaspar, etc.), who always took the part of Don

Juan's servant. There was much knockabout, word-play, would-be comic misunderstanding and so forth, an equivalent to the antics of Harlequin in the *commedia dell'arte* pieces, although, it may be suspected, less adroit and graceful, for the leading clowns of the *commedia* reputedly possessed great athletic charm. It may be noted that the type of dramatic counterpoint in which the serious action coexists with a comic sub-plot or parody *can* play an important part in such dramas, enriching their meaning and their implications. (An example would be Marlowe's *Dr Faustus* or even some of the popular plays which were derived from it and made known in German-speaking Europe by the so-called *englische Komödianten*, groups of itinerant players.) But, all too often, the clown's antics detract from the effect of what should be solemn and dramatic moments. This is very marked in the puppet-plays of Don Juan at the point where Hans Wurst is instructed to invite the Statue to a meal. In the Augsburg version, the coarse use of 'Fressen' (instead of *Essen*, *Mahl* or *Tafel*) combines with the meaningless jingle of 'steinerner Stein' to trivialize a fateful moment: 'Du, steinerner Stein, sollst heute Mittag zu meinem Herrn zum Fressen kommen!' (*Das Kloster*, iii, 720). In the Strasburg version, too, Hans Wurst describes the intended banquet as a 'Nachtfressen'.

There was also a very popular Don Juan ballet which is of more than merely historical importance since Gluck wrote the music for it. The scenario was provided by the Imperial ballet-master in Vienna, Gasparo Angiolini, and the work was first performed in that city in 1761. The action is a freely adapted and condensed version of the stock Don Juan plot. Angiolini, in his Preface of 1761, gives us the scenario in some detail. Don Juan visits Donna Elvira, his mistress, and is surprised by her father, the Commander. The two men fight and Don Juan kills his adversary (Act 1). The Second Act is a banquet scene in which the Statue of Don Juan's victim arrives uninvited (this is usual), puts an abrupt end to the festivities and invites Don Juan to supper. Act Three is closer to tradition: Don Juan appears in response to the invitation, refuses to repent and is engulfed in the flames of Hell (this is where the famous Dance of the Furies comes in).

There has been much debate as to Angiolini's sources. He himself talks of a Spanish piece ('une Tragicomédie Espagnole'), but this, in the absence of any conclusive internal corroboration, could simply mean 'originating in Spain'.[19] I would guess that popular

Italian versions provided the main impulse but, since the ballet represents such a truncated version of stock elements and since the unusual features seem to be of Angiolini's own devising, the question of sources is relatively unimportant. What *is* certain is that the ballet was performed widely in German-speaking Europe, in Italy, Paris, London and elsewhere. Surviving scenarios and playbills make it quite clear that Gluck's music was the constant factor and that the dramatic action varied considerably from performance to performance.[20]

For a century after Molière, there had been no further serious attempt to re-interpret the legend or to explain Don Juan's character. Instead, his story lived on in a variety of popular pieces (stage- and puppet-plays, ballet) which did little more than keep his name and the main events of his life and death before the public. These popular pieces are important as a stage in the transmission of the legend but cannot be regarded in any way as an enrichment of its inner meaning. However, they have a further interest for anybody who is concerned with the early stage-history of Mozart's opera, for, as we shall see, comic scenes from the puppet-plays were imported into many of the earliest German-language productions of that work.

# 2

## Don Giovanni
### The Opera by da Ponte and Mozart and E.T.A. Hoffmann's interpretation of it

*Il Dissoluto punito o sia il Don Giovanni* dates from 1787 and was the second of the three operas which Mozart created in collaboration with Lorenzo da Ponte as librettist. Da Ponte drew on various stage-plays, including Molière's *Dom Juan* and Carlo Goldoni's *Don Giovanni Tenorio* of 1736 (to which we shall have to return later and in a different context). In addition, there were already several operas in existence which dealt with the Don Juan theme, and it is certain that da Ponte was influenced by at least one of these, that by Bertati, for which Gazzaniga composed the music.[1] Since all these operas except Mozart/da Ponte are long forgotten, except to specialists in the field of operatic history, and since da Ponte wove the diverse strands (together with much of his own invention) into a unified whole, we shall concern ourselves here with this most famous operatic treatment only. It is only fair to mention that some critics, for instance Dent, find certain inconsistencies and confusions in da Ponte's libretto, especially as regards the time-span of dramatic events. But such things can be easily exaggerated when one takes a work under the microscope; when we experience the work in performance, we are unlikely to be worried by them.

The fundamental outline of the story, as given by da Ponte, is much as in previous versions. Since, however, so many later writers either borrow from him or allude to him when writing their plays or when theorizing about the 'Don Juan type', it can do no harm to give a brief summary here. Don Giovanni, in disguise, has made an attempt on Donna Anna's virtue. She pursues him from the house, determined to identify the intruder. The hubbub brings her father, the Commendatore, to the scene; he fights a duel with Don

Giovanni and is killed. After Don Giovanni and his servant Leporello have escaped, there is a scene between Anna and her fiancé, Don Ottavio, in which the latter swears to avenge the Commendatore's death. Now Donna Elvira, who has been loved and abandoned by Don Giovanni, arrives in search of him. He makes his escape and leaves her to Leporello who reveals the enormities of his master's past behaviour in the famous 'catalogue aria', in which he reels off the total number of Don Giovanni's conquests country by country. Next we witness Don Giovanni's designs on a rustic beauty, Zerlina. Such an episode was by now *de rigueur* and is, indeed, perfectly logical given the idea, just propounded by Leporello, that Don Giovanni wants all women, from all countries and of all types. Don Giovanni turns Zerlina's head and is in a fair way towards winning her from her bridegroom Masetto (the wooing reaches its climax in the duet 'Là ci darem la mano'), but is interrupted by the appearance of Elvira. The first act ends in confusion and turmoil after Don Giovanni has been routed in his pursuit of Zerlina and also identified by Anna as her would-be ravisher and the killer of her father.

The second and final act begins with a series of swift-moving incidents and impersonations, very effective when realized in Mozart's witty and elegant music, provided that they are staged with the necessary pace and deftness. Don Giovanni passes himself off as Leporello in order to woo Elvira's maid and, later, to outwit Masetto; Leporello, wearing his master's cloak, is left to deal with Elvira and evade or placate his master's pursuers as best he may. For there is by now no doubt in anyone's mind that Don Giovanni was responsible for the Commendatore's death. Now comes the dramatic scene in the cemetery, where Don Giovanni finds the statue of his victim and forces his trembling servant to read the inscription in which the Commander's killer is threatened with retribution. In wild and arrogant contempt, Don Giovanni mocks the Statue ('O vecchio buffonissimo!') and invites it to supper, again through the agency of Leporello, now half-dead with fear. The Statue first nods and then answers 'Yes!' There follows a scene in which Anna assures Ottavio that she loves him, but asks for more time before the marriage can take place. We now move to Don Giovanni's residence for the famous supper scene, where Don Giovanni, still in reckless good humour, brushes aside Elvira's last despairing attempt to move him to betterment. The Statue enters and urges him to repent; after repeatedly and obstinately refusing to do so, he is dragged down to Hell. The opera closes with a sextet, in which the other characters muse on the libertine's fate and reveal their own future plans: Zerlina and Masetto are reconciled, Leporello will seek a better master, Anna promises that she will marry Ottavio after a year has elapsed, Elvira announces her intention to end her days in a convent. It will be noted that, in da Ponte's version, the plot has been given a tighter construction and greater economy than in some earlier treatments; there is a peasant-girl (Zerlina), but no fisher-girl, and there is only one banquet scene.

Since, as we shall see presently, the grandeur of Mozart's music led many admirers of the opera to read things into both the story and the characters which are not justified by any objective scrutiny of the libretto, we must begin by looking carefully at da Ponte's characterization of Don Giovanni. Like most of his predecessors, Don Giovanni is both womanizer and defiant and blasphemous rebel. Although most of his actions are wicked and his past behaviour (if we are to believe Leporello's statistics) is a record of outrageous sexual licence, we are probably captivated by him to some extent by virtue of his flamboyant manner and his stubborn courage in the final encounter with the Statue. But he despises vows and promises – his own and other people's – if they threaten to cut across his plans, and he pursues his ends using a mixture of deception, cajolery, flattery, bullying, threats and violence. He will change his tune from one moment to the next, treating his social equals with politeness and a superficial gallantry, while browbeating or patronizing those from the humbler classes. This class element in the behaviour of successive Don Juans has sometimes been underplayed in critical accounts and historical surveys. Yet it is already present in *El Burlador* and is, as Brecht reminds us, strong in Molière. It is a terrible thing, says Sganarelle, when a 'grand seigneur' is also a villain.[2] Hans Mayer[3] points to similar implications in Masetto's judgment on Don Giovanni as 'quell'indegno cavaliere . . . quell'uom senza onore': Don Giovanni is a disgrace to his class. He justifies his promiscuity (when he bothers to justify it at all) by a simple appeal to the natural appetites. When urged by Leporello to give up women, he declines, more in surprise than indignation, no doubt:

*D.G.* Leave women? You know that they are more necessary to me than the bread that I eat and the air that I breathe.
*Lep.* And yet you have the heart to deceive them all?
*D.G.* All out of love. Whoever is faithful to one is cruel to all the others. My feelings are so boundless that I wish them all well.

(p. 174)

His toast to wine and women, when Elvira makes her final, futile appeal to him to change his way of life, is a restatement of the simplest and most direct *carpe diem* philosophy: 'Vivan le femmine! Viva il buon vino! sostegno e gloria d'umanità!' Although not himself given to more than an occasional laconic and slightly mocking defence of his conduct – and that only when challenged[4] – he would no doubt agree with the philosophy of nature by which previous Don Juans, such as those created by Dorimon and Shadwell, had justified their actions.

Since the idealization of the Don Juan type, prompted in the first instance by this opera, will be the subject of the following pages, it is as well to note that da Ponte's Don Giovanni, although very depraved, is by no means as appallingly so as most of his predecessors. There is no wronged father in this work and none of the indiscriminate and treacherous killings which occur in many earlier versions. Don Giovanni kills once, but 'honourably' in a duel and only after trying to warn off his opponent. His 'non mi degno di pugnar teco' ('I do not deign to fight with you') must refer to his challenger's age; it cannot possibly have anything to do with the only other imaginable reason why a Don Giovanni should refuse to fight a duel, namely the social rank of his potential opponent. Hence Anna's use of the word 'assassin' when she returns to find her father lying dead, while understandable, is not technically correct. The exchange between Leporello and his master immediately after the duel makes Don Giovanni *sound* merely like a callous libertine. 'There's a fine adventure', says the servant, 'ravish the girl and murder the father' ('sforzar la figlia ed ammazar il padre!'). But, as we shall see, it was only an attempted ravishment and Don Giovanni's comment on the Commendatore's death – that he wished his fate on himself ('L'ha voluto, suo danno') – happens to be true. Another thing which may temper our awareness of Don Giovanni's wickedness, although not this time detracting from it, is the fact that his conquests lie in the past, enshrined in Leporello's catalogue. What we actually witness is his *unsuccessful* pursuit of Anna and Zerlina. Furthermore, the final sextet suggests that all has ended well for Zerlina and Masetto and at least tolerably well for Anna and Ottavio. This is more than – or in addition to – the purely moral satisfaction referred to at the end of Molière's play. Elvira might be seen as standing for all those whose lives had been blighted by Don Giovanni, but her treatment by da Ponte (levity) and also by Mozart (touches of musical parody) makes it difficult for us to take her as seriously as her fate and actions might seem to demand. Moreover, Don Giovanni has the advantage of beautiful and seductive music to give him a degree of appeal to anyone who is not a tone-deaf and uncompromising moralist. As we shall see, turning him into a tragic hero involved taking very considerable liberties, but he is not such a totally impossible candidate for such treatment as, say, Rosimond's Dom Juan, let alone Shadwell's Don John or the murderous villains in the German puppet-plays.

In 1813, the German Romantic author and composer E.T.A. Hoffmann wrote a short tale which was to have radical and long-lasting effects on the conception of Don Juan as a type. The title is 'Don Juan. Eine fabelhafte Begebenheit, die sich mit einem reisenden Enthusiasten vorgetragen' ('Don Juan. A fantastic event which befell a travelling enthusiast'). A traveller stops for the night in an unnamed small town. To his amazement, he hears the sounds of an orchestra tuning as he sits in his hotel room. It turns out that a theatre adjoins the hotel and that *Don Giovanni* is being given that evening. He hurries into the special box reserved for guests, in order not to miss this 'opera of operas'. In the course of the first act, he becomes aware that someone has entered the box but he is too engrossed in the work to pay any further heed. When the curtain falls he looks round and discovers to his amazement that his companion is Donna Anna (or, more exactly, the Italian singer who is taking her part) whom he has simultaneously been watching on the stage. She reveals a mysterious knowledge of the traveller, in whom she recognizes a kindred spirit, and they talk about the opera. As the bell rings for the second act, she vanishes. That night, after the performance is over, the traveller writes a long letter to a friend, in which he gives his interpretation of the opera and of Don Giovanni's character in particular. As he finishes, the clock strikes two and he seems to be aware of the opera singer's perfume and to hear her voice again. Next morning he learns that she had died suddenly during the night, at two o'clock.

The 'fantastic event' just described is more than an excuse or framework for an account of the opera; its fantastic and doom-laden atmosphere sets the tone for the equally fantastic and doom-laden reading of Giovanni's and Anna's characters which forms the subject of the traveller's letter to his friend. The traveller's (or Hoffmann's) point of departure is a disparity, or supposed disparity, between the levels of significance of da Ponte's libretto and Mozart's music. Hoffmann's attitude towards the plot seems offhand and scornful:

> A *bon vivant*, who loves wine and women beyond measure, who has the temerity to invite the Stone Guest to a festive table – truly, there is not much that is poetic in this and, to be honest, such a man hardly seems to merit being singled out by the infernal powers as a prize exhibit for Hell.
>
> (pp. 82 f.)

This, it may be said, is the reaction of an out-and-out Romantic individualist. The reason why supernatural powers had bothered themselves with Don Juan had traditionally been that he was a sinner whose behaviour, if widely emulated, would disrupt society and threaten a divinely ordained moral order. Hence he had to be punished (and seen to be punished). But if, like Hoffmann, you looked on him as an individual and saw in him nothing but one reckless hedonist, you might well come to wonder what made him important enough to be warned and then dragged off to his fate in such melodramatic fashion by a visitor from the spirit world.

The question of whether Don Giovanni is regarded primarily as an individual or as an exemplary warning figure is crucial at this stage of his history. 'He was a numbers man,' says Barry Goldensohn, in a recent poem, 'Last Act: Don Giovanni'.[5] Now, unless we dismiss the 'numbers' as comic hyperbole (Leporello's catalogue-aria) or half-mad arrogance (as when Giovanni asserts that he will augment the list by ten names in a single night), they must suggest a pointless, repetitious, and vulgar way of life unless invested with some additional meaning. That meaning was provided in all early versions by a moral framework which showed the sinner as provoking Heaven and receiving his due punishment. But for a man like Hoffmann, who would regard that as tame didacticism conveyed in absurdly melodramatic terms, a more fitting 'sub-text' must be found, if Mozart's music were not to appear totally inexplicable.

So it is that Hoffmann voices his astonishment that Mozart could ever have composed such music to this trivial story: 'es [ist] kaum zu begreifen, wie Mozart eine solche Musik dazu denken und dichten konnte'.[6] To explain this supposed paradox, he seeks a deeper meaning in the work, an imaginative interpretation suggested by the music, without reference to the literal meaning of the librettist's text: 'wie mir in der Musik, ohne alle Rücksicht auf den Text, das ganze Verhältnis der beiden im Kampf begriffenen Naturen [Don Giovanni and Donna Anna] erscheint' (p. 85).

How, then, could the music suggest a meaning not present in the words? Not only is this Don Giovanni less outrageously dissolute than his predecessors; the music helps to minimize or gloss over his guilt in a number of quite specific ways. Leporello's catalogue aria is, if taken *au pied de la lettre*, an appalling record of philandering. But the infectious high spirits of the music make it very difficult for the hearer to take the crimes seriously. Similarly, the wooing of Zerlina is, objectively speaking, a cynical attempt to win a bride-to-be from her groom on the very day of her wedding by means of false promises. Yet the mellifluous beauty of the music given to Don Giovanni at this point makes him *sound* sincere. In the duet 'Là ci darem la mano', he sings the same tune as Zerlina does. If Zerlina sounds as if she is in the grip of strong feelings (as she is), we are hardly likely to experience Don Giovanni's delivery of the same notes as false and calculating. Nor would it be at all easy for the singer to imply any such thing. So our awareness both of Giovanni's past wickedness and of his present scheming is to some extent cushioned by Mozart's music. One could even take the point further and claim that, if the opera is played and sung with due beauty and elegance, virtually all Don Giovanni's discreditable characteristics – his flattery, his extravagant promises, his arrogant high spirits, his calculating gallantry, etc. – are transmuted by the music and made to seem more dashing, more sincere or more unaffectedly exuberant than they really are.

But the main factor which made Hoffmann's re-interpretation possible will undoubtedly have been the impact of the 'demonic' and supernatural parts of Mozart's score: the slow section of the overture, the treatment of the duel and the Commendatore's death, the churchyard scene and the dialogue with the Statue at the banquet. Even in our day, the effect of these passages is overwhelming enough; it is no wonder that Hoffmann was carried away by the intimations of horror and doom present in the music. There is abundant evidence to suggest that the effect on Mozart's early audiences was electrifying. Here is part of an anonymous poem, dating from about 1820, 'Zur Ouvertüre von Mozart's Don Juan':

> And so he stands there, the raving miscreant, accursed, but nevertheless great in his sins. So he goes hence into the torment of eternal flames. This picture, too great and terrifying for words, can only be mysteriously expounded by music, can only be painted by Mozart, the master of sound.[7]

This view, that there are emotions and ideas that music alone can express, was one shared by Hoffmann[8] and will have encouraged the quest for meaning beyond the words of the libretto.

It may be added that the tendency to separate words from music and to regard the opera as *Mozart's* achievement persists. The hero of Artur Brausewetter's novel *Don Juans Erlösung* (1915) maintains that there are four great tragedies of human destiny: the stories of Hamlet, Faust, Wallenstein and Don Juan. Of the last, he adds: 'Mozart created this tragedy in immortal sounds, but its poet . . . is yet to come' (p. 172). And a recent producer of the opera, Göran Järvefelt, argues that the music given to Donna Anna reveals things about her inner state which are not expressed in the libretto. Like Hoffmann, Järvefelt believes that Giovanni's arrival spoilt Anna's chances of a harmonious relationship (even if a tepid one) with Ottavio and awakened in her passionate desires which had until then lain slumbering. And, like Hoffmann, Järvefelt flatly declares that the words spoken and the sentiments implied by the music are two totally different things.[9]

To return to Hoffmann's day: another factor which helped to make the plot *seem* trivial is the circumstance that most early performances of this opera in Germany and Austria were in crude German translations, many of which incorporated extra comic scenes from the popular stage-plays and puppet-plays, usually an episode in which Don Giovanni outwits constables who are inquiring into the death of the Commander, and one in which he gets the better of a creditor; this latter scene had figured in Molière and quickly became a part of the popular German versions. In addition, there was often extra comic (or would-be comic) dialogue between master and servant, also imported from the puppet-plays. These interpolations, together with all the material which in the original had been in the form of *recitativo secco*, now figure as spoken dialogue; in fact, many of the playbills describe Don Giovanni as a *Singspiel*,[10] that is, a mixture of singing and speaking as in an English ballad-opera. There is probably no opera that has been so ill-treated as *Don Giovanni*, says Engel, referring to the liberties taken with da Ponte's libretto and with the composer's passages of *recitativo secco*. Although Hoffmann's tale is based on a performance in Italian, it is virtually certain that he will have known one or more of these trivialized German language versions. Otherwise, why should he affect surprise that a moderately sized German town should offer a performance of *Don Giovanni* in Italian? ('Also italienisch? – Hier am deutschen Orte italienisch?' – p. 75). There is no doubt that, if one allowed oneself to become too concerned with the surface extravagances and improbabilities of the plot, there might indeed appear to be a gulf between words and music.

What is this deeper meaning, hinted at in the music? Man, says Hoffmann, has intimations of transcendental values. The conflict between the real and the ideal, or between the demonic and the divine, is the very essence of terrestrial life. Don Giovanni comes to believe (or is made to believe by the powers of evil) that the ideal is to be found in love, that somewhere there must be a woman who could help him to achieve here on earth the highest happiness (which, in reality, man knows only as a vague longing and which can be realized only in another world):

> Through the wiles of the Evil One there came into Don Juan's mind the thought that through love, through the enjoyment of woman here on earth, that promise could be fulfilled which resides in our breast only as a Heavenly prospect and which is the infinite longing which brings us into direct relationship with the transcendental.
>
> (p. 84)

So Don Giovanni goes from one woman to the next, but is always disappointed because none lives up to the ideal. Finally he falls into cynicism and avenges himself, through his arts of seduction, on the sex which has, he thinks, failed him:

> always thinking himself deceived . . . in the end Don Juan necess-

arily found the whole of earthly life dull and flat. Despising humankind, he rebelled against the vision [of woman] which, in his eyes the highest thing in life, had disappointed him so bitterly.

(p. 84)

Anna is Giovanni's opposite, 'ein göttliches Weib', pure and incorruptible, destined by Heaven to be Giovanni's mate. But he finds her too late and so can only seduce her, arousing turbulent passions in her, so that she now thinks only of revenge. Although she had once thought that she loved Ottavio, she is now indifferent to him and her request for a year's grace is a mere excuse; she will never survive this year to marry him.

It must be recalled that this is an imaginative interpretation suggested by the music and not supported by the text. It cannot be insisted on too strongly that Hoffmann's Don Giovanni and Donna Anna are not da Ponte's. As we have seen, Don Giovanni is not (if we allow ourselves to be guided by the libretto) an embodiment of tragic *Zerrissenheit* and the demonic pursuer of an impossible ideal of womanhood, but an uncomplicated hedonist who possesses women in joyful gratification of natural appetites. In his interpretation of Donna Anna, Hoffman has freed himself just as radically from da Ponte's depiction. To begin with, although Hoffmann calmly informs us that Anna was seduced by Don Giovanni, there is not the slightest hint in the libretto that this was so. (If she *was* seduced, she lies about it most unconscionably.)[11] Da Ponte's Donna Anna is emphatically not a kind of Superwoman, predestined consort of the Superman, Don Giovanni. She is respectable and correct, conventionally shocked by Don Giovanni's advances. Da Ponte gives a convincing depiction of a young woman filled with grief over her father's death and obsessed by the desire to avenge him. There seems no reason to read anything mysterious into her reluctance to marry Ottavio without delay; her bereavement and her unwillingness, even inability, to fly in the face of social convention force her to keep Ottavio waiting despite the fact that she loves him: 'I greatly regret delaying a happiness which our souls have long desired. But the world's opinion . . .' (p. 254). This reference to public opinion, coupled with the protestation of love in the immediately following aria ('Non mi dir'), makes her position perfectly clear. It seems hard on da Ponte that he should have taken the trouble to create a Don Giovanni and a Donna Anna who make admirable sense as characters, only to have them dismantled and re-assembled in this fashion. Not only has the human psychology been 'rewritten' by Hoffmann for the sake of this interpretation; it may be added that a new meaning has been placed on the supernatural events. In da Ponte, inasmuch as the intrusion of powers from another world is not simply exploited in a sceptical spirit as an opportunity for a *coup de théâtre*, it has its traditional function of punishing the dissolute man, as is, after all, clearly stated in the opera's title. But Hoffmann's interpretation of the supernatural element is part and parcel of his concern with Don Giovanni's longing for a transcendental ideal and with the Devil's trick which deludes him into believing that this ideal can be achieved on earth, in and through woman.

As we shall see, this new conception of Juan and Anna affected literally scores of Don Juan plays, poems and novels and also coloured discussion of him as a type over many decades. Dédéyan roundly says that Don Juan was transformed into Faust by Hoffmann.[12] I would not go quite so far myself, but it is certainly true to say that, in Hoffmann's interpretation, Don Juan becomes a tragic and quasi-Faustian figure by virtue of his hopeless quest for something beyond normal permitted human experience. Thus Hoffmann's tale fuelled and encouraged the already present tendency to see Don Juan as a sort of 'second Faust', a rebel of the flesh where Faust was a rebel of the intellect.[13] The perspective from which he was viewed became increasingly important. In older treatments of the theme, he had been seen as one who wickedly transgressed against the moral norm. But according to the Romantic view of the world, a view which sees the man of imagination and sensibility as consumed by transcendental longings of which the ordinary man – the 'Philistine' – has no conception, the heroic rebel may be expected to act according to his own criteria. If these involve an unremitting and self-defeating quest, even one which harms his fellows, he becomes a tragic figure, but not necessarily, and certainly not primarily, a wicked one. We shall have cause to return to this question of the author's and reader's/audience's perspective when we come to discuss reactions against the new, romanticized Don Juan. As we shall see, Hoffmann, virtually single-handed, brought about a polarization of views: his followers accepted the notion of an idealistic Don Juan and played down the suffering of his victims accordingly, while others, taking the offences against God and humankind as their starting-point, rejected an interpretation which seemed to exculpate the criminal and libertine.

Very broadly speaking, we may talk of an agreed view of Don Juan before Hoffmann. According to this view, Don Juan's pursuit of pleasure was unscrupulous and sinful and his claim that he was entitled to 'be himself' was always presented as false and dangerous; implicit in such condemnation was the fear that chaos would come were this claim to self-realization to become widespread. Such differences as we encounter among these early versions (up to Mozart/da Ponte) usually concern the exact degree of Don Juan's guilt and the question of whether his rebellion is directed against a God whose existence he acknowledges or whether he is an atheist. But these differences are inessential compared with the common factor. This meant that early audiences were confidently expected to side with Don Juan's victims and with the moral and social order which he violated so flagrantly. Don Juan may claim a double standard according to which there is one law for the herd and another for the rebel, but neither authors nor audiences would agree for a minute. Hoffmann, with his postulation of idealistic motives and his implicit *tout comprendre, c'est tout pardonner*, quite destroyed the consensus which had reigned for a century and a half. Before we examine this schism, which is of central importance for an understanding of Don Juan's fortunes in nineteenth-century Germany and France, we must turn our attention to the most famous of English Don Juans and consider what Byron made of this figure.

# 3

# Byron

In England, Shadwell's version remained popular and was frequently performed until about the middle of the eighteenth century, when it gave way to a whole range of shallow dramatic entertainments (melodramas, 'tragi-comic pantomimes', burlesques, etc.). These were nourished by a variety of sources: Shadwell, French and Italian plays, even *El Burlador*, as we can see from the double invitation and the two supper scenes in the 1782 pantomime. (The anonymous author of the Introduction to this scenario ascribes the 'old Spanish play' to Calderón, by the way.) Sensation, lavish use of stage effects and broad comedy are the mark of these pieces. By the time we reach the 1780s, the pantomimes performed in London under such titles as *Don Juan or the Libertine destroyed* are relentlessly superficial in their treatment both of the legend and of the central character. A violent, lecherous and sacrilegious Don Juan is accompanied on his adventures by a clown-servant, much as in the pieces familiar from the *commedia dell'arte*.[1]

Later, a burlesque of the Mozart/da Ponte opera was staged; later still there was a farce in which Don Juan was brought back from Hell and reformed; also a sixpenny chapbook loosely based on Shadwell. Don Juan even invaded the English Punch and Judy plays. It seems that such famous legends may go through long periods of transmission in the most intellectually undemanding forms until such time as an imaginative and innovative writer rediscovers them and gives them new meaning and potential. An obvious parallel would be the case of the Faust legend in Germany up to the time of its reclamation by Lessing and Goethe in the late eighteenth century; another would be the story of Hero and Leander, which for some time was known in German-speaking countries mainly in the form of folk-ballads. It may be that the extravagances of the traditional Don Juan plot, its walking and talking statues and choruses of demons, made this theme unacceptable in the Age of Reason. Certainly the editor of the 1782 scenario, referred to above, says in his Introduction that the story is 'too improbable for a serious Drama' (p. 4). In the case of Don Juan in England, the literary rehabilitation had to wait until the Romantic era and, when it came, was in the form of a sort of picaresque novel in verse rather than a 'serious drama'.

Byron's *Don Juan* was written between 1818 and 1823 and published in stages between 1819 and 1824. The author had certainly seen a Don Juan pantomime and, indeed, refers to it in the opening stanza of the first canto, clearly assuming that this is the form in which the legend will be familiar to the bulk of his readers:

> I'll therefore take our ancient friend Don Juan,
> We all have seen him in the Pantomime
> Sent to the devil, somewhat ere his time.

In addition, he probably knew one or other of the older Don Juan plays and, of course, Mozart's opera. But his poem owes little to the Don Juan tradition as far as plot is concerned, unless we care to see some of the episodes as implied variations on, or ironic reversals of, traditional incidents. Byron's additional debts have been diligently investigated and it has been shown that he drew a great deal on travelogues, histories and other sources, above all to provide the adventurous, martial and exotic material for cantos 2–9.

For *Don Juan*, Bryon chose the rhymed eight-line stanza (*ottava rima*) which he had already used in the 'Venetian story' *Beppo*, written in 1817, and which had proved an admirable vehicle for a light and playful verse narrative. As in *Beppo*, so in *Don Juan*: Byron constantly draws the reader into events, chatting with him, appealing to him and teasing him. As in *Beppo*, too, the story is constantly interrupted by, and smothered in, digressions: assorted reflections on social mores, religion, philosophy, poetry and much else besides. Byron himself owns to the discursive manner with ironic self-deprecation: 'But let me to my story: I must own,/If I have any fault, it is digression' (*Don Juan*, iii, 96). Later, he even claims that the plot is there chiefly as a framework to carry the satirical observations (xiv, 7). The reader often finds the thread of the narrative abruptly broken off, sometimes at tense and dramatic moments. That is to say, Byron's *Don Juan* is not 'about' one man's life and character as previous Don Juan works had been; the hero's fortunes and situations are used as a spring-board for reflections on topics which have no obvious and direct reference to him. Indeed, in the later cantos set in England, Don Juan's role seems to be chiefly that of an outsider against whom the absurdity, artificiality, corruption and hypocrisy of English high society can be measured.

A vast amount has been written about this poem: its political and social content, its character as a picaresque travelogue, its style, the satirical techniques employed, its position both in Byron's oeuvre and as a landmark in English light verse, and so on. Our concern here, however, is specifically with the work as a contribution to the Don Juan legend and to the way in which its central character is to be perceived and morally evaluated. But since Byron's undoubtedly revolutionary interpretation cannot be analysed without reference to the plot, I will attempt the briefest of summaries.

Juan is brought up in an atmosphere of sexual prudery by his widowed mother. His sexual initiation comes when he is aged sixteen. But already we see that this is to be a new and different Don Juan; he is no unscrupulous seducer, for the young woman, Julia, is at least equally willing. We know that this episode was based on an actual event, with an acquaintance of Byron's playing the part of Don Juan (see Byron's letter to J. C. Hobhouse of 25 January 1819). But I find it impossible to believe that Byron shaped the event for inclusion in his poem[2] without wishing to imply a parody of a stock incident in the Don Juan tradition (perhaps also nourished by memories of *The Marriage of Figaro* or *The Merry Wives of Windsor*). For the episode culminates with the unexpected arrival of the husband. Juan hides but is presently discovered, a struggle ensues but Juan gets away without fateful consequences. In fact, the only blood to flow is from the cuckolded husband's nose. The superficial similarity to traditional episodes serves only to underline the difference: the wicked attempt on innocent virtue which had always had a tragic outcome is here replaced by an escapade in which Juan is comparatively innocent and the result comparatively harmless (except for Julia, who is despatched to a nunnery).

After a voyage, Juan is found shipwrecked on an island, where he enjoys an idyllic love affair with Haidée, the daughter of a pirate and slave-trader. This is Byron's equivalent to the shipwreck and fisher-girl episodes in the traditional versions, but again the link stresses the completely different conception of the hero, for this is no thoughtless and callous seduction; Byron treats the whole episode (which ends in tragedy for Haidée) seriously and sympathetically and makes clear that the young couple are genuinely in love. (So much so, in fact, that we presently find Juan twice resisting sexual temptation because of his memories of her.)[3] His fortunes change abruptly: he is wounded, is sold into slavery in Turkey, escapes and distinguishes himself fighting with the Russian army, becomes the favourite of the Empress Catherine in St Petersburg and is sent by her to England as Envoy. This is the section of the poem largely taken up with satire of English high society. At this point the work breaks off. But it is only the narrative that remains fragmentary; there is nothing inconclusive or incomplete in the author's view of Juan and of how he relates to his fellow-men (and women).

How, then, does Byron conceive of his hero? Juan does, it is true, become 'a little dissipated' (x, 23) and is mildly rebuked by the author for his inconstancy (ii, 208 ff.). But he is a far cry from Shadwell's Libertine, who commits a rape 'to pass the time', or from da Ponte's Don Giovanni, with his thousand and three victims in Spain alone. Leporello's catalogue implies a philanderer who is capable of being aroused by any presentable female; the contrast with Byron's exacting hero, who 'had not seen of several hundred/A lady altogether to his mind', who 'ne'er seem'd anxious to seduce' and even had a leaning towards marriage,[4] could not be very much greater. Despite Byron's confident assumption that we all know his hero as an 'ancient friend' from the pantomime, it is likely that contemporary readers will have been struck rather by the *lack* of resemblance, for this Don Juan is a 'modestly confident and calmly assured' youth, a 'gentle Spaniard' (xi, 52; xiii, 22) with nothing of the arrogance of previous Don Juans. Moreover, women are drawn to him by his handsomeness and winning ways, so that he has no need to develop the arts of seduction and deceit to any extent which would even remotely link him to his predecessors; in many of his affairs he is not the prime mover.

Superficially, then, Byron's hero is not much like a Don Juan at all. What links him to the type is that, for him too, nature is the only guide. Writing two years before the first cantos of Byron's poem appeared in print, Coleridge had mused on the Don Juan legend from its Spanish beginnings through to Shadwell and beyond and had picked on this appeal to nature as the chief way in which successive Don Juans had sought to justify themselves:

> Obedience to nature is the only virtue: the gratification of the passions and appetites her only dictate: each individual's self-will the sole organ through which nature utters her commands . . .
> (*Biographia Literaria*, chapter 23)

Seen in this light, Byron's Don Juan makes sense as a logical and consistent character; he enjoys women when they attract him, but can on occasion resist their advances. This does not happen out of an absolute ideal of constancy and certainly not out of religious or moral scruples; it comes about only if grief at losing one love is too fresh in his mind to permit him to be drawn to another woman (yet), even if she is to his taste. Thus he manages to forget Julia for Haidée, but renounces the opportunity of two easy conquests because of Haidée's memory. It would not be 'natural' to betray that memory while it is still green – but, as the sequel will show, neither will he be so 'unnatural' as to live forever faithful to his lost love, for that would be a different sort of betrayal, a betrayal of appetites implanted in him by nature. Here we see the link between Byron's conception of Don Juan and his attacks on society: a hero for whom 'obedience to nature is the only virtue' is shown first overcoming an unnatural upbringing, then enjoying an idyllic interlude in which unspoilt nature and unaffected love combine to make him happy, only to be pitchforked into a series of thoroughly artificial milieux (Turkish harem, Russian court, English *haut monde*).

Juan's childhood[5] is a denial of nature. His mother is, ironically, described as a saint, 'each eye a sermon and her brow a homily'.[6] The boy is permitted to read only edifying books:

> But not a page of any thing that's loose,
> Or hints continuation of the species,
> Was ever suffer'd, lest he should grow vicious.
> (i, 40)

The contrast between natural and unnatural attitudes and ways of life permeates the poem. It is at its clearest when we compare the brief love-affair between Juan and Haidée with Juan's later experiences in England. Alone save for the ocean and the stars, Juan and Haidée yield to love naturally and completely, without need for vows, protestations or artifice. The word 'nature' runs through these stanzas like a *leitmotif*:

> nature's oracle – first love . . .
>
> She loved, and was beloved – she adored,
> And she was worshipp'd; after nature's fashion,
> Their intense souls, into each other pour'd . . .
>
> And thus they form a group that's quite antique,
> Half naked, loving, natural, and Greek.
>
> (ii, 189, 191, 194)

But, in England, love is a saleable commodity, whether on the level of prostitution or in the marriage market of more respectable circles, where feminine accomplishments are bait for husbands (xii, 53) and eligible females are paraded like thoroughbred animals while matchmakers and 'needy honourable misters' cluster around (xii, 31 f.).

Yet this is deemed respectable, even moral, whereas Juan's intense love for Haidée would be branded sinful:

> Is not all love prohibited whatever,
> Excepting marriage? which is love no doubt
> After a sort . . .
> But love *sans* banns is both a sin and shame,
> And ought to go by quite another name.
>
> (xii, 15)

Byron might insist on the essential morality of his poem, describing it as 'a *Satire* on *abuses* in the present states of society, and not an eulogy of vice' (to Murray, Christmas Day, 1822), but it is not surprising that early nineteenth-century England took umbrage at a work which frankly owned the proximity of love and lust (ix, 77), treated Juan's illicit amours so calmly and zestfully portrayed him disguised as a female slave in a harem or being pursued by a lecherous female dressed up in a monk's cowl. That this Don Juan had few traces of that character's traditional negative features (arrogance, violence, treachery) will not have improved matters. It is no wonder that, despite the defence of Leigh Hunt, Shelley and others, there were attacks on the 'licentious', 'immoral' and 'irreligious' nature of the work.[7]

If we are to account fully and satisfactorily both for these hostile comments and for the author's somewhat pained reaction to them, we must consider not only the content of the poem, but the manner in which it is written. The impression created is casual and ironic: J. J. McGann has convincingly linked this style to the conversational manner of Horace and his 'English inheritor', Pope. There are, of course, many styles in *Don Juan*; Byron is capable of purple patches, especially when his social or political feelings are running high, he turns elegiac at the moments of greatest emotional intensity (Juan and Haidée), he has passages of great lyrical beauty . . . But the dominant note is one of irony or even flippancy: 'He learn'd the arts of riding, fencing, gunnery,/And how to scale a fortress – or a nunnery' (i, 38). That satirical use of zeugma certainly reveals that Pope was one of Byron's mentors.

As already in *Beppo*, Byron indulges himself in extravagant, ingenious, sometimes deliberately forced rhymes, as if making fun of the medium in which he operates and thereby playing a game with the reader by cheating more orthodox expectations of what rhyme ought to be and what it ought to do: 'oddest, he/modesty', 'passion/rash one' or even, impertinently, 'appendix/index'.[8] Puns abound, many of them likely to put the modern reader in mind of the facetiousness of mid- and late Victorian humour: 'if a man's name in a *bulletin*/May make up for a *bullet in* his body . . .' (vii, 21, Byron's italics). There are also joking references within the work to its style and form: thus Byron comments on the tyranny of rhyme(!) or the number of stanzas that should properly make up a canto.[9] The work is strewn with quotations and recondite allusions, often used to create a calculated dissonance between their normal (serious) associations and their present, more light-hearted or even burlesque, context. The mocking tone must have seemed to many of Byron's early readers to make mischief more mischievous by leavening Juan's immorality while simultaneously deriding respected English institutions, customs and moral values. Why, then, did Byron give this particular form to his thoughts on the Don Juan figure and on the relationship between society, morality and sexuality?

Not content with describing his poem as 'a little quietly facetious upon every thing' (to Moore, 19 September 1818), Byron even calls it his 'Donny Johnny' and defines his intention as to 'giggle and make giggle' (to Murray, 12 August 1819). His facetiousness will almost certainly have been a sort of protective covering, a donning of the cap and bells in order to claim the traditional jester's freedom to mock and, through mocking, to criticize; that is, the flippancy has a moral purpose. Frivolity of treatment may make the 'shocking' aspects of the poem slightly less shocking. Byron tries to enlist his public on his side, appealing to his 'kind reader' to share his views (ix, 23); elsewhere he defends himself against possible objections from the 'chaste reader' (iii, 12). Where all else fails and the reader proves hard to placate, the poet can, by implication, point to the light-hearted tone of his work: surely you will not take this to be a serious threat to morals? But, as we have seen, he did not escape whipping: 'Some have accused me of a strange design/Against the creed and morals of the land', he says ruefully, and again: 'a jest at Vice by Virtue's called a crime' (iv, 5; xiii, 1).

If we recall the intense moral earnestness and the obsession with correct behaviour (or, at least, the appearance of it) that were so widespread in Byron's day, we will not share his surprise. For many, he seemed to wink tolerantly at offences which respectable society abhorred, while 'jesting at vices' over which most people preferred to draw a veil. In his poem, Byron constantly returns to the theme of hypocrisy, obviously regarding it as the English disease and hence feeling (or pretending to feel) in duty bound to tell unwelcome truths (x, 84) and to expose the pretensions of the English to being a moral people (xi, 87). Ironically assuming the moral standpoint of his countrymen for a moment, he equates telling the truth with *im*morality:

> But now I'm going to be immoral; now
> I mean to show things really as they are,
> Not as they ought to be . . .
>
> (xii, 40)

Not until the 'Nietzschean' Don Juans of nearly a century later will this character be exploited to uncover such a radical clash of moral values (see chapter 8). At one point, Byron casts himself as Mephistopheles: not, that is, as tempter, but as ironic and disillusioned spectator (xiii, 7). E. D. H. Johnson[10] has argued that the indignation caused by the flippancy and apparent moral laxity of *Don Juan* came about because Byron had seriously misjudged the moral temper of English society. At the very least, he had underestimated the rage that would be felt among segments of the population predisposed to hostility towards him for political as well as moral reasons, and the prominence that such reactions would be given in some of the influential reviews. But even those who had prized his earlier works and were hence predisposed to react favourably, felt let down, believing that a great talent was here abused. That is to say, both the readers' disapproval and the author's half-amused, half-pained surprise were equally genuine; the ironical defence-mechanisms described above had proved inadequate.

*Don Juan* gave rise to many imitations, continuations and parodies.[11] These include genuine sequels which recount the hero's further adventures, one continuation which shows him as a reformed character, two critical reviews of the poem in the manner of the poem and a number of parodies in which the style and form of *Don Juan* are used as a vehicle for satirical reflections on anything and everything. In addition to these parodies, there was a play loosely based on episodes from Byron's poem (Buckstone 1828) and the indebtedness runs through to comparatively recent times, with Eric Linklater's novels *Juan in America* and *Juan in China* (1931 and 1937) and Humbert Wolfe's poem *Don J. Ewan* of 1937.

Linklater imagines a modern Don Juan, linear descendant of Byron's hero, transplanted to other continents. His two works are picaresque novels in which the erotic element is no longer of central importance. In fact, Linklater's Don Juan, like Byron's, is more of an Innocent Abroad than a Don Juan in the expected sense and, like Byron's Don Juan, the hero of *Juan in America* can resist a woman if memories of a past attachment are still sufficiently strong. There is, to be true, a rather tepid defence of sexual promiscuity, with a reference to 'normality' replacing the traditional appeal to 'nature':

'Is it normal to fall in love with a whole procession of women?'
'Yes, if they're all different, and all pleasant to look at, and amusing to talk to.'

(p. 232)

But this is a far cry from the daily and imperative need for women expressed and demonstrated by Don Juans of previous ages. When we come to *Juan in China*, we even find the hero living for 'three months of happy fidelity' in 'almost domestic contentment' (p. 21). There is thus little more than a name to link these Don Juans with traditional conceptions of that character. The tendency, already present in Byron, to use the name as an excuse for picaresque adventures and satirical observations, is simply taken further.

But apart from nineteenth-century parodies and twentieth-century updatings, Byron's *Don Juan* seems to have had no real successors among the hundreds of poems, plays and novels dedicated to this character since the 1820s. The reasons are not far to seek. The mixture of levity, indignation and moral earnestness, the loose and digressive structure which nevertheless acquires its own unity through the skilful way in which the author uses his hero as a stick with which to beat contemporary society, the virtuoso use of *ottava rima*, the light touch and the extraordinary variations in poetic tone: these things, failing the appearance of a second Byron on the scene, are inimitable (except briefly and for satirical purposes).

In Germany Byron's poem was lavishly praised. Goethe described it as a work of boundless genius ('ein grenzenlos-geniales Werk'); Platen and Hebbel were also numbered among its admirers.[12] But it did not have much influence on subsequent treatments of the Don Juan legend in Germany; as we shall see, the Germans, influenced by Hoffmann and also inclined to regard Don Juan as a 'second Faust', took a much more serious and romanticized view of the character.

With hindsight we can see that Byron's real importance, as far as the further development of the Don Juan theme in Western European literature is concerned, is much more general than any question of 'successors' or 'indebtedness' would imply. Byron had taken up the notion of a Don Juan guided and motivated by nature and, for the first time, had removed from it any stigma of wickedness. Previous Don Juans had certainly defended their conduct by asking why it was wrong to obey one's natural urges, but the authors had wanted and expected their audiences to reject this amoral claim by reference to religion or to plain social decency. By contrast, Byron's hero is clearly depicted as more admirable than society at large, which is shown as going against nature and as thoroughly hypocritical, both in sexual matters and in its general moral conduct.

Another departure from tradition is that this Don Juan is relatively passive and that women are often seen as making the running. This is conspicuous in the house-party episode which takes up the last cantos of the poem, for here three women (Aurora, Lady Adeline, the Duchess of Fitz-Fulke) are all shown as being, in their different ways, distinctly interested in Juan, without his having taken particular pains to attract their attention. The climax comes when the Duchess disguises herself as a ghostly monk in order to enter Juan's bedchamber (canto xvi). The incident is all the more forceful in that it is a reversal of the many traditional episodes in which the 'trickster of Seville' had resorted to disguise or impersonation in order to pursue a lady. This insistence on the active role of the woman was one more reason why Byron's work was considered shocking in its day. But the idea of Don Juan as the quarry, not the hunter, has lived on and figures in several later works, including Shaw's *Man and Superman*.

Weinstein, talking of the liberty with which Byron treated the legend, goes on to argue that he 'opened the way to what amounts to licence. Henceforth Don Juan becomes a name that an author may freely bestow on any hero, just so long as he has some adventures with women' (p. 81). There is much truth in this, in that many writers were to use 'Don Juan' as a label for a human type, divorced from the legend which had traditionally been associated with him (see below, chapter 9). But the next important step in Don Juan's history is dominated by Hoffmann's theory that he was driven on not by obedience to nature but by transcendental longings.

# 4
# Hoffmann's Influence

## GERMANY

Here, as we shall see, the new, 'Hoffmannesque' Don Juan rapidly became linked – almost confused – with the figure of Faust. The relationship had already been perceived eight years before the appearance of Hoffmann's tale by Franz Horn, writing in the periodical *Luna*. Basing his remarks on Goethe's *Faust* (the published 'Fragment' of 1790, that is) and Mozart's opera, Horn states that 'Faust and Don Juan are the peaks of modern Christian poetic mythology.'[1] As soon as Hoffmann's influence makes itself felt, the link becomes more obvious and more specific; the two legends come to be seen as 'peaks of modern Christian mythology' in the sense that both characters strive for an absolute (of fleshly indulgence in Don Juan's case, of total experience or perfect knowledge in Faust's), a striving which puts them out of humour with the restrictions of ordinary human existence. The link is very clear in what seems to be the first German Don Juan to have been influenced by Hoffmann, Eduard Duller's poem 'Juan' of about 1835.[2] (I have never found a satisfactory explanation of why it took so long for Hoffmann's influence to make itself felt in his native country. But neither, as far as I know, has anyone come forward with an earlier example. Considering the multitude of Hoffmannesque Don Juans which were to follow, this initial time-lag remains a minor mystery.)

The contrast between this new, idealized Don Juan and the traditional 'libertine' and 'criminal' must have seemed little short of vertiginous to Duller's first readers, even if some of them had been prepared for a change of approach from having read their Hoffmann. Duller's Don Juan seeks something far beyond what is normally vouchsafed to man: 'I grasp the immeasurable, it is mine. I must ransack the universe, experience ecstasy after ecstasy and feel myself as a god in every living being, finding this divine self in the highest and in the lowest' (pp. 151 f.). The parallel to Goethe's Faust, who wants to comprehend the secret unifying force that holds the universe together and who, gazing on the Sign of the Macrocosm, feels himself akin to a god, is manifest. The link becomes yet clearer if Duller's original German is set off against the relevant parts of Faust's opening monologue in Goethe:

| *Duller* | *Goethe* |
|---|---|
| Das Unermeßliche fass' ich, 's ist mein! | Wo faß ich dich, unendliche Natur? |
| Das All durchwühlen | Ich fühle Mut, mich in die Welt zu wagen, |
| Muß ich, Wonn' auf Wonne fühlen. | Der Erde Weh, der Erde Glück zu tragen. |
| In jedem Wesen mich als Gott empfinden . . . | Bin ich ein Gott? Mir wird so licht! |

Frustrated in his search, Don Juan concludes that the only reality is that apprehended by the senses ('Wirklich ist nichts, als was der Sinn erfaßt!', p. 152) and so devotes himself to a restless life of philandering. He approaches death, convinced that there is nothing beyond the grave but annihilation, but is promised salvation (by the Stone Guest!), since even his despairing progress through life has been a quest for God.

The scene in which the Stone Guest appears at Don Juan's banquet contains motifs which sound as if Duller were deliberately reminding us of the corresponding scene in Mozart's opera: '. . . as the reveller feasts to the accompaniment of sweet melodies . . . as the ground trembles under the Guest's steps like the Last Trump' (p. 154). This suggests in turn that, for Duller as for Franz Horn and Hoffmann, the demonic reading of Don Juan's character is linked to the impact of Mozart's music. Indebtedness to Hoffmann cannot be proven, but the depiction of Don Juan as a frustrated, quasi-faustian idealist, who turns to the life of the senses because 'the immeasurable' seems to be shut off to him, is too much like a fusion of Hoffmann's Don Juan and Goethe's Faust to be a coincidence. I find it unlikely that Duller would have effected this strange transformation in Don Juan's character without the pointer, so forcefully expressed in Hoffmann's tale, that there was more to the plot of Mozart's opera than the misdemeanours and punishment of a vulgar libertine.

Duller, of course, goes much further than Hoffmann and turns the traditional ending on its head. Hoffmann had been carried away by the awe-inspiring music which Mozart had provided to accompany the Stone Guest's terrible warnings, and had accepted the idea of Don Giovanni's descent into Hell, which he saw as retribution for a tragically misdirected idealism that had led to a career of obdurate sinfulness. Duller, yet more romantic in his approach, presents us with a Don Juan whose idealistic quest for the Divine here on earth is not less misplaced and deluded, but of such intensity that it merits salvation. The optimistic ending of Goethe's *Faust*, the completed version of which had been published three years before Duller wrote his poem and whose hero is redeemed mainly because he never ceased to strive (lines 11936 f.), will almost certainly have been an influence here.

The first German drama obviously and openly inspired by the new conception of Don Juan is, as far as I know, Braun von Braunthal's *Don Juan. Drama in fünf Abtheilungen* of 1842. Don Juan, at the beginning of this play, is already a hedonist, libertine and accomplished seducer. He is joined by a devil, Atheos, and the bulk of the play deals with their association and their adventures in Italy, France and England. The action ends, where it began, in Madrid, and culminates in Don Juan's death. (He is poisoned by Rosa, whom he had seduced and abandoned.) The ending hints that judgement rather than salvation is to come, as Don Juan concedes the destructive sinfulness of his way of life.

There seems to be an involuntary confusion of two quite different Don Juans within this play, where the idealism suggested by Hoffmann coexists with a straightforward appeal to nature as a warrant for sensuality. On the one hand, von Braunthal's Don Juan declares, in words which would have gained the approval of Shadwell's Don John or da Ponte's Don Giovanni, that 'we are given life to enjoy and its only truth is – enjoyment!' (p. 81). But this same Don Juan is also described by the author in his introductory verses to the play as obsessed by a dream of perfection. As his devilish companion puts it, with a most *un*devilish appreciation of high aspirations, Juan tries to track down the ideal as conceived by his imagination (p. 23). Elsewhere this ideal is likened to a painting which no woman of flesh and blood can rival (p. 31). Such a view is clearly incompatible with the simple creed that pleasure is the object of life and its only truth.

Braun von Braunthal's play is no doubt inconsistent and muddled, but we can, with hindsight, see that it signals a move from the old to the new conception of Don Juan. Even if von Braunthal cannot make up his mind as to which type he is depicting, the old 'libertine punished' will from now on give way to an idealized and idealistic Don Juan. In Nikolaus Lenau's *Don Juan: dramatische Szenen*, written about 1844 and published posthumously in 1851, we find the first eloquent and clearly thought-out dramatic representation of the new Don Juan in German. Lenau came to the material in the first place through a German translation of *El Burlador*:

> The legend of Don Juan is great, greater than that of Faust, which in its original form is nothing special ... I too have the idea of making a version of Don Juan and I would show him from quite a new angle.[3]

Than Lenau should place Don Juan above Faust is surprising at first glance, but he makes it clear that he is talking not of the character or the issues, but of the legend, the dramatic or narrative form in which the story is transmitted and in which, so to speak, it issues its invitation to successive writers. From this point of view, we may indeed place Tirso's well-conceived and well-constructed play above the potent but crude sixteenth-century chapbook which is the source, direct or indirect, of virtually all later works which deal with the exploits of Dr Faust.

Lenau's *Don Juan* is a fragment consisting of isolated episodes dealing with various of Don Juan's loves and his often violent escapades and culminating in a very free variation on the traditional supper-scene. The chief debt is to Tirso (from whom, unusually, the name of Don Juan's servant is taken) and there are also motifs and incidents clearly borrowed from da Ponte.[4] But Lenau's conception of his hero's character just as clearly derives from Hoffmann:

> My Don Juan must not be a hot-blooded creature constantly chasing after women. There is a longing in him to find a woman who for him is the essence of womanhood. Because, reeling from one woman to the next, he does not find this, he is finally seized by disgust, and that is the devil that carries him off.[5]

That original plan was modified and, in the process, made more tragic by the fact that, in the poem, Don Juan *does* find his incarnation of feminine perfection in Donna Anna, but only after he has lost his innocence: 'And yet she is so lofty and of such heavenly purity that I – don't laugh! – could wish to regain my innocence' (p. 423).

By degrees, Don Juan becomes totally disillusioned, bereft of desire and hope: 'Steintot ist alles Wünschen, alles Hoffen' (p. 441). At the end, far from toasting wine and women or planning yet more dastardly exploits, he longs for death as the only escape from a paralysing sense of futility and boredom. And so he virtually commits suicide, throwing away his sword in a duel: 'My mortal enemy is delivered into my hands, but this too, like the whole of life, bores me' (p. 448). If the law of your nature compels you to live by the senses and the only woman who might have satisfied you more than fleetingly is encountered when you are already morally destroyed by your past behaviour, nothing is left.

Lenau's *Don Juan* is a companion piece to his *Faust* of 1836. Like Faust, Don Juan wants to encompass all experience within himself, even resenting the trick played on him by time – for some future beauties are as yet too young for him, while others were in their prime while he was too young for them (p. 403). That is, like Faust, he would like to pass beyond the limits of what is humanly possible. Where he is caught in the trap of his restless sensuality, Faust is caught in the trap of his speculative urge, finding no answers to his questions, but temperamentally unable to stop brooding. Both figures are coloured by the author's intensely melancholy nature, above all by his conviction that we enter life full of idealistic and energetic hopes which are gradually betrayed, so that we end in disillusionment (see his sonnet 'Eitel nichts'). It is the ruthless logic with which this philosophy of disappointment and ennui is superimposed on the traditional story of Don Juan which justifies Lenau's claim to originality, for all his obvious indebtedness to Hoffmann.

Lenau's *Don Juan* is mainly composed in rhymed pentameters (with occasional excursions into tetrameters), the verse showing great suppleness and variety to match Don Juan's mercurial temperament, as he moves from philosophical self-examination to passionate wooing, from fiery and often arrogant recklessness to bitter humour, resignation and, at the end, despair. (It should perhaps be mentioned that, although the work itself is short, its time-span covers several years, so that the gradual burning-out of Don Juan's powers and desires does not seem implausibly abrupt.)

The work is fragmentary, no doubt, in that Lenau sweeps us on from adventure to adventure with many rapid transitions and some things left only half-explained. Nevertheless, he achieves a perfectly satisfactory poetic and dramatic unity. This is partly because the hero's motivation and gradual psychological disintegration are so clearly conceived and charted, partly thanks to a group of related motifs and images which recur, with slight variations, at frequent intervals. Lenau's (or Don Juan's) favourite images are nearly all drawn from the world of nature. He sees the world as a continually self-renewing act of procreation, governed by (and hence, for him at least, justifying) the principle of change and inconstancy, so that God is blasphemously cast as a sort of cosmic and elemental Don Juan, insatiably embracing the world: 'Der Gott der Zeugung ists, der Herr der Welt,/Die er, nie satt, in seinen Armen hält' (p. 406). So it is only logical that, in his wooing, Don Juan constantly appeals to the world of nature, seeing a willing and life-affirming ardour as akin to a natural law (p. 414). Thus, when Maria complains of his waning love on the grounds that *she* is unaltered, he defends himself by claiming that change is a law of existence: 'Doch wechseln muß im Leben die Gestalt' (p. 426).

The images with which he explains and justifies his behaviour are restless, dynamic and often violent: he likens himself to a beast of prey and his moods to tempests, fire, rushing torrents and – most frequently and most significantly – to the boundless and eternally restless ocean. This last image runs like a *leitmotif* through the poem, suggesting both the ecstasies and the hazards of yielding to love:

Dem Meer der Liebe . . ./Vertrau dich kühn . . . (p. 418)

Sie haben . . ./Die hohe See der Wonne nie befahren. (p. 422)

. . . wenn ich getaucht/Hinunter in das Meer der Lust! (p. 424)

Even when he dreams the impossible dream of recapturing his lost innocence, Don Juan still draws his imagery from nature, managing to suggest that the whole of creation is to be transformed into one huge Purgatory for his regeneration – an ocean is needed to cleanse him and only the fiery crater of Vesuvius could purify his soul (p. 423). The hyperbole is not as out of place as it might at first appear, for Don Juan's idealistic yearning for Anna is in itself an impossible paradox by his own stated criteria: by remaining constant in his love for her, he would be bidding the world stand still, denying the law of natural flux, seeking a perfection which, as Hoffmann had long since pointed out, is not of this world.

In this work, Lenau gives Don Juan's traditional appeal to nature cosmic reverberations and keeps it constantly before our eyes through the language, and especially the images, which he puts into Don Juan's mouth. This doctrine of mutability is set off first against a hopeless dream of fidelity to Anna, then against the petrifaction of despair ('Steintot ist alles Wünschen . . .'). The first, if achieved, would have lifted Don Juan out of his human status as he understands it; the second destroys him altogether.

If many a Don Juan before Lenau had worshipped all that was 'natural' and had used this concept as a means of justifying his conduct, and if many another since Hoffmann had dreamed of surpassing the limits that nature places on human experience, it is only Lenau who manages to show these two attitudes so inexorably at odds within the one character and to demonstrate with such merciless logic that such a man is doomed, Stone Guest or no Stone Guest. As we shall see, the brooding power of this version was later to inspire Richard Strauss to compose his musical portrait of Don Juan.

The list of Don Juans influenced in various ways by Hoffmann's interpretation is long and continues well into this century. The titles that follow give a representative selection only:

| | |
|---|---|
| E.W. Ackermann, 1845 | Otto Anthes, 1909 |
| Albert Möser, 1866 | Thaddäus Rittner, 1909 |
| Alfred Friedmann, 1881 | H. Bethge, 1910 |
| Julius Hart, 1881 | R. Heymann, 1921 |
| O.C. Bernhardi, 1903 | E. Kratzmann, 1939 |
| R. von Gottschall, 1906 | Rudolf Hagelstange, 1954 |

Julius Hart's blank-verse tragedy *Don Juan Tenorio* may be taken as typical. The hero has long and vainly sought an ideal beloved: 'Seit zwanzig Jahren such' ich/Nach einer Liebe, die mich ganz erfüllt' (p. 9). He believes he has found her in Anna, but this happens too late to bring them happiness; he can only destroy her world and cause her madness and death.

Most Hoffmannesque interpretations of Don Juan's character do not merely temper his guilt or try to exculpate him; they turn him into a hero, often taking issue quite explicitly with the traditional hostile view and hence with orthodox morality; the world may call him a sinner, but the poetic mind sees his tragic situation. 'I am unhappy; others call it sinful', says Bernhardi's Don Juan (p. 121). This gulf separating the common view of Don Juan from the poetic one is the main theme of Albert Möser's sonnet, 'Don Juan', in which the author addresses his hero thus:

> You do not enjoy a good reputation on earth; the mob is all too ready to vent its anger upon you because, faithless, you often fled from those sweet bonds of love which you yourself tied. But believe this: the poet understood you; you were intoxicated by the ideal.

This poetic 'understanding' may positively glorify Don Juan, as when Rittner sees him as personifying or manifesting the Life Force itself. According to this view, if there is expenditure of spirit, energy, talent, charm and resourcefulness, that is sufficient; the object is immaterial ('es ist doch gleichgiltig, wofür der Geist ausgegeben wird', p. 7). Indeed, the Don Juan of Rittner's piece cannot himself explain or understand the motive force behind his actions ('Ich suche es eben mein Leben lang zu ergründen', ibid.). The play is like an act of homage to an unconquerable erotic force personified in, and exercised by, one man.

We have seen how Hoffmann turned da Ponte's rather conventional Donna Anna into a personification of the ideal. Most writers who accepted his view of Don Giovanni took over his Anna as well. She appears in many works, explicitly represented as an ideal of womanhood, although under various names and playing various roles. Braun von Braunthal's Rosa is one reincarnation of this Anna; there is another in Lenau's Donna Anna, who, as we have seen, seems to reproach Don Juan for his lost innocence. This obviously reflects Hoffmann's view that Giovanni and Anna were destined for each other but met too late. Lenau's Don Juan makes an important distinction between Anna and all the other women in his life: 'with this woman, for the first time, I experienced in love the feeling that my ardour would never be extinguished in her divine body' (p. 424). In Paul Heyse's play *Don Juans Ende* (1883), Anna is again represented as Don Juan's only real love, the only woman with whom he might have enjoyed more than a fleeting relationship ('das einzige Weib, von welchem mich das Schicksal früher trennte, als ich selbst ihrer überdrüssig wurde', p. 7). But Anna is dead and Juan has turned libertine to dull the memory of her.

Such sentiments may seem strange in view of the fact that this character had traditionally been represented as believing that the pleasure of love *necessarily* lay in change. But they seem to proceed as a natural consequence from Hoffmann's view of Anna. Gautier, taking the notion to its logical extreme, argues that, had he met her in time, Juan would have been a model husband to her: 'son rêve réalisé, don Juan eût fait le meilleur mari des Espagnes.'[6] The supposition underlying the theory of Hoffmann and those who followed him is, of course, that the Superman turns into a monster only out of frustrated idealism and that, under different circumstances, he might have been a paragon. The implausibility of this is (unwittingly) demonstrated by Alfred Friedmann and Carl Sternheim in their plays of 1881 and 1909 respectively, two works in which Don Juan veers between sentimental (or, in Sternheim's play, near-mystical) devotion when fired by ideal love and the most cynical bestiality on all other occasions. The proposition that Mr Hyde the philanderer and Dr Jekyll the noble lover could inhabit the same skin may be theoretically conceivable, but these two examples, in which something of the sort is worked out in dramatic terms, suggest that it would be very difficult to make such a transition convincing and acceptable in practice. When Hoffmann raised Anna to the status of predestined soul-mate to Don Giovanni, he implied an absolute distinction between her and all the women on Leporello's list. No such contrast is present in any of the older pieces and it is not, by any objective examination of the libretto, to be found in da Ponte. Hoffmann invented it and, in so doing, created a potential difficulty for those who were to follow his reading.

Often Anna is the agent of Don Juan's salvation. Hoffmann does not, of course, talk of this possibility, but he must have given a hint to many a later writer when he described Anna as a divine woman over whose purity of spirit the Devil had no power. Could not such a woman win back the once noble Don Giovanni? Later, the influence of Goethe's *Faust* was to play its part here too; the oversimplified notion that Faust was saved wholly or mainly through the intercession of Gretchen became widespread in nineteenth-century interpretations. If Faust, why not Don Juan? For examples of Don Juans saved through love, one could cite Precht's poem 'Don Juan'

(1853), Bernhardi, Lembach's drama *Don Juan* (1912) and Trenck's 'passion', *Don Juan – Ahasver* (1930). Lembach has a number of very obvious stylistic echoes of Goethe's *Faust. Der Tragödie zweiter Teil*, intended to establish a parallel between Don Juan and Faust in the manner of their salvation.

Perhaps the most unexpected variation on Hoffmann's Don Juan is to be found in Rudolf von Gottschall's poem 'Don Juans hohes Lied' (1906). This Don Juan knows that the ideal does not and cannot exist on earth and is yet compelled to pass from woman to woman, trying to 'piece it together' in an unceasing and, by definition, futile quest: 'ich suche die göttlichen Trümmer zusammen.' Musing on Don Juan's fate nearly a century before, Hoffmann had seen the Devil's hand at work: man in his fallen state can be tricked and corrupted in such a way that his potentially divine striving for the highest imaginable good becomes diverted into destructive channels (p. 83). And so Don Juan, a victim of diabolical wiles ('des Erbfeindes List'), embarks on his career of seduction. From this notion, two conflicting, although equally logical, developments could flow: you could portray Don Juan as disillusioned to a point where death is a welcome release (Lenau), or you could see the divine potential, even if temporarily misdirected, as deserving of salvation. By contrast, Gottschall's Don Juan continues along his path in full awareness of the curse that is laid upon him (that is, the obsessive need to seek a reincarnation of Aphrodite in mortal woman), yet seems to find enough fleeting pleasure in each encounter to keep him from utter despair. Other writers had certainly managed to extract hope from Hoffmann's doctrine, but this hope had centred on salvation and fulfilment in another world; Don Juan's earthly life had been one of destructive passion and frustration. Hoffmann had indeed argued that Don Juan's longing, in common with all human yearning for perfection, could be cured only in the hereafter, stating plainly that his hope of attaining his ideal on earth was a delusion (see above, p. 30). Gottschall 'rewrites' Hoffmann in a spirit of cautious optimism: at least some fragments of the Divine ('göttliche Trümmer') are discoverable among the imperfections of mortal existence.

Rilke wrote two poems on the Don Juan theme: 'Don Juans Kindheit' and 'Don Juans Auswahl' (1908, both in part 2 of the *Neue Gedichte*) and presents the seducer in a new light. The second of these poems is specially characteristic of Rilke, in that a familiar theme is dealt with from an unfamiliar perspective; the stress is on Don Juan's victims, if 'victims' is the right word, for an angel appears to Don Juan and announces that it is his destiny and duty to lead women through love to loneliness. There is no direct link with Hoffmann's Don Juan, but the degree of seriousness with which Don Juan's career is referred to the order of the universe would be unthinkable, had there not been a long tradition of presenting that character in a serious, idealized and romanticized way. Such hints of this as Rilke possessed were probably picked up from the French poets rather than from German dramatists and novelists, for Hoffmann's impact in France was as great, or almost as great, as in his native country.

## FRANCE

After talking of the tragic idealist that Hoffmann made of Don Juan, Bévotte goes on to say that, in most of the works which the legend of 'el Burlador' inspired in France in the nineteenth century, one finds more or less direct reminders of Hoffmann (1911, i, 252). The German author was much admired in France and the Don Juan tale was one of the most highly prized of his works, following a translation in the *Revue de Paris* in September 1829.[7]

Hoffmann's interpretation seems to have brought about a quite abrupt change of attitude, as may be seen from a comparison of two contrasting views, the one dating from 1828, the other from 1832. Here is Gérard de Nerval, in the Preface to the first edition of his translation of Goethe's *Faust*:

> if Faust and Manfred presented us with the type of human perfection, Don Juan is no more than an example of depravity. How greatly Faust surpasses the vulgar *amours* of Don Juan!

But in 1832, in the second canto of his oriental tale *Namouna*, Alfred de Musset discussed Don Juan in terms that strongly contrast with Nerval's and unambiguously show how Hoffmann's notion of a vain quest for an ideal woman is beginning to establish itself in France:

> Was there not one, nobler or fairer, among so many beauties, who, from far or near, had at least some elements of his vague

ideal within her? All resembled her, but it was never she. All resembled her, Don Juan, and you passed on!

(ii, 47)

This new Don Juan was quick to catch the French imagination. In *La Comédie de la Mort* of 1838, Gautier represents Don Juan as seeking a transcendental ideal of womanhood. Where Hoffmann had been content to describe Anna as the embodiment of purity and incorruptibility, Gautier puts forward a curious – some of his early readers might have felt, an impious – combination of the erotic and the sacred, for this Don Juan dreams of 'a woman, such as no sculptor has ever fashioned, a type combining Cleopatra and the Virgin'. Ever denied satisfaction, he has been condemned to remain cold while others burnt with love for him, 'froid au milieu du feu' (p. 39). That last phrase takes up a hint from Hoffmann, who had talked of Don Giovanni's conquests as being a pleasure no longer, but 'sinful scorn' ('frevelnder Hohn'). But where Hoffmann had contented himself with showing the springs of Don Giovanni's libertinism and its destructive consequences, Gautier suggests an alternative, 'Faustian' path. For his Don Juan ends by cursing love because it obstructs the path to knowledge, which is the true end of life: 'Do not listen to love, for it is a bad master. To love is to be ignorant; living is knowledge. Learn, learn . . .' (p. 40). Hoffmann's logic, according to which constant disappointment leads to the rage of disillusionment, is here taken to the point of paradox. The paradox is compounded by the fact that Gautier has just shown Faust taking stock of *his* past behaviour and bitterly regretting time wasted on learning and speculation. Each of these characters is in thrall to an ideal which the finite world cannot satisfy ('jene unendliche Sehnsucht' of Hoffmann's tale). This accords with the interpretation widely placed on both Faust and Don Juan in the late Romantic era, but with the curious twist that each character sees the futility of his own way of life but (mistakenly) promises himself fulfilment from the other's.

Gautier returned to Don Juan in his *Histoire de l'Art dramatique* of 1858–9: 'Don Juan represents aspiration towards the ideal. It is no vulgar debauchery which thrusts him on; he seeks the vision of his heart with the obstinacy of a titan who fears neither lightning nor thunder.'[8] The phrase 'vulgar debauchery' is tantamount to borrowing Nerval's terminology ('vulgar *amours*') in order to refute

Nerval's view, and the whole passage is closely similar to that in which Lenau rejects the old conception of the wicked philanderer in favour of the new, Romantic interpretation (see above, p. 48).

Gautier now develops a point already hinted at in *La Comédie de la Mort*: that Don Juan's quest is at bottom a religious one; he believes that the ideal within him vouches for the existence, somewhere, of a personification of the ideal and that this, in turn, proves the existence of a Creator (*Histoire*, iv, 36). A perfect piece of orthodox teleological reasoning is resorted to in order to explain and justify Don Juan's womanizing! Only the terms have changed: the ideal is no longer a combination of Cleopatra and the Virgin, as in *La Comédie de la Mort*, but a vague memory of Eve, so that Juan's search for her is an attempt to recapture pre-Adamite perfection and innocence: 'Don Juan, c'est Adam chassé du paradis et qui se souvient d'Eve, avant sa faute, – d'Eve, le type de la beauté et de la grâce' (iv, 37). It may be recalled that Gautier is one of those who believed that Don Juan was an ideal husband *manqué*. And, since Don Juan has spent his life questing after ideals of love and beauty, adds Gautier prophetically, later authors will doubtless change the conventional ending, for such idealism is noble and does not merit damnation (iv, 38).

Examples of Hoffmann's (or, as we should perhaps now say, Musset's and Gautier's) Don Juan are not hard to find in the French literature of the mid- and late nineteenth century. E. Jourdain's *Don Juan. Drame fantastique* (written in 1855, published 1857) seems to take the conception to its ultimate conclusion; this Don Juan stabs himself because convinced that his ideals are beyond his grasp, that he has nothing to live for:

> Happiness? I have never found anything but its shadow; all the fruits that I touched turned into ashes and filled my mouth with bitterness. All the women whom I loved betrayed my hopes. I believe in nothing, neither in God nor the Devil . . . Oh! if I had ever loved, if I had ever found a woman's heart which responded to mine, I would reason otherwise.'

(p. 82)

Had the author stopped here, his drama would have formed an exact French companion-piece to Lenau's dramatic poem. But Jourdain has a surprise in store for us (and his hero), for, now that Don Juan is mortally wounded by his own hand, it is revealed that a young 'manservant' of his is in fact a girl who had loved him hopelessly and had disguised herself as a youth in order to be near him. Thus, ironically, he stabs himself minutes before finding the love that he had sought in vain. With his dying breath, he confirms that he can indeed 'reason otherwise' and overcomes his nihilism: 'Cela ferait croire à Dieu!' (p. 86). Thus the denouement of Jourdain's play anticipates by a year or two the teleological argument which Gautier was to put forward in his *Histoire de l'Art dramatique*.

Villier de l'Isle Adam's poem 'Hermosa' (1859) is openly indebted to Musset's *Namouna*:

> Well, this feeling that torments us without respite, this accursed ideal, this unknown factor, this dream to which human beings succumb one after the other, this hope which some seek in science, some in faith, others in power: for my part, I have sought it in love.
>
> (p. 89)

But he meets his ideal woman too late, when he is burnt out and incapable of love: 'Trop tard! je ne peut plus aimer' (p. 94). Like Gautier's Don Juan, de l'Isle Adam's sees this inaccessible ideal in terms of a lost Paradise: 'J'ai soif d'un paradis dont je suis exilé' (ibid.).

Since there would be no point in giving a catalogue of all the plays, poems and scattered remarks which betray Hoffmann's influence in nineteenth-century France, I will confine myself to a few examples. Armand Hayem was the author both of a Don Juan play (*Don Juan d'Armana*) and of a treatise on the Don Juan type (*Le Don Juanisme*), both published in 1886, although both were written somewhat earlier. Let us begin with the treatise, in which Hayem attempts to define what he sees as a recurring psychological type.

There is a particular 'race' or class of men with sufficient common features and attitudes for them to be labelled 'Don Juan', Hayem argues. They are robust, young in spirit, imperturbable, strangers to remorse or scruple, curious and audacious, finding their pleasure in novelty rather than in the intensity of any individual experience. Their immorality is leavened – or at least made tolerable to some extent – by a nobility and grace of manner. Don Juanism is a philosophy of life, an art and a mania. But Don Juan is easily bored, especially by women who have 'too much heart'. And so he never experiences a gradually ripening relationship, being condemned instead to endless repetitions of what is basically one and the same experience. As a consequence, his pleasure comes more from planning a campaign and from his sense of triumph at successfully carrying it out than from the actual sexual consummation, let alone from any emotional involvement. Yet he is idealistic in his way, adds Hayem. For he has within himself an indistinct but delightful image of an ideal woman whom all resemble in some characteristic without ever living up to the complete ideal. (This is pure Musset: 'all resembled her, but it was never she.')

*Don Juan d'Armana* consists of four acts. The first three show Don Juan's stratagems with different women; the fourth depicts his death at the hands of one of his victims. But, having already discovered that his powers as a seducer are on the wane, he quits life without regret.

In the treatise, Hayem argues that Don Juan is predestined by nature to his particular way of life: 'Some men are monogamous, others bigamous or polygamous, and that by *nature*' (p. 95, Hayem's italics). In the play it is Don Juan himself who puts the idea, linking it to his right to a personal morality: 'Everyone's destiny is in his blood. Everyone's morality is in his temperament' (p. 50). This is, of course, a claim made by many a Don Juan long before Hoffmann, let alone Hayem. What about the more specifically nineteenth-century proposition, also contained in *Le Don Juanisme* and, as shown, almost certainly taken over from Musset, that Don Juan is an idealist? This figures in the play at the moment when Don Juan envisages the possibility of marriage, if and only if he should succeed in finding an ideal woman: 'I would marry if a woman of my stature existed. – Have I not sought this woman all my life without encountering her?' (pp. 120 f.).

Hayem has woven Hoffmann's (or Musset's) notion of Don Juan into a complete and coherent view of the 'Don Juan type' more successfully than most writers to date. But his Don Juan is no longer quite what Hoffmann and his immediate disciples had envisaged. Hoffmann's point about Don Juan's disillusionment has a metaphysical foundation: absolute ideals are *by definition* unrealizable in an imperfect universe. Gautier's evocation first of the Virgin, then of Eve before the Fall obviously carries similar implications. But Hayem is less interested in metaphysics than in the psychological motivation of Don Juan:

I am not tempted by facile pleasures. I thirst after the impossible
... I feel within me a vertiginous sense of immense horizons
which recede as I advance. Insatiable, I go forward towards
nothingness or infinite light!

(pp. 24 and 48)

I cannot believe that *néant* and *lumière infinie* are intended to have any metaphysical reverberations when put into the mouth of this Don Juan; he simply means absolute disillusionment or utter fulfilment – the psychological consequences of either finally conceding that the ideal woman will never be found or the bliss of possessing her at last. There is certainly an indirect indebtedness to Hoffmann's ideas, but they have been robbed of all transcendental implications; the definition of the ideal and the agonizing over whether it can ever be realized are solely Don Juan's problems and preoccupations and no longer concern the powers, if any, that govern the universe. Salvation and damnation are psychological states.

Jean Aicard's verse-drama, *Don Juan 89*, is like Hayem's play in that it takes up the notion of an idealistic Don Juan and divests it of any metaphysical or cosmic overtones. But Aicard's interest is not primarily psychological as Hayem's had been; he sets up an idealistic Don Juan in order to pour scorn on an age which, he felt, had betrayed all ideals. (Hence the title: *Don Juan in the year 1889*.) In his Preface, Aicard says: 'Never has the human soul had a more profound feeling of the *inadequacy*, the *misery*, the *unreality* of life ...' (pp. viii-ix: his italics). He represents the late nineteenth century as being materialistic, corrupt, philistine and pretentious, dominated by cranks, swindlers and quacks. The implication is that a fastidious idealist like Don Juan will have been repelled by his age in all its public and institutional aspects and will have concentrated his efforts on a quest for private fulfilment in and through love, only to be disappointed in this too. Tired of life, he deliberately provokes situations in which he might be killed.

One critic places this drama among a group of nineteenth-century Don Juan works whose authors represent the hero as pursuing a wrong and chimerical ideal and who try to propose worthier, less self-centred outlets for his energies. Aicard, he argues, holds up involvement in social and political affairs as the solution (Weinstein, pp. 136 f.). This is true up to a point, but does justice to neither the gloom nor the irony of the work. Near the end, Don Juan holds a conversation with his Double in the form of an image in the mirror. This other self certainly urges Don Juan to devote himself to the cause of political liberty. But Don Juan cannot do this; his aristocratic and fastidious nature is revolted by the prospect of contact with the sweaty crowd ('la foule sue et pue', p. 453). So the play does not demonstrate the positive notion that the idealist, having misdirected his efforts, should rechannel them into more altruistic outlets, but rather the more pessimistic idea that such a haughty character as Don Juan will never succeed in doing any such thing.

A proud and disdainful Don Juan was to have been at the centre of Baudelaire's projected play, *La Fin de Don Juan*, of which only a fragment exists. This dates from about 1853 and was published posthumously in 1887.[9] We cannot form any idea of what the plot was to have been, but the general conception of the hero is clear. Baudelaire envisaged a contrast between Don Juan, consumed with ennui and melancholy, and his (unnamed) servant, who was to have embodied all the philistine characteristics of the bourgeoisie (!) – 'a cold, reasonable and vulgar person, who constantly talks of virtue and thrift. This is the future bourgeoisie that is about to replace the declining nobility' (p. 79). A somewhat similar view of Don Juan's servant is also present in Gautier's *Histoire de l'Art dramatique*, where Leporello is seen as acting out the part of Sancho Panza to Giovanni's Don Quixote (!) and as standing for 'prosaic reason' as against his master's poetic enthusiasm (iv, 37). A sense of caste had figured in Don Juan's character from *El Burlador* onwards, of course, often accompanied by contempt for lesser mortals: timid conformists (Molière, Shadwell) or the peasantry (da Ponte). It is a great pity that we shall never know how Baudelaire would have worked out his modern variant on the idea, to show the contrast between Don Juan's lofty feeling of apartness and the 'stupid' contentment of the bourgeoisie.

A tantalizing hint at least is provided by his opening scene, which was to have recalled the episode 'Vor dem Tor' in Goethe's *Faust*, in which Faust and his assistant, Wagner, mix with the citizenry and peasants. But the similarity only highlights the contrasting attitudes. Faust had shown a genial and tolerant sense of affinity with the people, witnessing with gratification the bustle and turmoil of their festivities and made fully aware of his humanity in such a context: 'Hier bin ich Mensch, hier darf ich's sein' (l. 940). But

Baudelaire's Don Juan despises the common people, even as he envies them:

> He speaks of his deadly boredom . . . He admits that he sometimes envies the naïve happiness of inferior beings. These bourgeois, who walk past with their equally stupid and vulgar wives, have passions which bring them suffering and happiness.
>
> (p. 80)

The 'calm hero' of Baudelaire's 'Don Juan aux Enfers' (included in *Les Fleurs du Mal*) is just as proud and disdainful. Don Juan's feeling of superiority to the mob, with its undemanding and conventional pleasures, also finds expression in a sonnet first published in 1866 under the pseudonym 'Fulvio' and generally attributed to Verlaine.[10] At first vilified, then vindicated through an appeal to transcendental idealism, Don Juan is finally glorified by the 'decadent' writers of the nineteenth century, who need no excuse for him and make no apology for labelling as heroic those actions which, according to the standards of the bourgeoisie, are wicked. For these writers, Don Juan's sense of apartness was one more indication of his superiority. This distinction between the free and bold individual and the 'mob' would later receive philosophical support from Nietzsche (see below, chapter 8).

But while Baudelaire banished a proud and unrepentant Don Juan to Hell, other French writers, like so many of their German colleagues, saved him from damnation through the agency or influence of Donna Anna or a similar pure and devoted woman. What is the 'mystical woman' Anna other than a voice which speaks to the 'infidel' Don Juan and reconciles him with Heaven? asks Blaze de Bury.[11] In this version, Don Juan is brought to repentance by Anna's assurance that heavenly beings experience a love that is untroubled by the restlessness and insatiability of earthly emotions (pp. 52 f.). So Juan gladly quits the body, which had cheated him with false promises of pleasure and satisfaction. But, despite the author's pious intentions, most readers will probably feel that Baudelaire's Hell is a more fitting – even a more dignified – destination for Don Juan than Blaze de Bury's Heaven.

We have seen, then, how many different implications were found in Hoffmann's tale. Don Juan's supposed idealism could attract because of its straightforwardly romantic appeal, by its 'Faustian' overtones or by virtue of its psychological fascination; the idealistic rebel could be used as a stick with which to beat the prosaic Philistine or could even be set off against a whole civilization which was regarded as corrupt and materialistic. Some writers were drawn to the possibility of showing how a notorious philanderer could be pulled back from the brink of damnation through the perfect love which he had hitherto sought in vain. Although virtually all the works mentioned in this chapter can be seen as resulting in some way (direct or indirect) from the view popularized by Hoffmann, that author might well have been surprised, could he have known of some of the conclusions that would be drawn from his theories.

# 5

# Reactions Against the Romanticized Don Juan

The idealization of Don Juan was bound to provoke a reaction, for the works which view him from this perspective still either show him performing wicked deeds or take such deeds for granted as the shared foreknowledge of author and reader. So Juan continues to act like a blackguard, but is motivated in terms which encourage the reader to admire him. His death is no longer represented as punishment, but as tragic and often heroic. Sometimes it even heralds salvation. George Sand's novel *Lélia*, first published in 1833, contains one of the earliest and most energetic of the objections to this process of whitewashing. After a violent attack on Don Juan's unscrupulous behaviour, Sand adds a cosmic dimension:

> Insolent fool! Where did you get those insane rights to which you have devoted your life? When and where did God say to you: here is the earth; it is yours and you will be sovereign lord over all families; all the women that you desire are destined for your bed.

In the second (1839) edition of the novel, the impact of that passage is strengthened by a new paragraph which talks of that age of 'inexplicable fantasies', in which Don Juan has become almost a divinity.[1] The human suffering caused by Don Juan, not his supposed motivation, is Sand's point of departure in this spirited onslaught.

In several works from the mid-nineteenth century on, we find the author taking revenge on the romanticized Don Juan. A neat example is Gustave le Vavasseur's *Don Juan Barbon* of 1848, a witty one-act play in rhymed verse. This depicts Don Juan in his respectable old age, now finding his only pride and pleasure in his daughter,

Dolorès. But she is in love with Don Sanche, a young libertine who, to turn the knife in the wound, has based his techniques of cajolery and seduction on Don Juan's. When he comes to claim Dolorès, Don Juan refuses her to him. They fight and the younger man wins. A further twist is given by the revelation that Sanche is a descendant of that same Commander whom Don Juan had killed in a duel. The situation is even worse in Erica Grupe-Lörcher's novel, *Der wiedererstandene Don Juan* of 1928, for here a *young* Don Juan is worsted by a rival, surely the ultimate humiliation for this proud conqueror of women.

Such works (and examples could be multiplied) take satisfaction in showing the biter bit. They would no doubt have met with George Sand's approval, but they do not explore the matter of guilt and punishment very deeply; they are, in essence, modern and secularized variants on the older works which had shown the 'Libertine punished'. Henry Roujon and Ferdinand von Hornstein go further and show how Don Juan's own devices and stratagems bring retribution on him.

The hero of Roujon's ingenious little novel *Miremonde* (1895) is a young nobleman, Pons des Liguières, a Don Juan in embryo, who attracts Leporello's attention by his physical likeness to Don Juan at the same age. One day des Liguières is amazed to receive a summons to supper with Don Juan, whom he, like everyone else, had supposed dead, dragged off to Hell by the Stone Guest. But in fact Don Juan is living quietly with his ageing servant and his memories in his castle, Miremonde, in southern France.

The two men – the original Don Juan and his younger copy – meet, and the elder of the two tells his story: how, as a youth, he had been initiated into the arts of love by the ladies at court and had become a rake by the age of twenty. In his adventures, love played no part, only desire, vanity and the wish to triumph over rivals. It is this cynical youth, then, who was wounded in a duel and brought to the castle of one Dona Andréa, there to be cared for. As a result of this, he met Andréa's daughter, Elvira. Struck by her beauty, youth, innocence and charm, he set about her conquest. But, since she *was* innocent and pious, he had to marry her in order to possess her, intending from the outset to abandon her. This he did shortly after the wedding, leaving behind a note revealing his true identity (for he had wooed and won her under the assumed name of Miguel).

He travelled and adventured, hoping to forget her, but was soon forced to doubt his own guiding premiss: that the only way to escape boredom is constantly to pass on to new conquests. And so he returned. But, sensing desire and arrogance rather than love, Elvira was chilled and terrified; she submitted to him, but only reluctantly and passively. Much later, when she was on the point of death, she wrote to him, making clear that, had he returned to her as Miguel, she could have received him with love. So here we have a complete reversal of the expected, a situation in which Don Juan is rejected by a woman even as she submits to him.

Roujon has taken up the traditional idea of Don Juan's role-playing and made it central to his plot and to his conception of the two main characters. In previous versions, the 'trickster of Seville' had often enough impersonated a bridegroom or a husband under cover of darkness or had in some other way borrowed an identity for an hour or two in order to achieve a seduction. But here the impersonation is much more radical: he abandons his 'Don Juan' side entirely and woos Elvira under the mask of an invented suitor. But the ruse succeeds only too well; he cannot forget Elvira and take up his career as Don Juan afresh, but neither can she endure his re-transformation from the phantom-figure Miguel, whom she had loved, into Don Juan, Miguel's cynical creator. In this version, Don Juan is not so much punished as self-punishing, for he disqualifies himself from the only love that might have given him lasting happiness.

Ferdinand von Hornstein, in his 'fantastic drama' *Don Juans Höllenqualen* (1900), clearly sees Don Juan's guilt as residing in, or symbolized by, the insincere hyperbole of his declarations of love. And so Hans, the Don Juan of this piece, is punished by having all his false promises and avowals become literal truth: 'Wahrheit soll werden/Don Juans Lügen' (p. 89). He promises a woman 'all he has'; she takes it and carts it off in his absence. He promises to love another 'unto death' and finds her lifeless in her bed when he goes to her. And finally he precipitates his own death when he declares to yet another woman that she makes him 'sick to death' ('du machst mich todeskrank', p. 164). Again we may say that he is his own executioner.[2]

Since the turn of the century, there have been four notable dramas which reject the romantic conception of Don Juan. Two of these (by Edmond Rostand and Henry de Montherlant) are comprehensive but fundamentally negative attacks on what previous dramatists and critics had made of the character; the other two (by George Bernard Shaw and Max Frisch) are more positive, in that they suggest new ambitions and a new way of life for Don Juan.

Rostand's verse-play, *La dernière nuit de Don Juan* (1914), shows how Don Juan is robbed of his illusions in the course of a long debate with the Devil. Firstly, it is shown that this famous lover did not dominate women as he claims; he gave them no unforgettable rapture and not even the intense experience of suffering. It had more than once been suggested in the romantic interpretations that the pleasure of being briefly loved by Don Juan outweighed the pain of abandonment (see, for example, Lenau, p. 422). But in Rostand the Devil maintains that the great 'romantic' experience was no more than a game for the women.

There now follows a specific refutation of the Hoffmann line of interpretation. Don Juan claims that his philandering was at bottom an idealistic quest: 'I have sought! I was he who believed that a treasure lies buried, that a blue flower exists on the top of a mountain' (p. 110). The reference is to the blue flower which is the symbol of the unattainable in Novalis's ultra-Romantic novel *Heinrich von Ofterdingen*; thus the link between Don Juan's idealism and a similar strain of longing for the impossible within the tradition of German Romanticism is made yet stronger. The Devil quickly sees this: 'What it is to have passed through Germany!' Don Juan is not allowed this comfortable feeling of having been the Great Quester for long, however. A ghostly figure representing this so-called unattainable ideal comes to tell him that he could, in fact, have found it in any woman, had he been prepared to bring a little love to the task: 'que dans chacune d'elles/Tu m'aurais pu trouver avec un peu d'amour!' (p. 117). But perhaps, suggests the Devil maliciously, you did not *want* to find your ideal – and Don Juan has to concede that this is at least possible: had he found her, he would have died of boredom (pp. 121 f.).

So Don Juan's legend is evoked only to be comprehensively debunked. But Rostand has nothing to suggest as a more positive, alternative motivation for Don Juan who, in this version, is simply stripped of all the romantic finery in which, for a century, he had been made to look resplendent.

Henry de Montherlant's three-act play, *Don Juan* (1956), is another attempt to cut the romanticized Don Juan down to size;

for all the superficial differences, it is, in spirit, a companion-piece to Rostand's play. In his accompanying Notes, Montherlant tells us that he has reacted against 'the mass of literature which had tried to make of Don Juan a complex person: a demonic being . . . a "myth" . . . I have relieved my hero of everything which the nineteenth century had made of him. Don Juan, in my play, is a simple character' (p. 177).[3] The brunt of the author's attack is contained in a scene (Act 3 Scene 2) in which three 'thinkers', caricatured figures, pontificate on the hidden springs of Don Juan's actions. The first two see him as an idealist, the third interprets him in psychoanalytical terms. (As in many such attacks, these views are rejected without much attempt at reasoned refutation.) So what does Montherlant have to offer in place of these abandoned hypotheses?

The 'simple' reading which he promises us is that of a straightforward hedonist for whom the pursuit of woman has become an obsession and a necessity: 'Each time that I seduce a woman, it is as if it were the first time. and I need to do that every day: for me, it is daily bread' (p. 16). Secondly, Montherlant's Don Juan means what he says with utter sincerity at any given moment, but is capable of contradicting himself roundly at the next. This interpretation of his behaviour is, of course, a perfectly tenable one, although not as original as the author seems to think; Pushkin's Don Juan is not very different, for example (see below, p. 99). But Montherlant is in any case wrong if he thinks that his reading automatically invalidates the other views which he satirizes in his play. For instance, the idealistic Don Juan, as envisaged by the Romantics, must be sincere in his initial wooing of each woman (since he at first hopes that she will turn out to embody the ideal), but has at last to reject her and go on to make equally sincere avowals as soon as he encounters the next possible candidate for ideal womanhood. Furthermore, if our introduction to Don Juan is through the Mozart opera, as it is for many people, our impression of the hero's ardent sincerity at any given moment will probably be reinforced. Leporello's catalogue and his master's cynical confidence that it will be augmented by half a score of names in a single night ('Ah, la mia lista doman mattina d'una decina devi aumentar', p. 110) certainly give the impression of the calculating and ruthless libertine – but it is hardly possible to *sing* 'Là ci darem la mano' or 'Deh, vieni alla finestra' except in tones of absolute sincerity, even if everyone, including the singer, knows that the passion will not last or will be swiftly transferred to another object if and when the present desire is satisfied.

Rostand and Montherlant, in their attempts to refute what they see as misguided readings of Don Juan's character, edge away from drama proper in the direction of dramatized literary criticism; in Rostand's case, certainly, Don Juan is reduced to something like a walking and talking visual aid in the critical process. Shaw and Frisch, by contrast, present us with three-dimensional characters and manage, although in widely differing ways, to integrate their case against the idealized Don Juan more fully into the dramatic texture.

In the 'Epistle Dedicatory' which serves as a preface to *Man and Superman* (1901–3), Shaw takes stock of the legend and of the picture of Don Juan that has emerged from it, tracing how the original 'monkish' disapproval of Don Juan, as expressed in *El Burlador*, has yielded to an heroic interpretation which sees Don Juan as a defiant challenger of the gods and of the dominant moral order. It is clear that he sees this idealization as largely due to the power of Mozart's music. In this he resembles Hoffmann, although the conclusions that he goes on to draw are quite different from Hoffmann's. For Shaw, the legend and its main characters are out of date: the legend because of its reliance on supernatural elements and on a literal belief in Hell, the characters because it is now woman who has the upper hand in the battle between the sexes.[4] So Shaw has written his modern variation on the story which negates both the original didactic message *and* the romantic-heroic reading. Into his play he has inserted what he calls a 'totally extraneous' dream-sequence set in Hell. But he is not doing himself justice; there are all manner of ingenious thematic links and cross-references which make clear how the play proper and the 'extraneous' act belong together conceptually and complement each other.

As is well known, the 'perfectly modern three-act play' referred to in the Epistle Dedicatory ironically updates the characters from Mozart/da Ponte, turning Anna and Don Giovanni into Ann and John Tanner, Octavio into the watery, helplessly adoring Octavius and Leporello into Enry Straker. In accordance with Shaw's drastic reversal of the traditional roles of the sexes, Ann has now become the pursuer, Tanner the quarry. And he knows this perfectly well: 'which of us will she eat?' Her purpose is Nature's purpose, her vitality a blind urge in the service of procreation: 'Sexually, Woman is Nature's contrivance for perpetuating its highest achievement. Sexually, Man is Woman's contrivance for fulfilling Nature's behest in the most economical way.'[5] Hence Tanner's exclamation when he finds himself unable to escape Ann: 'The Life Force! I am lost.'

In the Hell scene, that long and fascinating discussion-piece, Don Juan is made the spokesman for this new interpretation of his own legend. First, he demolishes the old idealistic notion of woman which had, since Hoffmann, so often been seen as the motive force behind his actions. For this worship cannot survive the realization that woman is a predator: 'this was not what I had bargained for. It may have been very proper and very natural; but it was not music, painting, poetry, and joy incarnated in a beautiful woman' (p. 666). And so the prey tried to escape. But the Life Force had other ideas, seizing him and throwing him into her arms 'as a sailor throws a scrap of fish into the mouth of a sea-bird' (p. 668). That last image is surely Woman's (or the Life Force's) revenge on more than one Don Juan who had equated his sexual gratification with the pleasures of eating and drinking. The motif is present in da Ponte, where Don Giovanni asserts that women are more necessary to him than bread, and is made much of by Grabbe, whose Don Juan describes kissing as the one dish of which he never tires and uses culinary imagery to justify sensuality as his way of praising God; the best praise for the cook is when one enjoys his dishes.[6]

But Shaw's Don Juan goes still further: he is disillusioned with all forms of pleasure and self-indulgence, everything that might divert him from his evolutionary path. For him, life is a constant urge towards higher things, a ceaseless process of experimenting and discarding. The ultimate object of the Life Force is to supersede all primitive forms of life and to work towards the highest good, which is intellect operating at its highest potential and concentration:

> I tell you that as long as I can conceive something better than myself I cannot be easy unless I am striving to bring it into existence or clearing the way for it. That is the law of my life. That is the working within me of Life's incessant aspiration to higher organization, wider, deeper, intenser self-consciousness, and clearer self-understanding. It was the supremacy of this purpose that reduced love for me to the mere pleasure of the moment,

art for me to the mere schooling of my faculties, religion for me to a mere excuse for laziness, since it had set up a God who looked at the world and saw it was good, against the instinct in me that looked through my eyes at the world and saw that it could be improved.

(pp. 679 f.)

This is the point at which Tanner and Ann come together under a sort of impersonal necessity. Each is serving the Life Force: Ann through her 'blind fury' of procreative zeal, Tanner through his intellectual aspirations as reshaper of society. His 'Revolutionist's Handbook' envisages, in clear indebtedness to Nietzschean ideas, a process of selective breeding by which a Superman will ultimately be produced out of a combination of brains and vitality. The creation of such a Superman is a social and political necessity, at whatever cost to existing institutions.

Max Frisch's comedy *Don Juan oder die Liebe zur Geometrie* (1952) is nearer in conception to Shaw than to Rostand or Montherlant, less concerned with debunking Don Juan than with showing a degree of self-awareness in him that forces him to revolt against his own Don Juanism – which anyway is more externally imposed than self-willed. The title gives us a clue: in a bold paradox, Frisch offers us a Don Juan who is irresistible to women because he prizes something more than women:

> His reputation as a seducer . . . is a misunderstanding on the part of the ladies. Don Juan is an intellectual . . . What makes him irresistible is entirely his spirituality . . . which is an affront, in that it recognizes goals that have nothing to do with woman.
> ('Nachträgliches zu Don Juan')

He is interested in and drawn to regions where truth is clear and demonstrable, less messy and turbulent than the realm of human emotions. Indeed, says Frisch, a modern Don Juan would probably be more interested in atomic physics than in womanizing. Hence Frisch shows his hero as having been pitchforked into libertinism and more or less forced to continue along that path through the power of his reputation; once he is widely held to be irresistible, he *is* irresistible. But he soon finds that he had been bamboozled by romantic expectations into believing in a love which is inseparably bound up with one particular partner, whereas he is at the mercy of a blind sexual urge that can drive him to love (or desire) more or less any woman. Hence he finds himself condemned to boredom: 'Hinter jedem Don Juan steht die Langeweile' (p. 319).

To escape into a more permanently stimulating world of intellectual satisfaction, Don Juan fakes his own death and descent into Hell, retreating into a secret and cosy imprisonment as husband of the Herzogin von Ronda. It is a witty touch that this Don Juan, who refuses to play the role that society tries to impose on him, must stage-manage a little farce of his own devising in order to *escape* from role-playing. It is also wholly fitting that a play which ironically turns the notion of Don Juan as passionate womanizer on its head should end with a travesty of the expected melodramatic climax. Although Don Juan chafes under the trivial annoyances and restrictions of his new life, he finds them a small price to pay for the freedom to pursue his studies. Irony is piled on irony: we have a libertine who prefers geometry to women, a fearsome and 'well-deserved' death which is a put-up job, marriage to a countess who was once a prostitute and who had found him attractive precisely because he had preferred chess to her allures – and finally a Don Juan who complains at the very fact that there are two sexes, talking of his

> resentment at Creation which has split us up into man and woman . . . What a monstrosity that the human being alone isn't a whole! And the greater his longing to be a whole, the more accursed he is, mortally exposed to the opposite sex.
>
> (p. 81)

So the Romantic admiration of Don Juan created its own Resistance Movement. It should be recalled that this romanticization had nearly always involved glossing over consequences in favour of motives. Each woman, says Musset, bore some resemblance to the ideal, but none satisfied it and so Don Juan passed by. The reader is clearly expected to accompany him and not to linger over the fate of the forsaken woman, whose only meaning for us, as for Don Juan, is that she is human and therefore imperfect. To savour the full extent of the change in perspective brought about by Hoffmann, we should perhaps return briefly to the older treatments. When Don Juan appealed to 'nature' as giving him an absolute right to self-determination, we may well have paused to wonder what had happened to the rights of his victims as fellow human beings; where he made new conquests to be duly recorded in his servant's catalogue, or likened his sexual needs to hunger or thirst, it may have struck us that women were being reduced to arithmetical units or comestibles in the process. By contrast, the later, idealized interpretation did not invite – or positively hindered – such reflections; our whole attention was deliberately directed towards Don Juan's monomanic pilgrimage.

Some writers could not accept this perspective, regarding it as over-indulgent towards Don Juan and callous towards his victims. The retribution which they visited upon him and upon those writers, whether dramatists or critics, who encouraged such views (for literature and critical observations on the literary type became necessarily intertwined) varied in nature and severity. Sometimes Don Juan is simply punished or humiliated for his effrontery and promiscuity. More subtly, he may be shown as his own executioner (as in Roujon and Hornstein). In Rostand and Montherlant, a Don Juan play is created in order to criticize the view of the hero suggested by previous Don Juan plays and their commentators. Rostand's work has the effect of turning what its author thought of as an absurdly romanticized Don Juan into a rather abject and pitiable creature. But the most interesting approach is that of Shaw and Frisch, each of whom in his different way dismantles the traditional notion of Don Juan and, simultaneously, the newer, romanticized conception, in order to present him as no longer either the despoiler or the idealizer of woman, but as her victim and, moreover, a victim who seeks and ultimately finds a more appropriate outlet for his energies. For few readers or playgoers can have at some time escaped the feeling that Don Juan possessed talents that could and should be employed less unworthily. Don Juan, says Coleridge, incorporates 'rank, fortune, wit, talent, acquired knowledge, and liberal accomplishments, with beauty of person, vigorous health, and constitutional hardihood – all these advantages elevated by the habits and sympathies of noble birth and national character' (*Biographia Literaria*, chapter 23).

There is another way in which Don Juan's quest can turn out to be self-defeating. We have heard Rostand's Don Juan admit that to have found his ideal would have sentenced him to boredom. Shaw presumably wished to convey something similar by depicting Donna A[n]na as a self-important and vainly conventional old woman in the Hell scene of *Man and Superman*. But it was Antony

Borrow, in his *Don Juan* of 1963, who made this idea central to his treatment. Here, Don Gonzalo, Ana's father, warns the young and passionately idealistic Don Juan of the dangers of achieving the ideal:

> I was a poet who had the misfortune to win my one true beloved, and to acquire the life-long companionship of the most divinely beautiful and adorable girl in the world; and I assure you that it was a very sobering experience.
>
> (Act 1 Scene 1)

The truth of this apparently cynical statement is brought home to Don Juan when he sees his 'divinely beautiful and adorable' Ana some ten years after the period of his first infatuation:

> *Juan* When I saw the body that the boy had thought so holy, I could not restrain myself.
> *Luis* Really?
> *Juan* I burst out laughing, put on my hat, and came home.
>
> (Act 2 Scene 1)

Yet – and this is the other horn of the dilemma – some sort of idealistic obsession is necessary if man is not to stagnate and degenerate: 'For we are real only to the extent that we are obsessed. A man without enthusiasm might as well lie down in his grave at once, for all the use he will be to himself' (Act 2 Scene 2). The trap is set: a tepid half-life or the pursuit of rich experience at the seemingly inevitable cost of disillusionment. A Catch–22 as neat and as inescapable as any devised by Joseph Heller, unless you turn Don Juan into an Evolutionist and social reformer (as Shaw did) or into a mathematician (Frisch) – that is, unless you devise an outlet for his enthusiasm which permanently involves him in exacting and self-renewing activity. Some might say that Don Juan thereby ceases to be Don Juan, but it is implicit in both Shaw and Frisch that the Don Juan stage of his career was a betrayal of his true nature. This is a drastic reversal of the long tradition whereby Don Juan tried to excuse himself by claiming that it was his nature that compelled him to pursue women so obsessively. That is to say: two of the most penetrating writers to treat Don Juan in this century have found it necessary to dismantle both the Romantic conception of him and the older notion that he was a simple hedonist, contented to remain a slave to 'natural' appetites.

# 6
## Links with Faust

The name of Faust has cropped up several times in this discussion; indeed, it would not have been possible to talk of Hoffmann's influence without making such references. But there is a great deal more to the story than this. Many a writer, whose conception of Don Juan was arrived at independently of Hoffmann or who was only marginally influenced by his views, perceived links between Don Juan and Faust. These are expressed in reviews, theoretical essays and casual jottings as well as being present, implicitly or explicitly, in plays, poems and novels devoted to Don Juan. The relationship may be stated in general terms of psychological affinity or contrast, or may involve unmistakable variations on specific motifs and episodes from the parallel tradition, most often drawn from Goethe's *Faust*.

Yet the linking may at first sight seem strange. We tend to picture Faust sitting gloomily in his study, surrounded by emblems of mortality and futile intellectual endeavour, bewailing his inability to rise above the human condition and, more specifically, to satisfy his curiosity for a range and intensity of knowledge and experience beyond what is vouchsafed to mortals. Unable to fulfil himself by legitimate means, he allies himself to the Devil, who undertakes to serve him on earth for a fixed period (usually twenty-four years) in return for Faust's soul when that period expires. Superficially, this brooding intellectual has little in common with the swashbuckling Don Juan. Two things helped to bring these contrasting figures closer. After the pact, one of the first things Faust does is to discover sensual pleasures and make up for lost time in the pursuit of women. This transition is very marked in Goethe's *Faust*, where no sooner is the hero rejuvenated in the Witches' Kitchen, than he turns from scholar into gallant and is presently seen accosting, pursuing, seducing and abandoning Gretchen. It is not wholly surprising that, to many, he seemed like a second Don Juan. At the same time, once Don Juan was no longer seen as a simple libertine, but as a quester after an ideal of feminine perfection, he was felt by many to resemble Faust: did not each try to achieve something not normally granted to man? Thus they could be seen as brothers under the skin for all their apparent differences. With the appearance of the Second Part of Goethe's *Faust* in 1832, a new factor entered: it became clear that one of the things contributing to the hero's salvation was the love and devotion of a woman who had originally fallen victim to his desires. For those who viewed Donna Anna as a quasi-divine figure and a potential agent of Don Juan's salvation, this suggested a further similarity. In more general terms, Faust and Don Juan came to personify the intellectual and the sensual sides of man taken to extremes of obsessive insatiability.

To link the two figures soon became a cliché of literary criticism. We have heard Franz Horn's version, written some years before Hoffmann's revolutionary account of *Don Giovanni*; here is a representative selection of comments, reaching from four years after the publication of Goethe's completed *Faust* up to this century:

> In Faust, the loneliness of the urge for knowledge is set off against the desire for pleasure in Don Juan. (Carl Rosenkranz, *Zur Geschichte der deutschen Literatur*, Königsberg, 1836, p. 148)

> Faust and Don Juan are the Middle Age's Titans and giants. (Kierkegaard, *Either/Or*, Part 1, 1843)

> Don Juan and Faust are not two different people at all, for every Don Juan ends up as Faust and every Faust as Don Juan. (Hebbel, Diary entry no. 5981, 1862)

> Don Juan is the Faust of music, a theme that challenges the limits of humanity, of finite existence. (D.F. Strauss, *Der alte und der neue Glaube*, Leipzig, 1872, p. 349)

> In a sense, every man is made up out of Faust and Don Juan. (F. Helbig, 'Die Don-Juan-Sage', in *Westermann's Jahrbuch*, xli, Brunswick, 1876–7, p. 650)

> In their awe-inspiring mystery, the two legends match each other; as for the original impulse that gave rise to them, they are

counterparts or opposites. (Karl Engel, *Die Don Juan-Sage auf der Bühne*, Dresden and Leipzig, 1887, p. 9)

We are here confronted with one of the most profound Christian themes, which, as in the case of Faust, is pervaded by a transcendental ethical element as its main constituent. (C. Adelmann, *Donna Elvira . . . als Kunstideal*, Munich, 1888, p. 8)

Mozart's Don Giovanni is the Faust of the senses; Goethe's Faust is the Don Juan of the spirit. (E. Lert, *Mozart auf dem Theater*, Berlin, 1921, p. 339)

E. Hirsch throws in the Wandering Jew for good measure: 'All three legends depict the unrest, the failure to find peace, the insatiability of the human heart which cannot satisfy itself with any earthly, heavenly or spiritual delight.'[1] And Max Frisch simultaneously associates Don Juan with Faust and distances him from Casanova.

This may strike us as singular at first glance, for there seem to be links between the notorious womanizer in real life and the notorious womanizer in fiction. Paul Nettl, a biographer of Casanova, recalling that da Ponte and Casanova knew each other, even toys with the possibility that the Don Giovanni of the opera might have been created in Casanova's image.[2] But any similarities are far outweighed by the differences. First and foremost, the notion that womanizing is a full-time job and a way of life is lacking in Casanova, who was certainly a scandalous libertine, if even half of what he tells us is true, but much else besides: traveller, writer, preacher, diplomat, spy, director of state lotteries, librarian . . . There may be superficial resemblances between some of his escapades and those traditionally associated with Don Juan, but he did not pursue women with Don Juan's utter single-mindedness. Nor, if the *Memoirs* – that strange mixture of gossip column, self-glorifying autobiography and picaresque novel – are to be believed, did he invariably tire of a woman as soon as he had possessed her; he seems to have been perfectly capable of a more lasting attachment at times. O.A.H. Schmitz makes two further distinctions in his treatise *Casanova und andere Gestalten* of 1905. One is a question of temperament: Schmitz sees Don Juan as a fundamentally sombre character, quite different from the gregarious and cheerful Casanova (p. 12). Secondly, Casanova lacks the 'sporting' attitude towards sexual conquest, which leads Don Juan to court danger and results in his deriving as much pleasure from the campaign as from the sexual experience itself. (See Schmitz, pp. 22–5: more on this in chapter 8, below).

To return to the original point: inasmuch as such disparate statements about the legends and characters of Don Juan and Faust have any common ground, they convey the sense that the two stories add to the corpus of Christian 'mythology', in that each of these two figures is trying in his own way to topple barriers erected by Christian law and morality. There are sufficient hints that, in Germany at least, the one character had come to be represented by the hero of Goethe's dramatic poem, the other by the Don Giovanni of Mozart's opera as interpreted by the Romantics. Behind all these pronouncements, there is a conviction that the opposites embodied in Faust and Don Juan are only apparent, that in a sense they merge, even if different writers define the merger differently. There were oddly few voices raised against this virtual fusion of the two figures, although most modern students of the subject would see at least as many differences as similarities. But Liszt queries Grabbe's wisdom in putting Faust and Don Juan together in a single play: 'Grabbe has also paid poetic attention to this good-for-nothing [Don Juan] and associated him with Faust, which might well dumbfound his Excellency von Goethe' (letter to Marie Lipsius, 10 June 1880).

Grabbe had indeed, in his *Don Juan und Faust* of 1829, brought the two characters together, presenting them as questers for an unattainable, even indefinable goal, however much their paths might diverge. If this theme were developed consistently and logically, there would be little to dumbfound Liszt, Goethe or anyone else; unfortunately, Grabbe's Don Juan is also made to justify his sexual conduct quite matter-of-factly in terms of natural appetites, as Shadwell's Don John and da Ponte's Don Giovanni had done. Hence he can mock Faust's pursuit of vain superhuman ideals:

*Don Juan*   Why superhuman when you must remain a human being?
*Faust*   What is the point of being human if you do not strive for the superhuman?

(Act 3 Scene 3)

This exchange ill accords with Don Juan's praise of ceaseless striving earlier in the play: 'Away with the goal – do not name it to me, even if I do strive for it . . . Happy the man who strives for ever;

yes, hail to him who could hunger for ever!' (Act 1 Scene 1). To present Don Juan as a quester brings him near to Faust; to depict him as perfectly happy with the human condition distances him again. The reference to eternal hunger is not much more than verbal sleight of hand, confusing hunger for the unattainable with the simpler appetites which Don Juan evokes when he declares, in that same scene, that the only food that one can never have enough of is kisses.

It is as if Grabbe had been unable to decide whether his Don Juan was to be motivated in the same way as da Ponte's Don Giovanni or re-interpreted according to Hoffmann. An opportunity is squandered in this interesting but muddled work. Eugène Robin's dramatic poem *Livia* (1836) achieves a clearer distinction between a Don Juan who lives unproblematically for each present experience and a Faust tormented by existentialist riddles. The contrast is caught up neatly as the two characters muse on the limits of the knowledge possible for humans:

*Faust*   What makes me suffer is that, knowing, I am ignorant . . .
*Don Juan*   Where am I going? How will this end? I do not know. And, after all, what does it matter?

(pp. 21 and 35)

The comparison of Grabbe with Robin seems to suggest that, whatever might be said on a theoretical level about the essential affinity between Faust and Don Juan, a creative writer probably has more chance of success if he presents the two figures in a way that dramatically underlines their differences. Works which place these characters side by side, whether to compare them or to distinguish sharply between them,[3] would be no more than curiosities, were it not for the fact that they illustrate in almost schematic form the close links which had grown up in people's minds.

At much the same time, it came to be felt that Don Juan, if he was indeed a sort of 'second Faust', might be shown as having a formal link with the Devil. In older works, he had certainly been *described* as a devil often enough. The idea occurs in the first of all Don Juan plays, where Catalinón, in an aside, laments that Aminta should have fallen into the Devil's clutches ('Desdichado tú, que has dado/en manos de Lucifer!', ii, 728 f.). This may be intended to cast Don Juan as the Devil, or to show him as Devil's agent or accomplice, but in any case the identification of Don Juanism with diabolical power or possession is established. 'C'est un Diable incarné', says Dorimon's Briguelle of his master (Act 2 Scene 4) and Sganarelle too includes this metaphor in the long list of derogatory terms which he applies to Dom Juan (Molière, Act 1 Scene 2). But such usage is no more than the convenient application of a hackneyed trope. With the growing tendency to link Don Juan with Faust, this developed into the more concrete notion of a pact with the Devil, similar in general terms and conditions to Faust's, but altered to fit Don Juan's particular desires. Faust, it will be remembered, is served in a variety of ways: the Devil answers his questions, provides him with wine, women and song (the old chapbooks use phrases like 'swinish and epicurean life') and puts magical powers at his disposal, usually so that he may avenge himself on his enemies or impress dukes and emperors. To adapt this agreement to Don Juan's needs, all that is necessary is to concentrate the Devil's services on procuring women and providing means of escape when danger threatens. The basic agreement (eternal soul as payment for temporal services) is common to both models.

The first example known to me occurs in C.A. Vulpius's novel *Don Juan der Wüstling* (1805). This work shows how the old conception of a thoroughly wicked Don Juan survives until shortly before Hoffmann made his contribution to the discussion. Vulpius's Don Juan is driven on by lechery and vanity, defending his inconstancy on the grounds that change is the law of nature (p. 179). He achieves his ends by all manner of ingenious and daring means: straightforward wooing, bribes, various wiles and fictions. In view of this, it is surprising to discover that a sinister and mysterious character who is his constant companion is, in fact, the Devil, with whom he had entered on a pact.

At the end of the novel, the Devil claims his prey:

'Here is the pact. I have fulfilled what I promised you. You lived for your pleasures as you desired. Women were yours; you never lacked money. Now you are mine. The time has run out.'
'The time has *not* run out,' cried Juan. 'I still have three days.'
'You haven't!'
'I have!'
'You haven't. You have forgotten to count the Leap Years.'
(p. 214)

The point of this exchange is that Don Juan had planned to cheat the Devil by repenting on the last day of his allotted time; a similar motif occurs in one of the puppet-plays of Dr Faust. In fact, the Faust tradition, like German Devil-lore in general, often demonstrates that an agreement entered on with the Devil may turn out to contain a hidden catch, usually turning on the exact interpretation of conditions regarding time and place. Here the catch – that the extra day contained in a Leap Year is not to be accounted a bonus – is made to reinforce the didactic point that to put off repentance until the eleventh hour is sinful folly; a motif from the Faust tradition has been brought in to strengthen a moral already present in *El Burlador*. It is this witty piece of borrowing that makes *Don Juan der Wüstling* something more than a trivial and sensationalist pot-boiler.

However, the situation in Vulpius's novel is fundamentally unsatisfactory. Although the Devil provides Don Juan with the necessary wealth to pursue his destructive career and rescues him from a tight corner or two, Don Juan achieves his conquests for the most part by natural means. The chief justification of the pact is of course to underline his villainy and to show the catastrophic results of his reckless procrastination, but the reader must nevertheless wonder why such a master of his disreputable trade needed the help of the Devil at all. Another author who fell into the same trap was Braunthal, whose Don Juan was likewise an expert seducer long before he took up with the Devil. Quite apart from their moral evaluation of Don Juan, these two authors arguably diminish his stature through their borrowings from the Faust tradition. For however we judge Don Juan, we certainly picture him as relying on his own contrivances and using (or abusing) his own gifts. The implied link with Faust is in these cases inappropriate, for Faust allies himself to the Devil to achieve something which is literally inaccessible to unaided human endeavour.

Another way in which Don Juan authors borrowed from the parallel tradition involved the figure of Gretchen, as created by Goethe. To understand how and why this came about, it is necessary to recall the early publishing history of Goethe's *Faust*. In the 'Fragment' of 1790 and *Faust. Der Tragödie erster Teil* of 1808, Faust's pursuit and seduction of Gretchen occupy a central place (although only the 1808 version completes the story by showing Gretchen ruined, shamed and half-mad as she lies in chains in her prison cell, awaiting execution). These early published versions inevitably led Goethe's readers to exaggerate the importance which Faust's libertinage was to assume in the general plan of the work. Not until a quarter of a century had passed would the publication of the Second Part permit a more balanced view. In addition, of course, the intense beauty and pathos of the 'Gretchen-tragedy' captured the imagination of Goethe's public much as Ophelia and Juliet have won a place in English hearts.

Some authors of Don Juan works obviously shared the impression that love (or lust, or gallantry) occupied a central place in Faust's career, and this enabled them to see Faust's pursuit of Gretchen as similar to the episodes in Don Juan plays and operas in which the philanderer seduced a girl from a humbler social class. This, in turn, encouraged a type of plagiarism, in which Don Juan is shown playing Faust's part *vis-à-vis* a young and naïve girl very obviously based on Gretchen. She has, as it were, been imported out of Goethe's play and inserted into Leporello's catalogue. That may make it sound like a very artificial process, whereby literature is spun out of literature, but this is not unfair, given the brazen poaching which was sometimes involved. I will take three examples, beginning with two cases of uninspired borrowing and passing on to a work in which the parallels can be seen to have important moral and psychological implications.

In Mallefille's *Memoiren Don Juans* (1847), Camilla is loved by Don Juan but abandoned when she becomes pregnant. The following exchange will show how close Mallefille is to his model:

> 'You see, there . . . there lies my child in its little grave – yes, it is dead – it was hardly born and I was hardly able to kiss it – and already it is dead! Sir, did I tell you that my child is dead?'
> 'Yes,' murmured Don Juan.
> 'Do not believe it! My child is alive. You hear, it is crying for its mother! I will lie down to rest and dream of him. He was a fine man. But he left me because I was carrying his child. You see, the child cannot be dead, for I must take it to its father.'
> (viii, 72 f.)

Anyone who compares that passage, in which the mad Camilla confronts her one-time lover, with the closing scene of Goethe's *Faust*, Part 1, will see the indebtedness at a glance. Mallefille's justification would no doubt be that he had already established a psychological affinity between Don Juan and Faust. Don Juan is 'inquisitive like Faust; he loves the marvellous, has a passion for the unknown and a thirst for the infinite' (i, 96). While still a boy, he climbs a high mountain and, when asked what he felt on reaching the summit, replies in truly Faustian terms: 'regret that I couldn't climb still higher and see more' (ii, 56). Unfortunately, these Faustian traits are buried under a mass of far-fetched picaresque episodes in the eleven volumes of this sprawling work, so that a mere act of plagiarism cannot save the situation.

W. von Königsmark is another who builds into his Don Juan novel (*Ein neuer Don Juan*, 1869–71) an episode modelled on Goethe's *Faust*. There is a piece of deliberate signposting by the author: when Oskar von Wildenberg, the Don Juan of this work, is attracted to a beautiful young flower-girl, Margarethe, he exclaims, 'Truly, just like Faust's Gretchen!' The justification for this almost over-explicit cross-reference is that von Königsmark is concerned to represent Don Juan (or von Wildenberg) as an uncompromising individualist, a man with an unshakable determination to be true to himself. Hence his story, like Faust's, demonstrates modern man's claim to self-determination. But to make such a comparison meaningful, it would be necessary either to distinguish between self-determination in the intellectual and sensual spheres or to show some true inner affinity between the two figures. Merely to hint at a similarity between Faust's courting of Gretchen and Don Juan's pursuit of a Zerlina type ensures that the link remains superficial. Moreover, any systematic attempt to motivate Don Juan soon gives way to a series of satirical attacks on contemporary urban life. The novel, with its subtitle *Ein Sittengemälde aus der Neuzeit*, is as much a picture of the manners and morals of the day as a contribution to an understanding of Don Juan; it is a German companion-piece to Aicard's *Don Juan 89*.

Sigismund Wiese, in his tragedy *Don Juan* of 1840, again makes open reference to Goethe's *Faust*, as if to force members of the audience to make the connection. (It should be recalled that Goethe's masterpiece remained one of the two or three best known and most discussed works of German literature throughout the nineteenth century, so that undisguised borrowings would not be missed by any reasonably educated person.) Here too, as in the previous examples discussed, we find virtual paraphrases of passages of dialogue between Goethe's Faust and Gretchen, culminating in a mad scene as in Mallefille. But here there is a much clearer conception of Don Juan as a Faustian idealist, one who strays to the very limits of human possibilities ('an der Menschheit Grenzen schweifen', p. 194). In fact, Wiese's Don Juan goes yet further: like a second Faust, he demands to experience utter perfection and – again like a second Faust – maintains that such a consummation, although denied to other mortals, is his right ('Berechtigt heisch' ich, was verweigert wird', p. 12). It is no coincidence that, in this same conversation, he is described by his companion as a 'superman' (*Übermensch*); the same term is applied, albeit scornfully, to Goethe's Faust by the Earth Spirit (l. 490).

Faust's ambitions have usually involved a desire to know or experience everything or to set the world to rights, to play God. In Wiese's play, Don Juan's attempt to be a superman hinges on the fact that unerring pursuit of his desires logically demands that he escape from the apparently inevitable human consequence: remorse. At first, he is always able to forget the fate of a previous victim in his pursuit of a new love. But the spectacle of one of his past victims reduced, like Goethe's Gretchen, to a state of madness forces him to realize that he cannot evade the human condition, just as Faust is made to concede that he cannot be omniscient or omnipotent. The sight of this poor demented creature is intolerable to Wiese's Don Juan, causing his whole being to rise up in revulsion against itself. He talks of her 'empty, terrible glance' which provokes feelings in him more agonizing than his nature can bear (p. 243). This phrase ('mehr als meine Menschheit trägt') recalls 'an der Menschheit Grenzen schweifen' and shows that Wiese is here concerned not only with the individual case (poignant though that is), but with the general question of whether the type of man who uncompromisingly pursues self-gratification and self-determination can throw off shame and remorse (see, too, chapter 9).

But, with the exception of Wiese's tragedy, works in which Don Juan is seen seducing a second Gretchen hardly add to our understanding and appreciation of either Don Juan or Faust. There were two authors, however, who were able to go beyond such obvious borrowings, setting up parallels to Goethe's *Faust* which genuinely enrich their treatment of the Don Juan type and our perception of him. These authors were Theodor Creizenach and Waldemar Bonsels.

Creizenach, in his play of 1836–7, draws on an episode which comes late in Faust's career in which Faust, now a very old man, reclaims land from the sea in order to create a community of free citizens where previously the chaotic and unruly elements had held sway (Goethe, Part 2, Acts 4–5). Earlier, Creizenach's Don Juan had been torn between his hedonistic urges and a restless idealism which sensed something beyond mere enjoyment. Moreover, he could become so infected by intellectual curiosity that, in the fascination of a debate with an eminent scholar during which he was led into 'profundities of knowledge' and 'treasure-houses of experience', he could even forget a rendezvous with a woman (Scene 3). The phrases chosen by Creizenach here inevitably remind us of Faust's speculative nature: 'alle Tiefen des Wissens, alle Schatzkammern der Erfahrung'. Don Juan's passion for speculation was combined with an equally passionate desire to attain for himself, and encourage in others, an ideal of freedom in thought, speech and conduct. Despite a temporary relapse when he was infected by Parisian frivolity,[5] it was the idealism which prevailed. And so, at the end, a reformed Don Juan had set sail for America in order to start a new life as a pioneer, serving the community and conquering nature.

This is the point at which the indebtedness to Goethe becomes unmistakable, for the portrayal of this new life is very similar to Faust's dream of a community living on land wrested from the elements. Here is Creizenach:

> Has not the stream left its banks, bidden by him [Don Juan] to surge along new paths, so that now towns lie along its banks and happy men have their dwellings there?[6]

If one compares this with Goethe's *Faust* (ll. 11559–78), it becomes clear that Creizenach is making a deliberate allusion. This accords with his conception of a Don Juan whose womanizing is not, as in Hoffmann and most of his imitators, the form taken by his idealism, but an aberration, a temporary diversion from his true destiny. The stress laid on intellectual curiosity sets up a resemblance to the Faust type in general, while Don Juan's espousal of an ideal of freedom and his ambition to master nature link him specifically with Faust as conceived by Goethe.[7] Creizenach's Don Juan discovers that sensuality cannot, in the long run, compete with intellectuality. But neither can this restless and dynamic character content himself with 'profundities of knowledge' in any abstract and meditative way: his insights and convictions must translate themselves into action.

Bonsels, in his epic poem *Don Juan* (completed 1914, published in 1919), borrows Goethe's idea of a wager between the Lord and the Devil, a wager that bears on the ruling characteristic of the hero. In Goethe's 'Prologue in Heaven' (*Faust*, lines 243–353), Mephisto is drawn to Faust because of his wild and insatiable longings; these, he thinks, will enable him to win Faust over. In Bonsels' variant, Satan mocks God for being the adored and trusted ruler of the weak (this clearly links up with Nietzsche's notion of Christianity as a religion for the enslaved and oppressed). But the strong belong to him, Satan: 'Dir folgt der Schwache, der dir leicht vertraut,/doch in dem Starken finde ewig mich!' (p. 15). If God will make over to him a truly strong man, one with the will and the capacities for the highest intensity of pleasure, let them see who will prevail. In Goethe, Faust will lose if he ever feels satiety and contentment, if he ever 'bids the passing moment stay' (lines 1699–702); in Bonsels, Don Juan is to possess all women whom he desires, but may not bide with or return to any of them.

In the end, like Goethe's Mephisto, Satan loses his bet; in this (still Hoffmannesque) reading of the Don Juan legend, the hero returns to Maria, the Donna Anna of this poem, and is saved, although 'legally' he would seem to have forfeited his soul to Satan and lost the wager for God. (There is another similarity to Goethe's *Faust* here, for Mephisto thinks that *he* has won his bet but is robbed of his prey: see Goethe, ll. 11825–35). Why then, to return to Bonsels, does Satan lose? Because, at the last, a sincere love turns Don Juan from his wickedness; despite all the Devil's threats, Juan has become unfaithful to his own unfaithfulness (Weinstein, p. 102) and has returned to God. Hoffmann's notion of a divine woman over whom the Devil has no power ('ein göttliches Weib, über deren reines Gemüt der Teufel nichts vermochte') is translated into action in the most direct manner.

Hence the similarities perceived between the two legends provoked a number of Faustian Don Juan works. Some are superficial, either adopting the facile device of giving Don Juan a pact and a devil as companion, or trying to create links between Faust's eroticism as displayed in the Gretchen episode and Don Juan's pursuit of a girl from the humble classes of society. But since Goethe's Faust is by no means promiscuous, whereas da Ponte's Don

Giovanni claims 231 victims in Germany alone, the linking is not in itself meaningful. There is more point if a true contrast (flesh/spirit, acceptance of life/questioning as to its purpose) is set up, or if it is implied that both figures are in their different ways idealists (Creizenach), or if the hero's fate is related to the world order as Faust's had been (Bonsels). Where we are offered little more than a 'second Gretchen', we are more likely to respond if the episode is made to illustrate a general point which hints at an essential inner link between Faust and Don Juan (as in Wiese).

There is an amusing postscript to this story, which relates to the transmission of the Faust and Don Juan legends in popular forms. The character and adventures of Dr Faust had first become widely known through an anonymous chapbook published in 1587, *Historia von D. Johann Fausten/dem weitbeschreyten Zauberer unnd Schwartzkünstler/ Wie er sich gegen dem Teuffel ... verschrieben/ ... biß er endtlich seinen wol verdienten Lohn empfangen* ('The Story of Dr Johann Faust the notorious Conjurer and Magician; how he made a Pact with the Devil, until he finally received his well deserved Reward'). This almost wholly fictitious account begins with Faust's upbringing and depicts him as arrogant, godless and dissatisfied. After a description of how he summons the Devil and makes an alliance with him, a long middle section shows the fruits of the pact (disputations, journeyings, the favour of the rich and powerful, magic tricks, the epicurean life), while the closing chapters show in harrowing detail Faust's last weeks on earth, his lament over his sinfulness and his gruesome death. In addition to stage works, there had been, since the end of the sixteenth century, a steady flow of chapbooks, ballads and popular novels, some drawing extensively on the *Historia*, some combining popular ingredients with ideas and episodes taken from famous literary works devoted to Faust. Now although Don Juan figures in many popular stage- and puppet-plays, there seems never to have been a German chapbook – an equivalent to the *Historia von D. Johann Fausten* – devoted to him. (This contrasts with the situation in England, where there was at least one chapbook, based on Shadwell's play.) In Germany, in the 1850s, there were two attempts to fill this gap and to synthesize something akin to the popular prose transmissions of the Faust story.

Norbert Hürte's *Wahrhaftige Historie vom ärgerlichen Leben des spanischen Ritters Don Juan und wie ihn zuletzt +++ der Teufel geholt* ('True Story of the scandalous Life of the Spanish Knight Don Juan and how he was finally carried off by the Devil'), dating from 1854, is a naïvely moralizing retelling of the legend 'for the people' – 'für's Volk erzählt', as the title-page tells us. The material is for the most part taken from da Ponte, with some additions by Hürte, these being mainly aimed at intensifying the impression of Don Juan's appalling depravity and thus driving home the warning message. Hürte's title is clearly copied from that of the old Faust-chapbook and his account of Don Juan's infamous way of life closely resembles the description of Faust's in the older work:

| *Hürte* | *1587 chapbook* |
|---|---|
| His lewd existence in opposition to God and all order . . . | And so Dr Faustus lives an epicurean life day and night and does not believe in God, Hell or the Devil . . . his devilish and godless existence . . . a swinish and epicurean life . . .[8] |

When Don Juan dies, both the justice and the horror of his end are underlined, as in the *Faustbook*, by terrifying and bloodthirsty details:

| *Hürte* | *1587 chapbook* |
|---|---|
| Like some monster, the miscreant lay on the floor in his own blood. With a fixed stare, his eyes started from his head. His swollen tongue protruded from between his teeth, his whole face was blue . . .[9] | His brains were sticking to the wall, for the Devil had hurled him right across the room. His eyes and sundry teeth lay all about, a horrible and shocking sight. |

If 'the people' had popular retellings of Dr Faust's story, intended both as sensational entertainment and a fearsome moral warning, why should not that other fascinatingly wicked figure, Don Juan, serve a similar dual purpose?

Friedrich Spießer's *Don Juan, oder: Der steinerne Gast. Seine Thaten und sein furchtbares Lebensende* ('Don Juan, or the Stone Guest. His Deeds and terrible Death'), which appeared in about 1857, is somewhat similar. The title again suggests a parallel to the Faust chapbooks and again the tone is heavily moralizing. Spießer's sententious 'for just punishment always waits on the godless sinner' (p. 8) is very close to 'until he finally received his well deserved rewards' on the title page of the first Faust-book. Spießer's fondness for expressions like 'the arch-villain and rogue' ('der Erzbösewicht und Schelm') corresponds to the constant denunciations of Faust's audacity, sinful curiosity, pride, arrogance, etc. ('Vermessenheit', 'Fürwitz', 'Stoltz', 'Hochmut') in the 1587 work. Since Spießer's account is rather different from Hürte's, it seems likely that these two authors conceived the idea of a Don Juan chapbook independently of each other, each drawing directly on the 1587 source.

What makes these two books more than minor curiosities is the fact that their authors saw the manifold parallels between the legends of Faust and Don Juan and the obvious similarities in the manner of their transmission in popular dramatic forms, but realized that the Don Juan story had nothing corresponding to the *Historia von D. Johann Fausten*. So they set about remedying the deficiency. There is no comparison to be made in terms of importance, of course: the *Historia* is the source, direct or indirect, of virtually all literary treatments of Dr Faust, while Hürte's and Spießer's works appeared when the Don Juan legend was very widely familiar and were without influence. But they are not simply attempts to plug a gap or to underline the parallels to the Faust legend in yet one more way. They are also, I believe, part of the revolt against the romantic idealization of Don Juan. If there was to be a Don Juan chapbook, a Don Juan 'for the people', then it must return to, and accord with, the moral consensus. An elitist appeal to the rights of the exceptional individual could clearly play no part in such a work.

Not only did Don Juan come to resemble Faust in various ways; there was a two-way traffic, in that the hero of many a Faust work shows Don Juanesque qualities.[10] The ground is prepared by the early popular versions of Dr Faust's story, in which sex is shown to be a major obsession, once the pact has been signed and the Devil's services procured. The underlying argument is that the learned Doctor has had no contact with women – indeed, no time for them – in his previous cloistered existence and now wishes to make up for lost opportunities. His loves have to be illicit loves, since the terms of the pact forbid him to marry.

In the nineteenth century, many authors of Faust plays show Faust abandoning learning in favour of love virtually before the ink (or the blood) has dried on the pact. This may have come about because of the prominence given to the pursuit of Gretchen in

Goethe's Part 1, for it is likely that not all Goethe's readers went on to master the full implications of the completed work, a matter of a further 7,500 lines. Or it may be that lesser spirits found Faust's womanizing easier to deal with dramatically than the more abstract philosophical and metaphysical themes associated with the legend. In such works, the supposed link with Don Juan's story is often underlined by more or less open references to episodes from Mozart/da Ponte, especially Don Giovanni's pursuit of Zerlina. But it is, of course, a gross oversimplification to label Faust a 'second Don Juan' on this score; the rival motive of intellectual speculation, which appears only rarely in the Don Juan legend, would be central in most people's conception of Faust's character, even if it was sometimes lost from sight by minor authors incapable of grasping it or of treating it dramatically. But where the theme of intellectual curiosity is not present, or is only fleetingly present, we tend to feel cheated. A Faust who throws off his intellectual concerns as soon as he catches sight of a pretty woman seems unworthy of his name, whereas Don Juan's move from the life of the flesh to that of the spirit can be, and has been, represented as a progress towards a worthier existence. That is: Faust is in danger of being devalued as he moves closer to Don Juan, whereas Don Juan, in approaching Faust, is likely to be ennobled, provided that the links go beyond the mechanical contrivances of Vulpius, Braunthal or Mallefille.

*1* 'Vengeance waits on my murderer': title-page of the piano score of Mozart's *Don Giovanni*, Vienna (Steiner), n.d.

2 The wooing of Zerlina (*Don Giovanni*, Act 1, no.7). Vignette by H. Ramberg.

3 'There will be ten more names on my list by tomorrow morning' – Don Giovanni at the height of his arrogance. Max Slevogt, *Das Champagnerlied*.

4 The doomed rebel. Ricketts, *The Death of Don Juan*.



5 Don Juan deified! An illustration to Byron, with all-too clear resemblances to a *pietà*. Ford Madox Brown, *Haidée and Don Juan* (Byron, *Don Juan*, Canto 2).

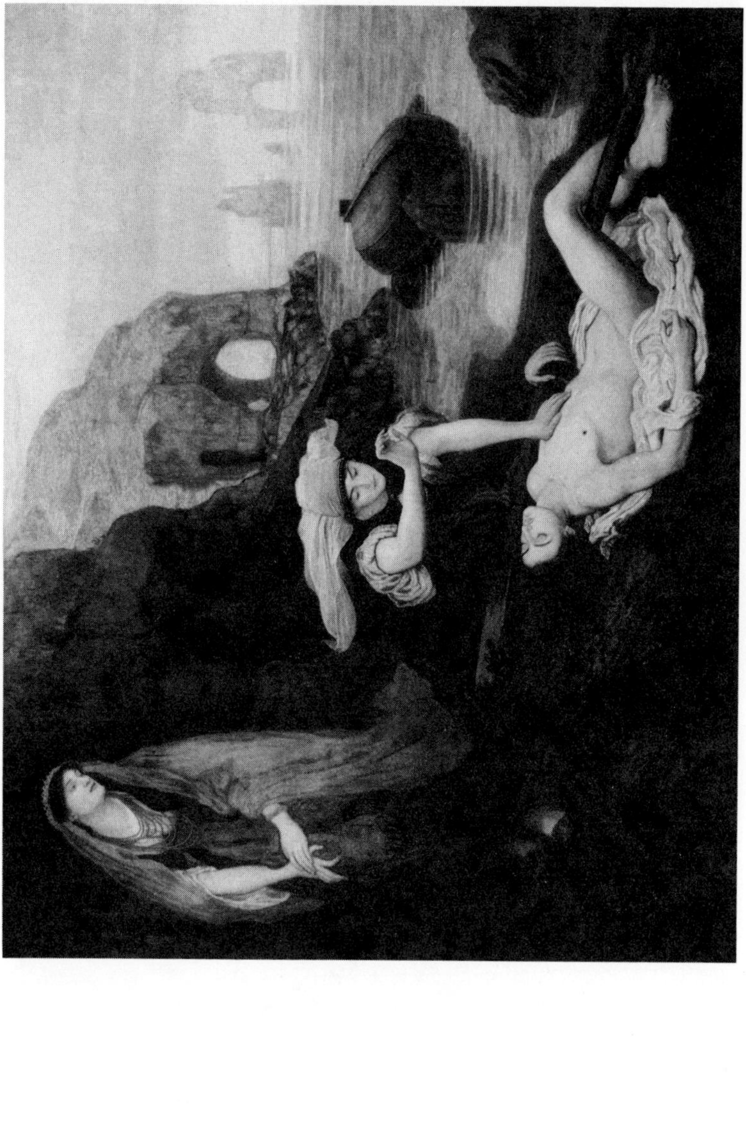

6   Don Juan's story as a fearful warning to sinners. Title-page of Friedrich Spießer's *Don Juan, oder: Der steinerne Gast*.

7  Title-page to Norbert Hürte's *Wahrhaftige Historie* (1854).

# 7

# The Mañara Story; Zorrilla; Two Contrasting Russian Don Juans

## THE MAÑARA STORY

In the nineteenth century, a further strand enters to complicate the picture by fusing Don Juan with a notorious Spanish profligate, this time a man who certainly existed and about whom a fair amount is known: Miguel Mañara, who was born in Seville in 1626. Despite a strict and pious upbringing, he drifted as a young man into a dissolute way of life but later repented, entering a monastery and ending his days in austere piety to atone for the sins of his youth. He died in 1679. There were even posthumous attempts to have him canonized. Soon legends grew up around him, some of which clearly derive from a confusion, intentional or accidental, between him and Don Juan Tenorio: thus it was said that Mañara was nicknamed 'el Burlador de Sevilla', that he was surprised in a girl's room by her father and fought a duel and that he kept a catalogue of his conquests. Esther van Loo believes that the historical Mañara knew *El Burlador* (the play, that is) and deliberately set out to emulate Don Juan Tenorio or even to outdo that notorious sinner.[1] Be that as it may, these parallels are important, since they help to explain the sometimes quite elaborate combinations of material from the Mañara and the Don Juan Tenorio stories in literary works nominally devoted to one or the other of these characters. One very distinctive accretion, however, is quite independent of the Don Juan Tenorio tradition and of very ancient origin: at a point where Mañara's profligacy has reached a climax of outrageousness, he has a vision of his own funeral, which so fills him with terror that it brings about his conversion.

This mixture of fact and fancy in which elements from two related tales had become intertwined was made familiar in France through Prosper Mérimée's short novel *Les Ames du Purgatoire* (1834).[2] Mérimée knows quite well that Miguel Mañara and Don Juan Tenorio were quite distinct from one another in their origins and devotes the first three pages of his work to a discussion of how he has gone about joining the two stories together: 'Regarding my hero, Don Juan de Maraña (*sic!*), I took pains to relate only those adventures which do not belong by prescriptive right to Don Juan Tenorio, who is so familiar to us from the masterpieces of Molière and Mozart' (p. 299).

Don Juan de Maraña is brought up by a fanatically pious mother who tries to fill him with a dread of damnation, using a painting of souls tormented in Purgatory as a sort of didactic visual aid. At eighteen, he leaves home to go to the University of Salamanca, where he falls under the influence of a corrupt companion, Don Garcia, and is drawn into a life of iniquity. One day, while ill, he amuses himself by drawing up a list of his conquests with details of the deceived husbands and their professions or stations in life. A comrade points out that one thing is missing from this list of cuckolds: the name of God (p. 370). So Don Juan blasphemously vows to remedy this deficiency, duly pursuing a nun and conquering her resistance. Two nights before the agreed elopement is to take place, he returns to the castle where he spent his boyhood. Trying in vain to sleep in the very room where the picture of Purgatory is still hanging, he spends a night of terror, surrounded by these images of retribution and suffering, although he does not yet repent or give up his project. Presently, back in Seville, he sees a funeral procession and, on asking who is being buried, is told 'Don Juan de Maraña' (p. 384). When he follows the procession into the church and asks the priest whose soul is being prayed for, he receives the same reply. He faints and, when he recovers, is purged of his wicked intentions and resolves to enter a monastery, where his devotion and austerity are as pronounced as his previous wickedness.

Mérimée's method, as he describes it in the prefatory remarks quoted above, sounds curiously synthetic, as if he were piecing together a jigsaw puzzle, fitting in some pieces and rejecting others. But it works well enough in practice. Incidents and motifs such as a variant on the Anna/Juan/Commander episode and the list of sexual conquests accord perfectly well with the middle stage in the hero's career; others which are too obviously and exclusively the property of the rival legend are shunned. These include the Stone Guest and the supper scene for self-evident reasons, but also the confrontation with the beggar and the alms-giving, familiar from Molière, who is one of the authors of Don Juan works singled out for mention by Mérimée. Clearly, this episode is omitted because the reckless atheism implied by it would run counter to Mérimée's conception of a character who is enticed away from virtue but is a potential candidate for repentance and rehabilitation. Mérimée plainly felt that most of his readers would be aware of the rival tradition through the works of Molière and Mozart/da Ponte and wished to make it quite clear where he stood and how he had proceeded.

The theme was taken up two years later by Alexandre Dumas the Elder ('Dumas père') and turned into a play: *Don Juan de Marana* (*sic!*). This is based on Mérimée, but with the addition of much sensational new material. The plot is too fatuous to retell: suffice it to say that this Don Juan is a dissolute character who is saved not as a result of long expiation, but through a last-minute repentance. Not only does Dumas combine the Mañara and Don Juan Tenorio legends; his play also contains a number of similarities to the Faust story. It may be added that, where many authors of Faust and Don Juan works were embarrassed by the supernatural events that they inherited, Dumas revels in them and even adds some of his own. There are good and bad angels, there is a dead man who returns from the hereafter in order to supply the missing signature to his will, there is a statue which comes to life, there is a meal served to Don Juan at which the wine is transformed into the blood of his victims and the water into the women's tears which he caused to flow. Much of this (especially the posthumous signing of the will) seems more appropriate to a *Ruddigore*-type extravaganza than to a play with a serious moral purpose; it is no wonder that a later writer felt impelled to simplify Dumas's piece. That writer was Arnold Bennett.

In 1923, Bennett published his slimmed-down version of Dumas, *Don Juan de Marana* (written in 1913). From the older play, which he describes as 'sprawling' and 'hastily and carelessly written', Bennett excises the Faustian trimmings and the more absurd magical elements and also replaces the eleventh-hour repentance with a period of atonement in a monastery, thus returning to Mérimée and, indeed, to the real-life Mañara. Without apparently knowing Hoffmann's interpretation of *Don Giovanni*, Bennett also introduces the motif of idealistic questing into his characterization of Don Juan, who 'restlessly searches for that which perhaps is undiscoverable' (p. 36) and 'is disappointed times without number; but ... still hopes' (p. 81). This gives the ending of the play a new meaning. The traditional Mañara story represents in the most straightforward but dramatic terms how a great sinner can still repent betimes and make good his misdeeds through expiation; in Bennett, the libertine achieves through the life of the spirit that ideal which he had previously sought in the flesh. Bennett combines this idealism with a much older ingredient of Don Juan's character, showing his hero as a Spanish grandee, very conscious of his dignity and honour:

> You have heard of that other Don Juan who went down into Hell and supped with the Commander ... I will be as great as he – greater. He was a voluptuary. I am more. I represent the tragedy of the grandees; I am the symbol of a doomed nation. And I will prosecute my ambitions magnificently.[3]

So this Don Juan, like Tirso's and Molière's, has a sense of honour and caste, still discernible through all his wildness and dissipation: he will never back away from a fight or any other danger and associates cowardice, lying and all petty dishonesties with the 'common people'. (This point is one that Nietzsche had made much of when defining the different attitudes underlying 'master morality' and 'slave morality'.) The pride and the aristocratic grandeur may have been suggested to Bennett by Molière or by Mozart, where it is only partially overlaid by *opera buffa* elements, for I have come across no hint that Bennett knew Tirso. Or this trait could have come from Byron's *Don Juan*, who has a strong sense of pedigree and a natural pride, for once untainted by arrogance. Franz Zeise, by the way, in his Don Juan novel of 1941, sees Juan as the last of the Spanish knights ('der letzte Ritter Spaniens', p. 126).

Other works based on or suggested by the Mañara story can be dealt with more briefly. Two novels, those by Delteil (1930) and Jelusich (1931) take up the story and combine it with elements of the Don Juan Tenorio legend, but with widely differing implications. For while Jelusich's Don Juan is still faintly but unmistakably related to Hoffmann's quester, Delteil sets out to refute any such reading, arguing that Juan has been no more than the plaything of the women, who have seduced him even as he believed that he was seducing them. Widmann (1858) and Haraucourt (1898) both take up the central episode of the Mañara story, the libertine's vision of his own funeral procession. Haraucourt, in deference to modern scepticism, represents it as an hallucination, thus getting the best of both worlds by combining a metaphysical shock for his hero with natural causation acceptable to his audience. Finally, Hartenstein's Don Juan novel of 1934 offers a reconstruction of Mañara's life as handed down by tradition, together with an imaginative interpretation of his character.

Thus the Mañara story enjoyed some popularity for a century (more, if one counts Antony Borrow's *Don Juan* of 1963, which has echoes of it).[4] Weinstein rightly sees it as one strand in the growing tendency to save Don Juan (p. 112). But it was a less important factor than Hoffmann's influence or that brought about by the near transformation of Don Juan into a second Faust. Weinstein probably exaggerates when he says that the Mañara story threatened to eclipse that of Don Juan Tenorio for a time (p. 116), unless he is thinking only of Catholic countries and/or authors. The Mañara legend undoubtedly owed much of its popularity to the genuine *frisson* provided by the incident in which the hero is a witness to his own obsequies.

More than one author who was attracted to the possibilities of the Mañara theme went out of his way to distinguish between this story and that of Don Juan Tenorio in order to spare his readers or audiences puzzlement and misunderstanding. Indeed, it is possible that some of the uninformed may have been taken aback by the works in which no such explanation was forthcoming, having, on the strength of the name 'Don Juan' on title-page or theatre-bill, been led to expect churchyard and supper scenes, Stone Guests and descents into Hell. For, ever since Mérimée had turned Miguel Mañara into 'Don Juan de Maraña', the hero's name had been a potential source of confusion.

## ZORRILLA

In twentieth-century Spain, the most familiar and popular work still to figure Don Juan is not *El Burlador*, nor Antonio de Zamora's melodramatic reworking of it (1744), but José Zorrilla's *Don Juan Tenorio* of 1844. Despite the title, this is again a combination of the two legends. Borrowings from the Mañara story include the blasphemous resolve to add a nun to the list of conquests and the sinner's vision of his own funeral. Zorrilla's Don Juan makes a bet with a friend as to which of them will commit more outrages in a year. He wins, killing thirty-two men and seducing seventy-two women. In the end, however, he is saved through a return to true belief and the love of a saintly woman.

One curious thing about this piece is what I take to be an unintentional link with the Faust legend. It is repeatedly suggested that such an appalling and successful villain must enjoy infernal help and protection; this idea runs like a *leitmotif* through the play. And when Don Juan invites the Statue, it is in order to discover whether there is another existence after life on earth or whether such ideas are only pious imaginings. Weinstein sees this change as a necessary modernization of the legend, in that a nineteenth-century Don Juan is bound to be more sceptical than his seventeenth-century predecessors[5] (although it should be recalled that Dorimon's Dom Jouan had issued his invitation for much the same reasons). Certainly, Zorrilla's Don Juan attempts to hold the supernatural at bay by trying to persuade himself that its manifestations are due either to trickery or to hallucination; only at the end does he concede that there is a world beyond this one.

It is this clash between a Divine world-order and an obstinate scepticism which gives the play its tension. But it must be admitted that Zorrilla's plot is extravagantly melodramatic. The work has, in fact, drawn on itself a good deal of harsh criticism from reviewers and from historians of the Don Juan legend. José Ortega y Gasset, writing in 1921, roundly condemned the play as vulgar. It seems to be a good example of the kind of piece which will find popular acceptance despite qualities which alienate the fastidious. Weinstein and others have pointed to this disparity and have put forward reasons for the play's undoubted popularity: the rapid succession of dramatic incidents, the dash and verve of Don Juan himself, the comforting moral that even the greatest libertine may find love and the greatest sinner mercy. Whatever the precise mix of reasons, the Spaniards seem to have adopted this play as 'their' version of 'their' legend.[6]

Zorrilla's *Don Juan Tenorio* became known in various European countries and was taken up and reworked by a number of authors. In one of these versions we may see an implicit criticism of the way in which Zorrilla's Don Juan was saved, for Christian Schneller (*Der Sturz*, 1948) takes over the plot but changes the ending completely. Schneller's Don Juan is urged to repent, but refuses, asserting his own will and identity as the only things worth clinging to: 'I have not become Don Juan Tenorio in order to praise the destroyer of my dreams with harps. . . . I won't let myself be saved; I am not weak enough to be saved!' (pp. 48 and 50). Schneller has here gone back beyond Zorrilla to a more defiant conception of a Don Juan who values truth to self more highly than life, whether on earth or in the hereafter.

## TWO CONTRASTING RUSSIAN DON JUANS

There are two notable Russian treatments of the Don Juan theme, very different from one another in almost all respects: the plays by Alexander Pushkin and Alexis Tolstoi. Pushkin's short drama, *The Stone Guest*, was conceived in 1826 and written in 1830. Since, despite its great interest and the fame of its author, it is not well known or easily available in translation, a brief account of the action follows.

Don Juan has been in exile after killing Doña Anna's husband in a duel. He returns to Madrid, homesick. Meanwhile, Anna has raised a statue to her husband and visits it each day to mourn. Don Juan catches sight of her and resolves to make her acquaintance. (This is the first time that he has seen her; that is, the duel with the Commander, her husband, was *not* the result of an abortive attempt on her virtue. Indeed, we are not told the reason for the duel.)

There is a switch of scene. Laura, an old flame of Juan's, is entertaining Don Carlos, the brother of the late Commander. When Juan enters, Carlos insists on a duel there and then. He is killed, but Don Juan, aflame with desire for Laura, makes love to her while the corpse is still lying on the floor. That matter can be disposed of later:

*Laura*       My beloved!
              But stop! . . . before the dead! . . . Where can we put him?
*Don Juan*    Why, leave him there – before the dawn I'll take him
              Beneath my cloak and carry him away
              And lay him on the crossroads.
                                                          (p. 142)

Having got rid of the body in due course, Juan disguises himself as a pious hermit, both for his own safety and as a means of approaching Anna, who has been living in seclusion since her husband's death. He gradually breaks down her resistance and makes an assignation for the next night. There follows a variant on the traditional invitation scene: Don Juan invites the Statue to stand guard at Anna's door while he visits her. It may be noted that this is an even more defiant temptation of Fate than the traditional invitation. Previously, Don Juan had simply invited the Statue to supper; here he is challenging his one-time victim to keep watch while an attempt is made on his widow's virtue – the spirit of the dead husband is being asked to connive at an act of posthumous cuckoldry. And there is a further, less obvious affront: the erstwhile nobleman and Commander is being cast in the role of a servant or a watchman.

In the final scene Don Juan continues his wooing of Anna, disdaining to shelter behind an assumed name and instead voluntarily revealing his identity and his guilt. Such are his charm and eloquence that Anna cannot find it in her heart to hate him. But, as they take an affectionate farewell of each other with an agreement to meet again the next day, the Statue arrives. Anna faints, Don Juan gives the Statue his hand and, as in most traditional versions, the Libertine and the Stone Guest disappear from sight.

However much Pushkin's plot may owe to tradition, his Don Juan is an original conception, 'a poet of passion', as Pushkin's translator, Avril Pyman, expresses it.[7] In courtship, he improvises like a musician:

> How to begin? 'I make so bold . . .' or, no!
> 'Señora . . .' bah! I had best not rehearse
> But say the first thing that comes to my mind,
> Even as I improvise my songs of love.'
>
> (p. 143)

And that is, in fact, exactly what happens when he approaches Anna; he achieves something like a state of auto-intoxication. The following exchange shows how apposite was his use of the word 'improvise'. 'What would you ask of me?' demands Anna and Juan, reacting to the question as a musician might take up a scrap of melody on which he has been challenged to extemporise, replies:

> My death!
> If only I could die now at your feet
> Then my poor body might be buried here,
> Not near that one you love, not here, not even
> Close by, but somewhere further from the tomb.
>
> (p. 146)

The flood of improvisation released by Anna's question grows more and more passionate, reaching its climax with a vision of the weeping Anna at his grave. At this, she breaks out with 'I think/You are demented.' And this new idea sends Don Juan off into another tirade: 'Is it then a sign/Of madness, Doña Anna, to crave death?' – and so on for another ten lines. It is as if he were a poetic and romantic dramatist who creates love-scenes in which he will play the wooer's part – but it is a part which he will make up in a state of self-hypnosis and in which he will be carried away by his own rhetoric. This state, so different from the conscious treachery and deceit employed by previous Don Juans, does not last, however; in moments of calmer reflection, Pushkin's hero is perfectly aware of what he is and what he does. In a conversation with his servant, he laments over a past love, now dead:

| | |
|---|---|
| *Leporello* | What of it, others followed. |
| *Don Juan* | That's true, too. |
| *Leporello* | And if we live, there will be others yet. |
| *Don Juan* | And that. |

(p. 131)

This conception of Don Juan as a man who means what he says when he says it, however inconstant he may turn out to be later, does not seem to owe anything to Hoffmann. But Pushkin's Anna shows fairly clear traces of da Ponte's Anna as re-interpreted by the German Romantic. She was married to Don Alvar (until Don Juan killed him), but this was a *mariage de convenance*, forced on her by parental pressure (p. 153). It is at least arguable that her ostentatious show of grief is in obedience to convention: 'A widow should keep faith beyond the grave' (ibid.–cf. da Ponte's Anna: 'ma il mondo ...'). Although she speaks of Don Alvar's love for her, she says nothing of her love for him. Pushkin's Don Juan pursues Anna with the utmost urgency, claiming that the risk of death is of no consequence when weighed up against his love for her. And he certainly professes to see in her an ideal woman who seems to reproach him for his past debauchery:

> ... it is true
> That I was long apprenticed to debauch
> But – so it seems to me – since I first saw you
> I've been as one regenerate, reborn.
> In loving you I fell in love with virtue.
>
> (p. 157)

Here, he is very like Lenau's Don Juan, who laments his lost innocence at the sight of Anna. The difficulty of deciding whether, in Pushkin, this really adds up to a unique passion for an ideal of virtuous womanhood is bound up with the author's characterization of his hero. Juan certainly makes these protestations and scorns risks in his pursuit of Anna – but, as we have seen, it is an essential ingredient of his character that he says *and means* the most extravagant things in the moment of passion.[8]

In Alexis Tolstoi's *Don Juan* (1860) we have one of the most ambitious attempts to work motifs from the Faust legend into a Don Juan drama. The play has a Prologue in Heaven, modelled on Goethe, which sets out to define the relationship of the Divine and the Satanic as they affect the created universe and human destinies and which makes Don Juan's fate the subject of a bet very similar to that in Goethe's Prologue. For Tolstoi, Satan is the negation of the Divine:

> I am the minus-sign in mathematics; the philosopher calls it the reversal of the Divine. In short, I am a nothing; as you know quite well, I am the constant negation of existence.
>
> (p. 11)

This is exactly like the terms in which Goethe's Mephistopheles defines his nature to Faust – he too represents a 'minus-sign' in the cosmic arithmetic:

> I am the spirit who constantly denies, and that with justice, for everything that comes into being deserves to be destroyed. And so it would be better if nothing ever came into being.
>
> (ll. 1338–41)

But, again as in Goethe, it is the Devil who spurs men on to activity, so that Tolstoi's Satan, no less than Goethe's Mephisto, is from the outset in a paradoxical and self-defeating situation:

> I am mankind's physician who galvanizes men in order to cause tension. And if there were no Devil in the world there would be no saints either!
>
> (Tolstoi, p. 17)

In Goethe, it is the Lord who first defines Mephisto's role in almost exactly similar terms:

> Human activity can all too easily slacken off. Man soon comes to love absolute peace. And so I am pleased to give him a companion who provokes and incites to action and works as a Devil.
>
> (ll. 340–3)

– and it is left to Mephisto himself to point out the cosmic paradox that is the logical consequence of his role: if activity is a good and necessary part of human nature and passivity the greatest ill, he, by goading men to action, must conduce towards the good, however much he may will the bad. (ll 1335 f.)

The good spirits mention Don Juan as singled out by God for his purposes, just as the Lord singles out Faust in Goethe:

> His course leads him to lofty deeds; the world will ring out with his praise! Angels guard him, you, Satan, keep away from him! You will not seize him, seek your prey elsewhere!
>
> (p. 14: cf. Goethe, ll. 308–11)

But Satan proposes to destroy Don Juan through his pride, through the obstinacy with which he seeks the ideal. Each woman will seem like this ideal until she is once possessed but then he will see her for what she is (p. 15). So Don Juan is made the subject of a wager in Heaven: if he ceases to be discontented with each experience as it comes his way, if he recognizes the ideal in any woman, Satan will have won. This is Tolstoi's 'donjuanesque' equivalent to the wager in Goethe, where Faust will lose if he ever bids the passing moment stay. In each case, the bet is bound up with the ruling characteristic of the hero, the insatiability of his desires.

At the beginning of the play proper, Don Juan is twenty-five, already a libertine and already falling prey to disillusionment, as

Satan had foreseen. Now comes his meeting with Doña Anna. She loves him and, in order to be able to marry him, breaks her engagement to Octavio, persuading her father with some difficulty to agree to the new match. But Don Juan is only half inclined to believe that Anna is different from all the rest, fearing that she too will disappoint him in the end. So he affronts her honour and that of her family by publicly serenading a notorious whore on the very day on which the engagement is announced, hoping to evade the marriage and still patch things up with Anna afterwards, thus getting her without marrying her. The engagement is broken off, of course, and first Anna's father and then Octavio are killed by Don Juan as they try to avenge Anna's honour. Don Juan does eventually possess Anna, but only by taking advantage of her while she is unconscious. Yet this does not break her spell over him as, according to his theories about women, it should. The end of Tolstoi's play is a variation on the conclusion familiar from traditional Don Juan pieces. The Statue, whom Don Juan had invited to supper in a mood of bravado, arrives to reveal that Anna has committed suicide. Don Juan, realizing too late that he had really loved her, refuses to repent, falling into wild despair. The Statue is about to claim his victim for Hell when he is repelled by good spirits: 'Back, you blind power! Away! leave him who has faith and loves!' (p. 126). An Epilogue shows us the death of the lay brother Juan after years of repentance.

It has been made clear to us that Don Juan's search for an ideal of womanhood is his way of seeking God and that only repeated frustration has turned him into a rebel against the Divine order. This is why it is worthwhile for Satan to stake so much of his prestige on the career of someone who is, on the face of it, a mere womanizer; it is also why Don Juan turns to the Church in the end. For Anna 'proves' the ultimate attainability of the ideal and hence the goodness and rightness of the universe.

No other Don Juan version took up and dramatized Hoffmann's ideas so closely and faithfully, says Heckel.[9] Simultaneously, Tolstoi relates the hero's fortunes to the world-order through his variation on the Prologue to Goethe's *Faust* and bases his Epilogue just as openly on Mérimée.[10] From a coldly logical point of view, the strands fit together with perfect coherence. Goethe's wager is restated in terms fit for a Don Juan, so that the faustian Prologue and the Don Juan play complement each other. Meanwhile, the long period of austerity and expiation suggested by *Les Ames du Purgatoire* is Tolstoi's attempt to make Don Juan's salvation morally acceptable, following his violation of Anna.

Yet the result is unsatisfying. For Heckel, the salvation seems like a denial of Don Juan's innermost being (p. 75); for the secularist, the very idea of salvation for this man may seem morally repellent, however long the lay brother Juan may spend on his knees. Yet others, familiar with Goethe's *Faust*, will see Tolstoi's version of the wager as narrow and trivial, compared with Goethe's grandiose conception which depends on whether Faust will find *any* human experience satisfying for more than a passing moment. Nor do years of secluded repentance, however austere and fervent, accord with the promise of 'lofty deeds' contained in Tolstoi's Prologue. The combination of motifs and ideas from Hoffmann, Goethe and Mérimée certainly makes this version one of the most elaborately idealized readings of Don Juan's character in the nineteenth century, but most people would, I imagine, prefer the reckless and defiant Don Juan created by Pushkin.

# 8

# The 'Sporting' Don Juan; The Conquest of Remorse; Don Juan and the Philosophers; Don Juanism as a Vocation

Don Juan's fortunes change sharply through the centuries. At first regarded as an appalling villain, he is later abruptly transformed into a tragic idealist. From the early nineteenth century onwards, these rival views coexist: while many writers stress the heroic quality which they see in the idealism, others, failing to see why a man who had created such havoc should be made into a hero, take their revenge on him.

That brief recapitulation obviously takes in an interconnected series of important developments in Don Juan's history and shows a general pattern into which many works, familiar and unfamiliar, readily fit. The pendulum swings with seeming inevitability between obloquy and admiration. The picture is tempting, but far too neat to be more than a part of the truth; where so many authors have contributed plays, novels, poems, critical articles and treatises, we cannot expect the result to lend itself to an orderly exposition of trends. Since few seem to have found it possible to write about Don Juan in a spirit of objective detachment (even clinical psychologists show the cloven hoof of prejudice from time to time), it will be found that the interpretations which I will try to summarize in the following pages nearly all imply value-judgements and bolster up one side or other in the long-running debate as to whether we should despise, admire, pity or even mock Don Juan. I should like to begin with the – at first sight slightly paradoxical – notion of Don Juan as a 'sportsman'.

By the term 'sporting' in this context, I imply an attitude towards seduction which takes as much pleasure in the hazards and difficulties of pursuit as in the conquest itself, an attitude similar to that of an angler who uses light tackle to pursue specimen fish and who would scorn to 'haul them in' with coarse line and big hooks. Many critics see the beginnings of this sporting Don Juan already in *El Burlador*, whose hero seems to delight in his skill at trickery as much as in the ensuing sensual gratification. Indeed, Margaret Wilson[1] says roundly that the play is fundamentally about trickery and the wages of sin. That is oversimplified, for the trickery is a means to an end, which is seduction, and the wages of sin are the punishment for that career of seduction and the other offences against God and man which it entailed. But Wilson's view is a salutary reminder that the actual enjoyment of women may give Tirso's complex hero no more, or little more, satisfaction than the stratagems of conquest. He does, after all, revel in his nickname 'the trickster of Seville'. In the subsequent development of the legend, the relative stress placed on these two factors of pursuit and possession will vary very considerably. But the delight in hazardous trickery *almost* for its own sake becomes a common motif. It is one of the few redeeming traits in Shadwell's infamous Don John: 'The more danger the more delight: I hate the common road of pleasure' (p. 33).

The sporting instinct is very prominent in the hero of Pushkin's play of 1830. It will be recalled that this Don Juan first contrives a meeting with Anna by impersonating a holy recluse. Within minutes, he confesses that he is no monk but a lover, assuming the name of Don Diego de Calvado. But at his next assignment with her, he scorns even this degree of pretence and reveals his true identity, even though Anna has just informed him that, should she meet the slayer of her husband, honour would oblige her to kill him. Not content with having manufactured this difficulty for himself, Don Juan goes on to deny any remorse for his deed. Since Anna had been on the point of yielding to 'Don Diego', this is indeed giving the quarry a fair chance. However much he may desire Anna, Juan is not interested in satisfying that desire by any means and at any cost. Charles Corbet goes so far as to maintain that this Don Juan brings a *purely* sporting mentality to his affairs.[2] In late nineteenth- and twentieth-century Don Juan works, a similar sporting mentality is not hard to find:

Daring attracts me more than winning, the struggle more than the booty.

(Paul Heyse, 1883, Act 1 Scene 5)

> I am tempted by what is forbidden; I am drawn to danger, anger, jealousy, things stolen, whether secretly or openly. Fruit that falls into my lap doesn't attract me!
>
> (Bernhardi, 1903, p. 18)

> I venture on the ocean because I find my pleasure in storms and dangers, not because I want to sail from one harbour into the next.
>
> (F. Thiess, 1950, p. 28)

This last Don Juan warns Octavio that an attempt is to be made on his fiancée's virtue and fights the Commander left-handed in order to ensure a more evenly balanced contest; like Pushkin's hero, he creates dangers if the situation is not already difficult and hazardous enough, thereby satisfying his honour and pride.

The notion of a sporting Don Juan is taken to its logical conclusion – some might say, its *reductio ad absurdum* – in a novel, *Don Juans Puppen* (1923), by Max Glass. Here we encounter a Don Juan for whom the chase is all and the achievement nothing. Tired of seduction in itself, he finds that his only remaining pleasure is to prepare the ground for the conquest and then abandon the woman at the very moment of her surrender:

> Now love is for him only the setting in motion of his powers of ingenuity in the arts of seduction ... It is no longer the physical possession which gives him pleasure, but the mental effort. He does not pluck the fruit.
>
> (pp. 37 f.)

The angling parallel suggests itself again: having landed his fish, he throws it back into the water.

This conception of Don Juan has been taken up in at least two of the treatises devoted to him: those by O. A. H. Schmitz and Hayem. Here is Schmitz: 'He is attracted by the difficulties of seizing possession and the dangers that this entails, only secondarily by the woman herself.'[3] Hayem is perhaps more interesting, for he both defines this trait in his theoretical work and shows it in operation in his drama. Having argued in the treatise that 'it is resistance that gives pleasure its piquancy', he shows in the play how Don Juan refuses to take advantage of a woman while she is lying unconscious and defenceless.

This sporting element, allied to Don Juan's intrepidity, is

undoubtedly one means by which successive writers have tried to make him less unattractive than he would have been, had he adopted purely Machiavellian tactics. The adjective is not unjustified, for the link between Don Juan and Machiavelli has been made more than once, most recently by Walther Mönch.[4] There is an obvious basis for the comparison in that both Machiavelli and Don Juan in their different spheres see the end as justifying the means and scorn conventional moral values. But it would never occur to Machiavelli to suggest that unnecessary risks might add spice to an undertaking; the whole thrust of his treatise is that the end is absolutely paramount and hence must be pursued with the swiftest, most efficacious and most relentless amorality. There is nothing 'sporting' about his declaration that a ruler will not prosper unless he is prepared to break his word or his conviction that the appearance of virtue and moderation is more important than the qualities themselves (*The Prince*, xviii-xix). If Don Juan were purely Machiavellian, he would forfeit most of whatever grudging admiration his flamboyant daring might otherwise command. For instance, if we disregard the dash and the seductive beauty of Mozart's music for a moment, the Don Giovanni created by da Ponte cuts a sorry figure in his pursuit of Zerlina, relying as he does on flattery, hypocrisy, false promises and aristocratic browbeating; Pushkin's hero, who refuses to shelter behind an assumed name, even if abandoning it may put at risk what he is within easy reach of achieving, is clearly more sympathetic.

We have seen how Wiese's Don Juan tried to exempt himself from remorse in order to pursue his goals single-mindedly and without scruple. The question of whether or not a Don Juan can escape this seemingly inevitable reaction to the suffering which he has inflicted on others occurs in many works, usually bound up with the hero's claim to untrammelled self-determination and, whether or not he says so in as many words, to a status above that of the common run of humanity. The desire to be freed from remorse would receive philosophical justification from the traditional appeal to 'nature': should Don Juan be sorry for his deeds if his whole way of life is in obedience to the dictates of nature? Later, this line of self-defence was reinforced by Nietzsche's argument that the strong and exceptional individual has his own morality (*Jenseits von Gut und Böse*, §260).

It is no coincidence that more than one of those who put forward a 'sporting' Don Juan also postulates freedom from regret as another of his characteristics. He has, after all, given the opposition a fair chance; why feel pity? Hayem argues that Don Juan, if he is to be a Don Juan at all, must be callous with regard to the suffering he causes: 'To be cruel, one must not suffer from the evil that one does . . . If he were not cruel, Don Juan would soon be a slave' (*Le Don Juanisme*, pp. 13 and 79). Bernhardi's Don Juan (1903) couples his conquest of remorse with his identity as a Don Juan and with his defiance of God: 'Let no word of remorse pass my lips: I was and will always be Don Juan! I defy Hell and God eternal!' (p. 198). The rebellion against God is seemingly no longer, as in older versions, a sinful refusal to repent or to believe, but a psychological act of self-assertion which sees true strength in never regretting what one has done. In Bernhardi, not for the first or the last time, Don Juan sets himself up as the Strong Man in contrast to the weak-willed and mediocre ('mittelmäßige Köpfe, Dreiviertel-Menschen, schwache Herzen', p. 141).

The most radical attack on remorse comes from the hero of W. van Vloten's novel *Don Juan empor!* of 1922. This Don Juan is quite aware that he causes suffering, yet continues in his way of life; it is his nature to be a Don Juan, the woman's nature to suffer:

> And yet it tormented him to see a woman whom he had once loved suffer so. It is a fault of Creation, he thought, that woman's love usually lasts so much longer than man's . . . You women fulfil your destiny by grieving and suffering over love and I fulfil mine by being driven against my will to cause you suffering. The Creator witnesses this pitiless and tragic love-struggle between man and woman just as unfeelingly as He listens to all the other millions of agonized groans on earth. I will strive to be similar to God and to be just as unfeeling as He!
>
> (pp. 26 f.)

He achieves this condition only after a struggle: 'I feel compassion for the abandoned women. But my lust for life quickly overcomes this compassion. My reason, too, resists it. Reason says: suffering is a normal part of women's life; you are fitted to it by nature' (p. 145). So this Don Juan vanquishes his natural contrition thanks to some rather specious metaphysical reflections: suffering womankind is part of the plan of Creation, so that Don Juan is no crueller than the cat that plays with the mouse or the fish that eats its young.[5]

But where Vloten's Don Juan is shown as successfully conquering remorse in his ambition to be 'similar to God', it is more common to find Don Juans who attempt this, but fail. It is significant that Stendhal, who stipulates freedom from self-reproach as a precondition of any successful Don Juan, promptly adds a word of doubt as to whether such a state is possible: 'In order to be happy in crime, one must feel no remorse. I do not know whether such a person could exist.'[6] Von Braunthal's hero illustrates the point. He originally claimed success: 'The trust which I had so often murdered left no feeling of horror in my breast' (p. 26). But just before dying he is forced to admit that this no longer holds true: 'the poisonous serpent of remorse gnaws at my heart' (p. 177). Forty years later, Lipiner makes the same point in his tragedy *Der neue Don Juan* of 1880. If we bear in mind that *Menschliches, Allzumenschliches* had appeared between 1878 and 1880 and that, in it, Nietzsche had made much of his ideal of the Free Spirit, we may be justified in seeing Nietzschean traits in Lipiner's Don Juan figure, Count Arwid Holm. For the Count claims absolute freedom, mocks virtue as weakness and regards most of his fellow-men as pygmies. Of a lesser mortal who has the temerity to lay claim to happiness, he says: 'Happy! Pah! Happiness is something great and has no place in such petty souls' (p. 43). 'Petty souls' – thus might Nietzsche's Free Spirit talk of common humanity. And it should not be overlooked that elsewhere Nietzsche cites remorse and shame as the last vestiges of common humanity which the Superman must cast off if he is to be truly great: 'What is the sign that one has achieved freedom? That one is no longer ashamed of oneself' (*Die fröhliche Wissenschaft*, §275). But Holm cannot live up to (or down to) this ideal; if 'freedom' must include freedom from remorse, he cannot achieve it: 'I deluded myself into thinking I was free, permanently removed from all pangs of conscience, all the servile folly of these people [less bold and free spirits]! And now it's nesting in me, somewhere in my soul, eating away at me!' (p. 21). The setting-off of 'servile' (*knechtisch*) against 'free' again hints at a link with Nietzsche's ideas. But the implication is that Stendhal was right, that Nietzsche's imagined consummation is a psychological impossibility, quite regardless of whether it is morally defensible.

There is both a connection with, and a contrast to, the Faust tradition here. Faust also attempts to storm through the world without a backward glance and is often shown as failing in this. In

A. Lenburg's *Faust* of 1860, for instance, the Devil urges Faust to be ruthless, but Faust cannot overcome what he sees as part of the human condition: 'I am still a human being and without doubt will remain so. I am affected by perfectly commonplace remorse.'[7] And presently the Devil taunts this weak and self-reproachful Faust: 'Wretched man! are you tempted towards remorse? Then you should have shunned the Devil' (p. 94). This is not dissimilar to Mephisto's taunt (in Goethe's *Faust*) that Faust should have fought shy of allying himself to the infernal powers if he was going to dissolve in compassion over a mere fallen woman (see the scene 'Trüber Tag. Feld' in Part 1). Faust's efforts to escape the pangs of conscience are part of his haughty desire to be more than man; Don Juan's are more limited – he certainly wants to be a Superman in his freedom from ordinary moral restrictions, but not a god. Even Vloten's Don Juan is only an apparent exception: his use of *Gottähnlichkeit* ('similarity to God') refers solely and specifically to the conquest of remorse and is thus nowhere near as far-reaching in its arrogance as Faust's 'yet art thou still but Faustus, and a man' (Marlowe) or 'bin ich ein Gott?' (Goethe).

Mention of Nietzschean views on morality naturally raises the question of whether and to what extent conceptions of Don Juan have been subject to changing ideas about morality or to new developments in philosophy. In the early Don Juan pieces, as we saw, serious attempts to explain Don Juan's wickedness (where such attempts were made at all) showed it as based on a philosophy of nature.

Some modern Don Juans have been shown as similarly motivated. Hans Bethge's hero justifies himself thus: 'I live as I must! It is an impulse, a natural act of willing, at once sweet and unhappy – it is an urge which I obey as a child obeys its nurse' (1910, p. 8). The hero of Charles Leyst's *Don Juans Mission* (*c.* 1921) not only lives according to a philosophy of nature, he tries to 'educate' others, to uncover and correct what is unnatural in people's emotional relationships, so that basic human emotions may come into their own. Since, according to this philosophy of nature, truth to one's own self and obedience to one's impulses are the prime virtues, it is not surprising to find Nietzschean echoes here too, as in the works of Bernhardi and Lipiner just discussed. For the right of the exceptional person to pass beyond received notions of good and evil in order to 'be himself' was one of the main lessons that Nietzsche's admirers extracted from his writings on morality.[8]

Vloten's Don Juan, whom we have already encountered, is another example, claiming, as he does, that his prime duty is to realize his personal potential to the highest degree. In this ambition, he is logically bound to place himself outside conventional morality: 'Good? evil? ... I have never been particularly interested in this antithesis. I just acted as I had to' (p. 236). So, like the 'Nietzschean' heroes in the novels of Vloten's contemporary, Hermann Hesse, this Don Juan can represent himself as one of those rebels and sinners who are reviled by society but without whom the world would petrify in harmony: 'For this reason, those who despise the law and create dissonance, the great sinners, are just as necessary for the good of the world as those who are active in the cause of duty and strict morality' (Vloten, p. 240). Similarly, the hero of *Don Juans Puppen* by Max Glass claims the right of the strong and clear-sighted man to act as he wills.[9]

The transformation of Don Juan into a hero has thus entered into a new phase. Byron had implied that the battle between self-indulgence and conformity was part of a wider conflict between natural and unnatural attitudes in human conduct and society; the German Romantics and the Hoffmannists in France had valued Don Juan as a man activated by transcendental idealism. Nietzsche's followers regarded Don Juan as a Strong Man whom the world needed even as it denounced him as a reprobate; someone whose uncompromising desire to be himself inescapably led him to revalue conventional moral standards ('Umwertung aller Werte', to use Nietzsche's own phrase). An aggressive nonconformity was seen as estimable: by the Romantics because the 'ordinary man' was regarded as unimaginative and materialistic, by the Nietzscheans because that same ordinary man was a stunted being who passively submitted to moral conditioning to a point where he was unable to think or act for himself. Simultaneously, however, a rival view of Don Juan gave him a more passive and impersonal role, seeing him as victim or instrument of biological forces.

This rival theory – that Don Juan is not so much set on a course of assertive individualism as unwittingly in the grip of a force stronger than he (the Life Force) – receives philosophical sanction from Schopenhauer. It matters little whether the Life Force manifests itself in and through Don Juan himself or whether he is the prey; the essential thing is that the human being is reduced to the status of an agent or tool. Schopenhauer had argued that the joys and pains of love, which had so obsessed poets through the ages, were important only inasmuch as they were the means to a broader end, the propagation of the species. Hence, he adds (nearly a century before *Man and Superman*), it is in Nature's interest to throw together such partners as will produce strong and able offspring:

> Nothing is so much in Nature's interest as the conservation of the species and of its true representative; to which end sound, vigorous and strong individuals are the means: only such as these concern her. Indeed, she regards and treats individuals just as means to an end.[10]

If they are employed or exploited in this way by Nature (or the Life Force), it is irrelevant whether individuals find happiness in love or not. In fact, they are likely to be caught in that cheerless trap to which Schopenhauer returns time and again in his philosophy: the ceaseless alternation of painful desire and boring satiety. The Don Juan of Jelusich's novel (1931) describes this experience in terms that are pure Schopenhauer: 'And so I was tossed to and fro between desire – nausea – and renewed desire – an eternal plaything of passion' (p. 261).

As far as works devoted to Don Juan are concerned, then, Schopenhauer and Nietzsche seem to provide the main philosophical impulses in the late nineteenth and early twentieth centuries.[11] Since these philosophies are, respectively, passive and assertive, they complement each other and bolster up two quite distinct interpretations of Don Juan's character. For an author who sees him as conscious, strong, determined and out of humour with the restrictions dictated by conventional social *mores*, there will be much attraction in Nietzsche's idea of two moralities, one for the free spirit and one for the slave. Those who see Don Juan as directly or indirectly in the grip of the Life Force can find authority for this in Schopenhauer's wholly impersonal and somewhat resigned interpretation of the sexual urges. I find it surprising that there are not more Schopenhauerian Don Juan works, in which the hero is shown to be the slave of life, helplessly oscillating between desire and boredom until he is forced to wonder whether the game is worth the candle, whether extinction might not be preferable to this purposeless swing of the pendulum. (Jelusich's novel, referred to above, evades this question by encompassing Don Juan's salvation in a singularly contrived and sentimental way.)

However Don Juan may be motivated, his way of life is shown to be a full-time occupation, almost a vocation. This is already clear in Molière's Dom Juan, who, like a second Alexander, longs for new worlds to conquer (Act 1 Scene 2). The universality of Don Juan's desires is made tangible as soon as the notion of the servant's catalogue takes root. It might be pointed out here that many writers (Max Frisch is one), having Leporello's 'mille e tre' in mind, speak of a thousand and three conquests, but these are in Spain alone; the grand total is two thousand and sixty-five. 'The poor man hasn't had a holiday in years.'[12] Vloten's hero makes sexual fulfilment his career; Erich Kästner's Don Juan has such an obsessive desire to possess all women that lesser womanizers seem like amateurs vainly competing with a professional. Sylvia Townsend Warner's Don Juan has 'a vocation as irrevocable as the vocation of a St John of the Cross',[13] while the hero of F. K. Becker's *Don Juans Anfang* (1925) expresses the same idea through the image of a multiplicity of hearts, one for each beautiful woman: 'Ich habe viele Herzen. Jeder schönen Frau schenke ich eins' (pp. 85 f.).

The changing forms which this idea of 'vocation' takes on over the centuries is yet another clear indicator of changing attitudes. In Molière, Dom Juan gives an impression of arrogance, with Sganarelle voicing the expected and conventional objections. In Mozart/da Ponte, our reaction would be one of deep disapproval if we allowed ourselves to take the catalogue and the circumstances in which its contents are revealed to Elvira at all seriously. The contrast with Warner's religious phraseology or Becker's 'viele Herzen' is too obvious to need spelling out.

Yet it is probably this single-minded pursuit of something both reprehensible and, in the end, often boring and self-defeating that sets up a resistance to Don Juan in many readers. The spectacle of an exceptional man who does nothing but chase and seduce women was certainly a major factor which led many authors to seek a deeper motive behind the debauchery. But even an obsessive carnality in no way redeemed by idealism can be made to seem a little more palatable if Don Juan's rivals are portrayed as emotionally tepid, for the rudest attempt to come between husband and wife or between a man and his fiancée will have a perverse attraction by virtue of its daring and its intensity if the officially sanctioned union is represented as lacking passion. The contrast between such correct but lukewarm relationships and the ardour of Don Juan's illicit designs is brought out in work after work, often in ways that clearly show the influence of the Anna/Octavio/Giovanni triangle in Mozart/da Ponte. In Wiese's tragedy of 1840, Don Juan robs two prospective husbands of their brides-to-be, and in each case it is plainly stated that the engagement had been contracted without any real warmth of love on either side; this fact assuredly makes Don Juan's intervention seem less despicable than it might otherwise have been.[14] Pushkin also represents Anna's marriage as having been wished on her by her mother for financial reasons. But it is Shaw who makes the point most radically and in a way that, provided we do not brush his remarks aside as Shavian naughtiness, cannot but affect our judgement of Don Juan.

Marriage, says Don Juan in *Man and Superman*, is a licentious institution, a mantrap camouflaged by pretence and hypocrisy: 'The confusion of marriage with morality has done more to destroy the conscience of the human race than any other single error' (p. 670). But, since marriage is society's chief means of propagating the human species, women, as the servants of the Life Force, demand it and withhold their favours unless the man's intentions are 'honourable':

> On inquiring what that proviso meant, I found that it meant ... that I desired her continual companionship, counsel and conversation to the end of my days, and would take a most solemn oath to be always enraptured by them:[15] above all, that I would turn my back on all other women for ever for her sake. I did not object to these conditions because they were exorbitant and inhuman: it was their extraordinary irrelevance that prostrated me.
>
> (pp. 676 f.)

And so he always replied 'with perfect frankness' that he could not possibly answer for his feelings until the end of his life. Here the debate is taken far beyond a contrast between dutiful emotion and unlawful passion to a point where society, in having thus institutionalized marriage, is shown as hypocritical, and it is the 'arch-deceiver' Don Juan who is the honest man, refusing to lend himself to social pretence and romantic delusions. Ana and her father, both pillars of respectable society during their lifetimes, emerge as notably less honest than Don Juan in the Hell-scene, as do Ann and Ramsden in the play proper. This is yet another ironic reversal of the audience's expectations in this most surprising of Don Juan plays, for, with very few exceptions, it had previously been inseparable from Don Juan's character that he should cynically exploit the conventions by making promises that he did not mean to keep[16] or even marrying with the set intention of abandoning his bride as soon as he had possessed her.

Gwyn Thomas, seemingly the only one of his countrymen to have treated so un-Welsh a theme, published a Don Juan novel in 1958 under the title *The Love Man*. One does not have to have read very far into his works to have encountered the thesis that the life-enhancing urges have been stifled by puritanism. What Thomas has done is to show Juan as a victim of outraged morality and he has used Spanish Catholicism as a stick with which to beat Welsh Nonconformism. Don Juan has tried to 'give back to life some of the shape that's been taken from it by all those footling clowns, the chaste, the submissive and the weak, the predestined pall-bearers and mourners at the vast interment of joy which is the business of so much living' (p. 39). Thomas's novel occupies a niche as a spirited example of those works which take issue with the 'monkish' moral of the original Don Juan play (which Thomas, as a student of Spanish, knew). Witty, vigorous and, at times, moving, *The Love Man* deserves to be more widely known.

# 9
# Don Juan as a Type

In many discussions of Don Juan's character, he gradually comes to stand for a human type who can be described and analysed more or less independently of the literary works in which he figures and which, strictly speaking, alone create and define him. The trend starts in the early nineteenth century, with Stendhal's *De l'Amour* of 1822.[1] Stendhal sets off Werther and Don Juan against each other as opposite types of lover and reaches the rather surprising conclusion that Werther is the happier of the two because his love is idealistic, making his soul receptive to all that is beautiful. His passion transfigures reality, whereas Don Juan makes passion into something ordinary and kills love by planning his adventures like military campaigns.[2]

Kierkegaard offers a quite different interpretation. He, like Hoffmann, was led to reflect on Don Juan through Mozart's music; indeed, he repeatedly declares that the Don Juan legend is the musical theme *par excellence* and finds its best expression in music. (This is in the long disquisition on 'the Erotic' in the first part of *Either/Or*, 1843.) After a very abstract discussion of erotic sensuality, Kierkegaard traces its various stages in such characters as Cherubino and Papageno through to Don Giovanni. That is to say, he is not interested in tracing a chronological development in Mozart's works, but in charting the gradual intensification of the erotic urge as displayed, stage by stage, in the various characters just mentioned. When we reach Don Giovanni, he argues, the sexual drive has become irresistible and demonic. Here he insists, rather strangely, that he is not talking about desire *in an individual*; he sees Don Giovanni as standing for an impersonal and elemental force. Presently, however, he seems to hedge his bets by saying that Don

Giovanni 'hovers between being idea – that is, power, life – and being an individual'. But soon he returns to the transcendent and, as it were, de-personalizing capabilities of music, which expresses the elemental power residing in this character and so ceases to present him – or, at least, ceases to present him solely and unambiguously – as an individual person.[3]

To move nearer to our day, Camus[4] sees Don Juan as a man who accepts and lives life, but entertains no delusions or hopes. His genius resides in the fact that he 'knows his frontiers' (p. 98). Thus, since he expects from life nothing which it cannot give, he avoids the trap into which the idealist falls. In fact, says Camus, it is ridiculous to think of Don Juan as an idealistic quester after some absolute of erotic intensity. He is not an eternal malcontent like Faust.

Many of the discussions of the 'Don Juan type' in the present century have come from psychologists and psychoanalysts. For Gregorio Marañon, Don Juan's indiscriminate pursuit of women is not proof of virility, but of emotional and sexual immaturity, even of a *lack* of virility. He has a rudimentary and adolescent sexual instinct which can find its puny satisfaction with any woman. Hence, although he is in his limited way in love with Woman, he is incapable of truly loving any individual person. Each and every woman is simply the means to sex ('le moyen d'arriver au sexe').[5] Adolescent, too, is his tendency to boast about and exaggerate his conquests; the servant's catalogue is the tangible sign of this.

The most discussed interpretation of Don Juan from the point of view of psychological theorizing is that by the Freudian, Otto Rank, who had the dubious distinction of being singled out for attack by Montherlant.[6] After summarizing Freudian views of Don Juan which, needless to say, cast the Commander as a father-figure, Rank goes on to argue that a cluster of very ancient and persistent mythical beliefs have found their way into the Don Juan legend and given it much of its force. Chief among these is the widespread conviction that the dead may be invested with magic powers and return to take vengeance on the living. This will doubtless have helped to account for some of the fascinated horror with which early audiences of Don Juan plays and operas will have watched the stalking figure of the Stone Guest.

Rank's more contentious theory involves the notion of the Double. Using the Mozart opera as his frame of reference, he begins by claiming that Leporello is Don Giovanni's double in a physical sense, pointing out how master and man impersonate one another and play each other's roles.[7] But they are not only physical doubles, adds Rank; they are the two halves of a divided personality. That is to say, Don Giovanni (or Don Juan, for the discussion does not confine itself to the opera) has cast off his conscience and his scruples – everything that could inhibit him in his career as a successful libertine – on to his servant.[8] For Rank, Don Juan is a latter-day reincarnation of a godlike or heroic figure for whom possession of women would previously have been a right, freely and willingly given. But Christianity has turned him into a monster, if not a devil. So now he must acquire by force or cunning what was formerly his by privilege.

These theories cannot be laughed out of court. The haughty and imperious claims on each and every woman which have been made by successive Don Juans do indeed suggest some sort of quasi-divine right; it is as if Don Juan felt that his very nature granted him a *jus primae noctis* over all women. This was the chief basis for George Sand's attack, as we have seen. Georg Trakl, if the Prologue to his projected Don Juan drama (1906–8) is a reliable guide, had a somewhat similar conception in mind; his Don Juan was to have inherited the defiant hedonism of a vanished dionysian age. In further support of Rank, it does often appear that the servant must carry the burden of all the conventional scruples from which Don Juan has liberated himself and placate those people whom his master has outraged.

For instance, da Ponte's Leporello can be seen as embodying decent and conventional sides of human personality and conduct which his master rejects and dispenses with – even if the point is occasionally obscured by comic business or weakened by the fact that the servant connives at the master's projects (for this connivance is not always dictated by fear or otherwise enforced). If one goes outside the opera, and the ageless terms in which Rank conducts his discussion certainly justify this, one can find other evidence which would support the theory, including the characterization of the servants in *El Burlador*, in Molière and other French pieces of that period and – from the point of view of a writer who scorns conventional morality – in Baudelaire's sketch.

But Rank's theory of Don Juan as god-turned-monster is unprovable and could in any case be no more than a vague and half-conscious tribal memory in the mind of dramatist or audience. Furthermore, the notion of master and servant as two halves of a split personality is possible only if one selects the evidence or knows only a very small proportion of the works devoted to Don Juan. For many of the servants are quite different from Rank's conception: some are almost as evil as Don Juan himself, some are would-be Don Juans or thoroughly willing accomplices who derive pleasure from their master's exploits, basking in 'black beams of vicarious sin', as Heath-Stubbs puts it (1965, p. 3). Others veer between outrage and connivance. Henri de Regnier (1908) perceives this and gives his Don Juan two servants, one of whom, Sganarelle, tries to dissuade Don Juan from a particularly disreputable and heartless escapade, while the other, Leporello, abets his master. This division of the *servant* into two distinct halves seems rather more plausible than the dissociation postulated by Rank.

Psychological examinations of the 'Don Juan type' nearly always have a basic limitation; the theory is either developed on the basis of selective evidence, or the evidence is selected *post hoc* in support of the theory – or the theorizing may simply abandon any foundation in specific literary works, however tenuous or selective. In such cases, the basis on which a definition of the Don Juan type is erected will presumably be a combination of clinical data or pure theorizing on the part of the writer; literature will simply have provided him with the name of Don Juan as a label and with a framework of reference for his and the reader's convenience. For Marañon, it is only a 'literary mirage' that enables us to see Don Juan as virile: 'à mon avis, seul un mirage littéraire autorise à considérer Don Juan comme l'archétype de la virilité. L'erreur est manifeste' (p. 22). But who is the Don Juan of whom Marañon speaks, if he is thus to be divorced at will from his incorporations in literary works? Rank too is highly selective; his theory of the Double is based largely on Mozart/da Ponte and, for the rest, he sees virtue only in those works which seem to support his views. Those which trouble the waters are written off as 'decadent'.[9] Brigid Brophy, in what starts as an analysis of the Mozart/da Ponte opera, is also inclined to remove the hero from his context in order to relocate him in a psychologist's casebook.[10] But the most extreme manifestation of this tendency known to me occurs in G.R. Lafora's essay 'The Psychology of Don Juan': 'I propose to study the real Don Juan from the medical and psychological standpoint, free from all literary prejudice.'[11] But the conception of Don Juan must have come in the first place from one or more of the literary works devoted to him, however much he may thereafter have shifted in the author's mind towards a type. The circularity of this method is demonstrated by the fact that Lafora, like Rank, refers with approval to various Don Juan works which happen to reinforce his theories. (These he would regard as literary evidence, no doubt, not 'literary prejudice'.)

I find the views of Stendhal, Kierkegaard and Camus more valid and more thought-provoking than the fantasies of Rank and Lafora. But they too are limited, as so often in discussions of the 'type', by the narrow range of Don Juan works to which they can reasonably be applied. Against Stendhal it must be urged that the 'happy' Werther professes a gloomy philosophy of life and is thoroughly disillusioned by most of his fellow human beings, at least in fashionable society. After going through an emotionally fraught and artistically unproductive period, he commits suicide, while by contrast, in the great majority of Don Juan works, the hero clings obstinately to life, even if erotic experiences continue to disappoint him. The objection to Kierkegaard is simpler, almost a matter of tone. The notion of Don Juan as someone who expresses and puts into practice the genius of sensuality is not exactly wrong, but far too abstract; to transport such a flamboyant and sensual character into the rarefied atmosphere of philosophical speculation and to discuss him as if it were uncertain whether he is man or idea seems inappropriate, to put it no more strongly. The shortcomings of Camus' interpretation are again those of narrowness; his view, like Stendhal's, must logically exclude all those Don Juans who have been motivated by any sort of idealism, leaving us only with the uncomplicated hedonists: da Ponte's Don Giovanni, rather than the re-interpretations of him inspired by Hoffmann, if one cares to put it in those terms.

It must be conceded that there is a genuine difficulty here. Let us take the hypothetical case of an interested and cultivated – but non-specialist – lover of music and literature who knows the Don Juan plays by Tirso de Molina, Molière and Shaw, together with Mozart's opera. The characterization of Don Juan differs from work to work: is he pursuer or quarry? what are his redeeming features? does he believe in anything beyond his own right to self-gratification? There are obviously also motifs and incidents which are not common to all four works; for instance, the important scene with the beggar occurs in Molière alone. Where Tirso and Molière give roughly the same sequence of events, Shaw departs wholly from the traditional plot, only referring to it in the Hell-scene in order to give his contemporary events an historical and legendary dimension. But for all the differences of plot and characterization, a certain picture of Don Juan will have been created, according to which some actions and attributes are appropriate for him, while certain others (for instance, a display of arrant cowardice) would be barely thinkable. From here it is not unnatural that one should go on to conceive of Don Juan as a human type who has, no doubt, gone through a series of literary incarnations and transformations, but who can also exist independently of these literary works and may be encountered and recognized in real life, even if his social class and milieu and the details of his adventures are different from anything come across in play or opera. He has so outgrown the work in which he first appeared, says Rogers, that he has taken on 'some kind of independent existence' (1977, p. 9). Michel Berveiller, in his study *L'éternel Don Juan* of 1961, even devotes a chapter to 'Le Don Juanisme avant Don Juan', suggesting that the type was there and waiting on literary treatment. In the sense that neither Tirso nor anybody else can create in a vacuum, this is true; it is certainly a salutary reminder that the two strands (Don Juan in real life and in literature) coexist, intertwining and influencing each other in people's consciousness. This is the point at which Don Juan in art and 'Don Juan' in actuality can easily become confused, so that it is difficult to write about him in such a way that the reader will know exactly what lies behind the name.

Having said that, however, I cannot escape the feeling that the procedures adopted by Rank, Lafora and, to a lesser extent, Stendhal and Camus are dangerously ambiguous. And Ronald Grimsley seems almost excessively polite when, talking of Kierkegaard, he maintains that 'any particular aesthetic illustration of a subject is ultimately inseparable from a viewpoint which extends beyond art to the more complex reality of human existence.' Possibly, but the location of the frontier that divides the two realms should always be made as clear as possible to the reader. The psychologists in particular blur this frontier by alternately referring to Don Juan in a literary (or operatic) context and removing him from it in order to discuss him as a type. Since the range of literary allusions is necessarily selective in such discussions (and, indeed, sometimes has to be deduced from the writer's depiction of the 'Don Juan type'), the reader's uncertainties multiply.[12]

In popular parlance, 'Don Juan' has become a synonym for womanizer. This applies to English, French, German, Italian, Spanish and, to a lesser extent, Russian. Hence many writers use his name for catchpenny purposes in the titles of works dealing with a rake or libertine, works which neither draw on the traditional elements of the legend, nor contribute in any way to a serious investigation of Don Juan's character and motives. A. von Schaden's crude and sensational novel *Der deutsche Don Juan* of 1820 is an example, as arc the one-act plays *Don Juans Ende* (1896) and *Die Waffe des Don Juan* (1902) by W. Weigand and Rudolf Strauss respectively, and O.J. Bierbaum's short story 'Don Juan Tenorio' of 1898. In two cases, the name of Don Juan furnishes a mere excuse for a pornographic romp ('Fernando del Castillo', *c.* 1870; Apollinaire, 1911).

As commentator after commentator has pointed out, the conception and story of Don Juan are very firmly rooted in seventeenth-century Spain. But, as the story spread over Europe and became more and more popular, the tendency to set Don Juan in new and, to each given audience or set of readers, more familiar localities became irresistible. Why should Seville or the never-never-land of *opera buffa* enjoy a monopoly? Hence 'local' Don Juans proliferated and we encounter him in towns and cities all over Europe.[13] Often, exact local detail and colour are provided in order to make his exploits seem convincing. But Don Juan, for a variety of reasons, does not always transplant happily into new localities. The dangers are clear in Ludwig Engel's novel *Der Don Juan vom Jungfernstieg* of 1922, set in Hamburg. The traditional figure brought into the modern age, the exotic events transferred to a familiar German setting: all this is obviously central to Engel's intentions. But the contrasts work to his disadvantage. Here is this modern Don Juan going about his work of seduction, tempting his prospective victim into a bar: 'Sie schritten an einer Bar vorüber . . . "Kommen Sie, mein Fräulein, trinken wir einen Schnaps!" ' (pp. 32 f.). There is nothing intrinsically ridiculous or trivial in the bar or the schnaps; it is simply that the reader, having had the figure of Don Juan put into his mind, will almost inevitably think of 'Là ci darem la mano' or 'Deh, vieni alla finestra, o mio tesoro!'

Similarly, the statue of Don Juan's victim seems somehow less awesome when transported to Trafalgar Square (Flecker, 1925) or Hyde Park (Levy, 1937). Again, as in Engel, the incongruity derives in part from the setting, in part from the form of words. In Flecker's play, Don Juan and a friend comment on how lifelike the statue is: 'I swear if I asked it to look in this evening it would nod its head' (Act 3 Scene 1). 'Look in this evening' – that sounds a little flat after Don Giovanni's imperious 'Digli che questa sera l'attendo a cena meco.' Here is another manifestation of that ambivalence which surrounds the figure of Don Juan. As soon as the author of a new version produces his variation on traditional motifs and incidents, the informed member of the audience (or reader) will make the connection and judge the one work against the other; this is likely to be particularly strong in drama, where the events are actually unfolding before his eyes. Here he will experience the new play as a play and will simultaneously respond to it as a contribution to a literary tradition. If the older, familiar work, with which comparisons are implicitly invited, is a great masterpiece, these can only fall out in one way, unless the author of the new work has a very sure touch. I would say that, despite very occasional lapses, Shaw and Frisch succeed; Flecker certainly fails.

Perhaps the task becomes easier when the theme is treated in a thoroughly light-hearted spirit, as when Don Juan is transported to Vienna and made into a petit bourgeois of uncertain means, who is encountered as he pursues the shopgirls of that city.[14] The transmutation of setting and social class and the absence of the potentially embarrassing traditional episodes (above all, the encounter with the Statue) make such works less vulnerable than the rather uneasy efforts at adaptation and modernization by Engel, Flecker and Levy. But the legend *can* be successfully transplanted to other ages and countries and treated with seriousness and respect. To illustrate the point, I would like to consider two works which have not yet made an appearance in this account: those by Melchior Meyr (1867) and Jean Anouilh (1955).

Meyr's novel *Der schwarze Hans* is played out among the peasantry in a remote German village; it is something like a companion piece to Gottfried Keller's village Romeo and Juliet (*Romeo und Julia auf dem Dorfe*). Meyr's Don Juan ('der schwarze Hans' of the title) has the traditional reputation of an unscrupulous womanizer and the traditional qualities of effrontery, courage and restlessness. After many conquests he is drawn to Kathrine, the village beauty, whom he eventually wins away from her fiancé, Heinrich. He soon tires of her, however, and abandons her, by which time she is pregnant. In the end he is stabbed to death by the infuriated Heinrich.

Meyr's hero scorns the 'miserable fear' ('elende Feigheit') that prevents conventional folk from grasping pleasure when it offers itself, and he justifies his abandonment of Kathrine with the familiar argument that he must act in accordance with his character (pp. 171 f.). Like his ancestors in novel and drama, he needs no other excuse. Heinrich plays the part of a Don Ottavio: devoted, goodhearted, but thoroughly unexciting (in fact, his *crime passionel* at the end comes as a surprise). It is no wonder that Kathrine comes to prefer the more virile and dashing Hans, as he plays Don Juan's traditional card by claiming that she could never marry a milksop like Heinrich ('so ein erbärmlicher Mensch verdient dich nicht', p. 44). There is even a hint that Kathrine is a sort of Anna figure, absolutely different from all the other women, who *had* to be abandoned because they fell short of Hans' exacting demands (p. 141). But – and here Meyr is perhaps shrewder than some writers who took up the conception of Anna as Juan's ideal – Meyr's philanderer tires of his Kathrine once she becomes available and compliant.

This is emphatically not one of those versions where embarrassing memories of traditional and familiar works constantly intrude themselves. It is a genuine village metamorphosis of Don Juan's character and story. The wooing is a village wooing, the characters and customs are firmly rooted in the daily realities of nineteenth-century rural life. Instead of duels, we have rowdy brawls and struggles in inns and on woodland paths; instead of rapiers, the weapons are knives and cudgels. Don Juan's end, when it comes, is certainly represented as divine vengeance on his misdeeds. God is not mocked, says Heinrich; one day He will light on the sinner like a thunderbolt (p. 184). But this turns out to be no more than a prophetic metaphor. Divine vengeance, when it does come, uses Heinrich's knife as its instrument, allowing Heinrich to represent himself as God's agent (p. 195). This is a good deal more convincing than the situation in Flecker and Levy.

Jean Anouilh's comedy *Ornifle ou le courant d'air* of 1955 is totally different from *Der schwarze Hans* in every respect: light and witty where Meyr is serious and even mildly sententious at times, urban as opposed to rural, as profoundly French as Meyr is profoundly German. But, like Meyr's novel, Anouilh's play is a recognizable variant on the Don Juan theme, even if specific similarities of plot are tenuous and at times only implied.[15]

Ornifle is a poet who has prostituted and commercialized his talent to churn out popular song-texts. Successful and famous, he is here encountered in middle age, still pursuing his career as a Don Juan and still capable of exercising power over women. The piece ends with his death (from natural causes – see below, p. 131), even as he plans a new conquest. As is usual in such freely updated versions, it is the conception of Don Juan's (or Ornifle's) character that is of central interest. He is a hedonist, indignantly rejecting the notion that pleasures are vain, accepting and following his own nature ('je suis ce que je suis' – p. 271). Regarding true and deep emotion as a rarity, he prefers lighter loves, although he is also prepared to savour the subtler pleasures of a longer, more persuasive courtship. He equates physical pleasures with pleasures of the soul and prefers to enjoy life rather than reflect on it. We are placed on earth to dance, not brood: 'La vie est trop légère pour réfléchir . . . Nous sommes sur cette terre pour danser' (pp. 270 f.). Even that brief description will show how the piece resonates with memories of previous Don Juan works. But since Ornifle seems to have no belief in the likelihood of finding true love and prefers to accept easier pleasures, he seems to come near to Camus' notion of a Don Juan free from illusions and unaffected by idealism.

Of the works mentioned in the last two chapters, it is the discussions of Don Juan as a type, especially those by the psychologists and psychoanalysts, that seem to reduce his stature by turning a character who has, throughout his literary incarnations, always been an out-and-out individualist, into an archetype. In virtually all other cases the scales are further tipped towards sympathy. A Don Juan who is portrayed as occupying a position 'beyond good and evil' is, at least in the eyes of most of the writers who thus conceived him, admirable in his rebelliousness and more vital than those against whom he rebels. Sometimes even, the affirmation of natural appetites in the face of society's hypocrisy (Shaw) or the pressures of the Church (Gwyn Thomas) show Don Juan to be more honest than the forces and interests that oppose him, however destructive his actions may be in their consequences. Furthermore, of course, a 'sporting' Don Juan at least has the saving grace of daring, even as he pursues his traditional career as despoiler of women.

# 10

## The Legendary Framework
### *An Aid or a Pitfall?*

A story as familiar as that of Don Juan can go through innumerable metamorphoses, as we have seen. Some writers took over the main ingredients from tradition and worked out their new interpretations within that framework; others abandoned the legend almost entirely; yet others ironized it. As some of the examples in the previous chapter may have shown, we can respond to the new variation on the old tune with delighted surprise or slight embarrassment, depending on the originality and technical skill of the writer. Was then the existence of a ready-made framework of events and a firmly established central character an advantage or a pitfall for the unwary? Meyr's *Der schwarze Hans* and Anouilh's *Ornifle* suggest the former; Ludwig Engel and Flecker certainly provide examples of the latter. If we are to look at this aspect of Don Juan's fortunes in more detail, it is necessary to go back to the beginnings.

The Don Juan legend, like the story of Dr Faust, grew up in an age in which the supernatural events forming part of it seemed perfectly possible and the Divine retribution which those events signalled was conceived as literal reality. Hell was a genuine threat. But both legends were to outlive this general credulity and would continue to exert imaginative power on generations who had lost much or all of the belief in the supernatural. With Faust the case is simple: by the time that the story was reclaimed for serious literary treatment in the latter part of the eighteenth century, hardly any educated people in Germany believed in the literal possibility of a pact with the Devil or of performing magical deeds with his assistance. It is Mephistopheles himself who, in Goethe's play, wryly admits that the Devil has been banished into story books (l. 2507); from now on, he and his magic will either be regarded as emblematic of Faust's more-than-human ambitions or will be treated ironically – or both. One would expect to find something similar happening at about the same historical moment in treatments of the Don Juan theme. But the first sign of rebellion against the supernatural aspects of the traditional story comes somewhat earlier and for a different reason.

Carlo Goldoni's *Don Giovanni Tenorio o sia Il Dissoluto* of 1736 has already been briefly mentioned as one of da Ponte's sources. Goldoni was, as far as I know, the first to reject the idea of the Statue as agent of Divine retribution. His play is thus unusual in that it contains most of the expected ingredients: wooing of a peasant-girl, Don Giovanni's pursuit of Anna and the resultant death of her father, the Commander, in a duel, etc. – but no perambulating Stone Guest. Instead, Goldoni's Don Giovanni is killed by a thunderbolt. Why? 'Everybody knows that poor Spanish play that the Italians call *Il Convitato di Pietra* and the French *Le Festin de Pierre*', says Goldoni in his *Mémoires*, also calling the traditional Don Juan plays an 'ancient piece of buffoonery'.[1] In the Preface to his own version (L'Autore a qui legge'), he makes merry over the 'farcical' ending of the existing plays, adding that he cannot let this dissolute man go unpunished but wishes to make his punishment credible and thus to arouse terror and penitence in the audience. The thunderbolt was chosen because it can be seen as instrument of God's wrath but is also explicable in terms of natural laws (i, 176 f.).

What happens in Goldoni is this. When Don Giovanni woos Elisa, he vows to make her his wife:

*D.G.*    I swear by the spirit that reigns over Heaven and earth that you will be my wife.
*Elisa*    And if not?
*D.G.*    May a thunderbolt fall from Heaven and plunge my faithless soul into Hell.

(p. 232)

Later, after persisting in his wickedness and rejecting all calls to repentance, he is trapped by his pursuers before the statue of the Commander. In his defiant words, we may hear an echo of Goldoni's scorn for the conventional, 'farcical' ending:

Commander, what are you doing? Why do you not come and avenge the shedding of your blood? Why doesn't that marble statue hasten to descend and carry me with it into the Underworld? ... Deceitful gods, I challenge you to take vengeance. If it is true that the heavens wield power over mortal man, if there is justice above, let a thunderbolt fall on me! Strike me, kill me and send me forever to Hell.

(pp. 278 f.)

At this blasphemous outburst, a thunderbolt does indeed strike him dead.

This, then – however implausible the coming together of Divine and natural laws at precisely the right moment may be – is acceptable, whereas a statue that walks, talks and visits mortals at the supper-table is not. Goldoni is not concerned with banishing the supernatural from his play; he simply wants to make it seem dignified. The perambulating statue will not do because it is as much a part of the 'absurd and vulgar' popular tradition as were the comic antics of Don Juan/Giovanni's servant (also omitted from Goldoni's play). The first modification of the supernatural part of the Don Juan legend came about not because of an author's scepticism, but because of his desire for theatrical reform and didactic effectiveness. Heaven's vengeance still lights on the sinner in spectacular fashion.

But, from the early part of the nineteenth century onwards, the supernatural elements began to constitute an embarrassment in themselves, with the result that they were often dispensed with altogether. This is, of course, easier to do in the case of Don Juan than with the Faust legend, for, with Faust, magic pervades the whole story and helps to give it its characteristic shape and meaning, proceeding step by logical step from the conjuration of the Devil to Faust's descent into Hell. But, in the parallel tradition, the supernatural enters into the story only at the point where Juan chances on the statue. All that was needed was to bring about the libertine's end in a way that did not offend against natural causation, while at the same time satisfying the requirements of poetic justice and dramatic psychology. And so we find Don Juan inviting death by throwing away his sword in a duel (Lenau), or actually committing suicide (Heyse). Or he may be killed by one of his victims (O.A.H. Schmitz, 'Don Juan und die Kurtisane') or by the father or bridegroom of a girl whom he had wronged (Lipiner, Meyr).

Don Juan's virtual suicide in Lenau is the most revealing

example. This disappointed idealist has no need of supernatural adversaries; as Hiltrud Gnüg points out,[2] his retribution comes from within as an inescapable psychological consequence of his way of life. Or, as Lenau puts it, disgust is the devil that carries him off (see above, p. 48). Don Juan does, it is true, talk of Heaven's lightning, but this turns out to be only a metaphor. A metaphor, moreover, which – far from making the abstract notion of punishment more sharply defined and more convincing – reveals only scepticism. *Perhaps* a lightning-stroke from regions I despised has paralyzed me, says Don Juan, but *perhaps* my feeling of emptiness is simply a result of my having burnt myself out (pp. 441 f., my italics). So the lightning-stroke is not only merely an image for whatever caused Don Juan's inner state; it is just one of two hypotheses and the regions whence it came (or might have come) are thrown into doubt by Don Juan's method of alluding to them.

In Barbey d'Aurévilly's short story 'Le plus bel amour de Don Juan' (1874), it is the visitation of the Stone Guest which has been demoted to the status of a metaphor; it has come to symbolize the approach of old age which will spell death to Don Juan's career, even if not to his life: 'It was the hour of the terrible supper with the cold, white marble Commander, after which there is nothing but Hell – the Hell of old age' (p. 101). Sometimes the supernatural is simply explained away as the product of credulous minds or the invention of priests, anxious to stress the dreadful end that awaits the libertine: there are examples in H. Roujon, 1895; E. Haraucourt, 1898; Otto Brües, 1957 and Gwyn Thomas, 1958. Since *El Burlador* was the invention of a monk and did have a didactic function, these authors have done no more than take up what was a motivating idea in Tirso's mind and make it part of the fabric and theme of their works which thereby become both a variation on, and critique of, the original play. In their effect upon readers or audiences, such versions are obviously similar to those Faust works in which the pact and the scholar-magician's gruesome end are claimed to have been put about by the Church in order to warn and deter the faithful. A witty variation occurs in Frisch's Don Juan play where, as we have seen, an unwilling libertine stages his own 'death', satisfying popular morality and providing himself with a means of escape at one and the same time. Or, of course, the supernatural can simply be treated as a joke. This occurs, in a spirit of jovial codding, in Shaw's *Man and Superman* and, rather more uneasily, in

## THE LEGENDARY FRAMEWORK

Ben Levy's play of 1937. In Montherlant, the apparition of the Statue turns out to have been a carnival trick played on Don Juan.

Anouilh, in his play *Ornifle*, simultaneously manages to introduce the idea of divine justice and to show Ornifle's death as proceeding from natural causes. Ornifle himself is in no doubt that Heaven is preparing his punishment ('polishing the thunderbolt', p. 271; it is surprising how often, since its literal use in Goldoni, thunder or lightning has been used as a metaphor for divine vengeance in Don Juan works). So Ornifle hardly needs the traditional warning. He knows that he may win a trick or two but that God holds all the aces. This, together with the idea of punishment delayed, is adroitly worked out. Ornifle is constantly under threat, but each time the danger seems to pass him by. His natural son tries to kill him, but the pistol is not loaded. Now more insidious forms of punishment seem likely to overtake him, ennui and jealousy: ennui because at length all experiences are disappointing, jealousy on account of his son's happiness with a young and beautiful girl. But he devises a method by which he hopes to win the girl, thus removing the cause of his jealousy and, since this will have to be a long and subtle campaign, overcoming his boredom. A further threat – the diagnosis that he has a weak heart – appears to have been a false alarm. Three tricks to Ornifle! But Heaven has been waiting patiently and now plays its ace. The illness was, in fact, genuine and grave; Ornifle collapses and dies just as he is preparing to put his latest campaign into motion.

So Anouilh's play has a perfectly natural ending in that this Don Juan suffers the consequences of a life of indulgence (wine, women and tobacco in his case; his songs are sung by others). The conventional metaphor of Heaven's thunderbolt does not merely carry its traditional meaning that pleasures always have to be paid for and that the moment of reckoning will come on us unexpectedly; it also conveys the additional point that the price, at least in the offender's eyes, may seem to be inordinately high.

At the risk of labouring the obvious, one must make a distinction here, as far as audience- or reader-reaction is concerned, between more or less realistic and updated versions and the older treatments of the legend. We accept the perambulating statue in seventeenth-century plays in the same spirit in which we accept Faust's pact in the old chapbooks or the presence of demons in paintings of the Temptation of St Antony. Over and above this, the dramatist – if he knows his job – will be able to convince us on an imaginative and aesthetic level through the way in which he achieves a combination and interaction of character and events, so that the coming to life of the Statue will seem logical and satisfying to us both as a dramatic climax and as poetic justice. With Mozart's opera, our reactions will probably be more complex. Firstly, the medium itself distances events from everyday causality; we expect opera to be exotic and irrational. In addition, the music, especially in the churchyard and banquet scenes, is likely to carry us along to such an extent that considerations of intrinsic possibility simply vanish from our minds. (It is a pity that we cannot put this to the test by experiencing a revival of a lesser eighteenth-century opera on the Don Juan theme.)

But, as soon as Don Juan is transported to a nineteenth-century German village or to the streets of Hamburg or London in our century, we come to expect that his adventures will carry plausibility in terms of that setting and era and we are bound to be alienated if the author resorts suddenly and incongruously to magical events in order to bring about Don Juan's end, unless this is manifestly done in either a symbolic or an ironic way.

As we saw, authors of some Don Juans borrow the idea of a pact with the Devil from the Faust tradition. Two of these obviously want to have their cake and eat it by evoking the pact as a notion or symbol and simultaneously denying its literal possibility. Thus Gobineau's *Don Juan* (1844) expresses his willingness to make a pact with the Devil if such a being existed (p. 63). The idea of infernal assistance underlines Don Juan's wickedness and godlessness, but a concession is made to modern scepticism. Similarly, in Richard Mansfield's play *Don Juan* of 1891, the pact – Faust's pact revamped to suit a Don Juan – turns out to have been only a dream (pp. 56 f.).

Many authors construct plots which bear obvious and deliberate resemblance to one or other of the familar versions of the legend, but which exclude all mention of anything supernatural (examples: Jourdain, 1857; Friedmann, 1881; Hayem, 1886; Bethge, 1910). It is in fact true to say that the great majority of late nineteenth- and early twentieth-century Don Juan works either dispense with the supernatural or ironize it.

But the supernatural is only one element – albeit the climax – in a traditional story which has come to form a shared background for the author and his readers or audience. The legend involves not only the Stone Guest, but also the master/servant relationship, the wooings and impersonations, rustic episodes, duel, etc. Some authors have obviously regarded all of this as superannuated or inhibiting and have abandoned the incidents of the legend altogether, taking over little more than the figure of Don Juan in order to exploit a common awareness of what the name may be expected to signify. This has the effect of channelling responses into an examination of exactly how the modern work adapts and varies the human type as familiar from tradition. Here one could instance the novels by A. Brausewetter (1915), Vloten (1922) and A. Schirokauer (1932), as well as Heimerdinger's cycle of ballads (1933). Shared knowledge is always assumed in works which describe a single episode in Don Juan's life and in poems where the object is to capture the essence of his character and in which any retelling of his exploits would obviously destroy the work's economy.

A different kind of 'collaboration' between author and reader is involved in those versions which ironically cite traditional characters and incidents in order to underline the fact that this is going to be a new interpretation or a critique of established ones. We have seen how this happens in widely different ways in Shaw, Rostand, Montherlant and Frisch.[3] Since Shaw's exploitation of the legend shows both the possibilities and the hazards of such a procedure, it might be profitable to return to *Man and Superman* for a moment and to look at it specifically from this point of view, putting ourselves in the position of members of the audience.

The first hint in the play, as opposed to the 'Epistle Dedicatory', that this is a variation on the Don Juan story, comes at what is otherwise a wholly light-hearted moment in Act One. Ann has been both rebuked and petted for her use of nicknames and her generally casual way of addressing people. Tanner, in his new position as her guardian, thinks (or pretends to think) that he is entitled to a more formal mode of address than his mere Christian name:

*Tanner*      I think you ought to call me Mr Tanner.
*Ann* (gently)   No you don't, Jack. That's like the things you say on purpose to shock people. . . . But, if you like, I'll call you after your famous ancestor Don Juan.
(p. 555)

Famous ancestor? Until now the play has seemed like a modern comedy of social satire. The only indications thus far of a serious or half-serious theme concern Tanner's authorship of a book so subversive that it must be thrown into the wastepaper basket. That is to say, the play promises to develop along fairly familiar lines in placing a 'shocking' innovator within a conventional social setting; members of the audience who do not happen to know in advance that *Man and Superman* belongs to the corpus of Don Juan plays might well be expecting a more light-hearted Shavian variant on a type of play familiar since the Naturalists. But from this moment on, they will be aware that what follows will somehow be related to Don Juan and that, moreover, Jack Tanner has been identified as the updated hero. As an automatic consequence, Ann and Octavius cast themselves as Shaw's equivalent to Donna Anna and Don Ottavio. Since the dramatic *events* have no resemblance to the traditional ones, it is also immediately clear that the relationship must concern the characters and the issues. And soon there are hints that this is to be a reversal of any expected reading of the legend. Within a minute of her reference to Don Juan, Ann(a), who would normally be thought of as the quarry, is labelled the predator; not long after, we find Jack/Juan scoffing at 'romantic tomfoolery' and declaring that 'moral passion is the only real passion' (p. 571). From here on, our reactions to the happenings on stage become complex: even as we follow the fortunes of the twentieth-century characters, we are invited, if not forced, to consider how they relate to their 'famous ancestors' and, simultaneously, whether they confirm or negate the expectations that we carry over from previous works devoted to them.

But this enrichment of the dramatic texture and philosophical meaning carries its own danger: that of facetiousness. Shaw, never one to resist the opportunity for a wisecrack, falls into this trap in the Hell sequence:

*The Statue*   Do you remember how I frightened you when I said something like that to you from my pedestal in Seville? It sounds rather flat without my trombones.
*Don Juan*   They tell me it generally sounds flat with them, Commander.

(p. 652)

It should perhaps be stressed that this flippant exchange comes at what is otherwise a profoundly serious moment, for Don Juan has just embarked on his eloquent defence of Heaven as the realm of reality and striving.

An ingenious exploitation of the legend occurs in Sylvia Townsend Warner's novel *After the Death of Don Juan* (1938), which is set in the eighteenth century. In this work Don Juan, finding it convenient to disappear for a while, engineers his own 'death' with Leporello's help. When he turns up again, his father explains why he had never believed that his son was dead: just such a legend concerning the Tenorio family had been circulating in the village for many generations; Molière had even written a play about it (p. 35). The chronology is apt; the Age of Enlightenment was indeed a time when educated people increasingly questioned the truth of fantastic and supernatural tales. It is, in fact, the period in which the magical content of the Faust legend was coming under critical scrutiny. Warner, far from finding the tale of Don Juan's miraculous death embarrassing, makes it an integral part of her wittily updated version.

The situation in Thaddäus Rittner's drama of 1909 is more serious but equally ingenious. The work, entitled *Unterwegs*, has a main character who is clearly meant as a modern reincarnation of Don Juan. In trancelike moments, he has dim memories of that previous existence:

> *Baron* And she was also engaged . . . I was disguised as Anna's fiancé. . . . Afterwards, in the garden, I fought with her father, the Commander Don Gonzalo.
> *Professor* (startled) What sort of crazy tomfoolery is this!?
> *Baron* . . . And unfortunately I killed him.
>
> (p. 32)

The play ends with the death of this modern Don Juan and with a hint that the Donjuanesque spirit will be reborn. So the references to past events from the legend have the effect of suggesting that Don Juan lives on in every insatiable lover just as, for many Germans, Faust is reincarnated in every restless striving spirit and, for Rilke, Orpheus comes to earth afresh in every true poet.[4]

So the range of possibilities is wide. The legend may so embarrass the author that he feels compelled to ironize its supernatural ingredients or dispense with them altogether. He may produce a free variation on the chief characters and events, assuming that his readers or audience will have at least a basic familiarity with the theme that underlies the variation. In Anouilh's *Ornifle*, which has already been mentioned as a modern transformation of traditional elements, the variations are often so free as to verge on the elusive. One can see something of Leporello's or Sganarelle's criticism of his master carried over into the attitude of Ornifle's secretary, Mlle Supo; there is an ironic modern equivalent to the traditional catalogue when Ornifle's son, having set a detective agency on his father's trail, confronts Ornifle with his disreputable past (Act 3); there is, as we have seen, a reference to the traditional notion that divine justice will strike down the sinner. But the only direct quotation (or, more accurately, a deliberate misquotation, only to be appreciated by those sufficiently knowledgeable and alert to pick it up in the course of Anouilh's fast-moving dialogue) comes when Mlle Supo asks Ornifle whether there is anything that he believes in. 'Je crois que deux et deux ne font pas quatre' is the reply. This is the author's way of ironically signalling an important difference between his Don Juan and Molière's. Ornifle, far from being filled with overweening certainty, is constantly aware of the puzzles and inconsistencies of life. His answer may also reflect his conviction that Heaven's retribution, when it comes, will outweigh the crimes – something that would upset the neat arithmetic of perfect moral justice.

In a minority of cases, then, the author will succeed in giving his work an extra dimension by setting off the old Don Juan against the new, the past events against his newly contrived plot, our expectations against his (unexpected) reality. Needless to say, there are also many Don Juan plays in which the characters make more or less facetious references to the literary tradition in which they stand and which they are developing, even as they speak. It is as if, through his characters, the author were giving his audience a knowing wink: 'We know our Mozart' (or Tirso, or Molière). Since it would be pointless to dwell on such sterile examples, I have concentrated in these few pages on writers who have seen the legend either as posing a genuine problem which had to be surmounted, or as offering genuine possibilities for exploitation (or both). The sense of opportunity and an awareness of the burden of tradition are nicely balanced in Max Frisch, whose Don Juan makes a brief appearance in another play by that author, *Die Chinesische Mauer*, in order to complain of all the writers who have destroyed his character; the Hell to which he has been despatched is the 'Hell of literature'.[5] But Frisch rescues him wittily enough, as do Shaw, Anouilh and some others referred to above. This, rather than an apotheosis through some sentimentalized reincarnation of Donna Anna, is perhaps the true salvation of Don Juan.

# 11

# Richard Strauss and Don Juan

The only famous musical work since Mozart's opera to be concerned with Don Juan is the tone-poem by Richard Strauss: *Don Juan. Tondichtung (nach Nicolaus Lenau) für großes Orchester*, opus 20. This was composed between 1887 and 1889, first performed in 1889 and published as an orchestral score in 1890. Reductions for piano solo and piano duet followed, although these give only the skimpiest impression of the richness of the original. From the beginning, this tone-poem has been widely seen as a triumph of Strauss's early maturity, bold and innovative, involving ambitious instrumental writing, ingenious polyphony, opulent harmonies and bold dissonances, together with lavish orchestral colour.[1] In fact, Strauss's father, in a letter of 14 November 1889, accused his son of over-indulgent use of orchestral effects. In a reply dated the next day, Richard defended himself against the charge – and subsequent critical opinion has tended to side with him and has seen the rich orchestration as one of a complex of musical resources serving the central, expressive intention.

Strauss prefaces his tone-poem with three extracts from Lenau's *Don Juan*. In the first of these, Don Juan wishes to possess all women in a storm of pleasure; the second concerns his absolute need for constant change in love, his inability to 'build temples out of ruins'; the final passage speaks of the death of all his hopes and desires, his weariness and disgust at life. Here are the passages in translation:[2]

> 1. I would like to pass in a tempest of enjoyment through the immeasurably vast circle of beautiful women with their various charms and die of a kiss from the mouth of the last. Oh, friend, I would like to fly through the whole of space wherever

beauty is in flower, to kneel down before each and to conquer, even if only for a few moments.

2. I fly satiety and the weariness of pleasure and keep myself fresh in the service of beauty, causing the one woman pain in my enthusiasm for the whole species. The breath of a woman, today the aroma of spring, may perhaps oppress me tomorrow like the air of a prison. When I wander in constant change through the multitude of beautiful women, my love for each is different. I do not wish to build temples out of ruins. Yes, passion is forever new. It cannot be carried over from one woman to another; it can only die in one place to be reborn in another and, if it knows itself truly, it knows nothing of remorse. Just as every beauty is unique, so too is the love that pleases her. Up and away in search of new conquests as long as the fiery pulse of youth beats!

3. It was a splendid tempest that drove me on. It has spent itself and silence remains. All wishes, all hopes are dead as stone. Perhaps a lightning flash from regions above which I despised has struck a mortal blow to my powers of loving, so that my world suddenly became a gloomy desert. Perhaps not – the fuel is all consumed and the hearth becomes cold and dark.

The passages are widely separated in Lenau's dramatic fragment. The first two are part of an opening dialogue in which Don Juan explains his behaviour and motivation to his disapproving brother; the final passage comes, as might be inferred, shortly before Don Juan's self-willed death. The dramatic action which, in the poem, separates the last extract from the first two, is taken up with a succession of erotic adventures and their often violent or tragic results. A variety of women are involved, one of whom (Anna) inspires Don Juan with genuine love and with regret for his lost innocence (see above, p. 49).

One of the incidents takes place during a carnival ball in which the merry-making and flirtation come to an abrupt end when Don Juan is told that one of his former conquests has died of a broken heart. This episode is hinted at by Strauss in an impassioned section built around a motif which sounds like a grotesque variation on a light-hearted dance:

Distorted recollections of tunes associated with Don Juan's eroticism are evoked, only to fade away to a long-sustained *pianissimo* pedal.

The gentler and more romantic themes in the tone-poem obviously stand for various of Don Juan's loves, with the celebrated oboe melody probably hinting at his greatest and most idealistic passion, that for Anna:

For the rest, the main emphasis in Strauss's work is, as his chosen quotations from Lenau would lead us to expect, on Don Juan's changing moods and his final descent into despair. His presumptuous and insatiable striving is magnificently conveyed in the opening bars of the work, while the triumphant horn theme is probably intended to communicate a vainglorious pleasure in conquest. But it is clear from the composer's treatment of his material that Don Juan's strivings and his emotional excitement always end in anticlimax or worse: the triumphant or amorous themes constantly reappear in plaintive or distorted forms, moments of fulfilment dissolve into gloom or foreboding. Neither triumph nor tenderness lasts; the music faithfully mirrors the predicament of Lenau's hero, caught up in a cycle of alternating satisfaction and disillusionment, as one day's 'aroma' turns into the stifling air of a prison by the morrow. The ending of the tone-poem gives a very faithful musical equivalent to the last of the three Lenau quotations. The 'tempest'

which has driven Don Juan onwards is recalled through echoes of the opening bars. These lead to a *stringendo* and a long series of chords of the dominant seventh, as if to force the listener to ask 'What now?' But, as we know from Lenau, the tempest has spent itself and what follows that long build-up on the dominant is in fact a bar's silence with a long pause indicated. It may not be fanciful to imagine that, in the two bars that now ensue, Don Juan's notion that Heaven's vengeful lightning may have destroyed his powers of loving is represented musically by the way in which an F natural from the trumpets cuts discordantly into a quiet A minor chord. Thereafter, as befits Don Juan's description of his world as a cold and dark wilderness, the music dies away towards its close, *pianissimo* and bleak.

This brief account of how Strauss portrays a character and its disintegration may help to explain the frequent references, in letters written at the time of the composition, rehearsal and early performances of *Don Juan*, to the poetic content of his work and the extra-musical impulse which had given rise to it (his favourite phrases are 'poetischer Inhalt', 'poetische Idee' and 'poetischer Vorwurf'). He constantly emphasizes the need for a proper understanding of this poetic content, demanding a chain of communication reaching from composer, via conductor, to audience. (This is not unlike the old eighteenth-century theories of music as expression and communication of mood, here applied to programme music and extended to involve the conductor in the concert hall rather than the singer or player in the drawing-room.)

But 'poetic content' does not here imply a detailed programme, according to which each important character, idea or incident in the literary work has its corresponding episode or motif in the music. The first person to seek such a programme in *Don Juan* was, as far as I know, Wilhelm Mauke in 1897, and several commentators have followed suit. But the composer never invited such attempts and did no more than tolerate them. It seems very significant that his jottings on *Don Juan*, contained in a sketch-book from the late 1880s, characterize musical themes strictly in terms of the hero's *moods* (ecstasy, suffering, longing, disillusionment) and at no time mention incidents in Lenau's dramatic poem. Were we in any doubt, we find Strauss's position regarding the 'programme' at this stage in his career made quite unambiguous by the way in which he applies the notion of poetic content as readily to the late works of Beethoven as to his own tone-poem; Beethoven's pieces could never have come into being without a 'poetic plan', he insists.[3] The implication is, if I understand him correctly, that *Don Juan* certainly has a programme, but rather in the sense that Beethoven's opus 81a piano sonata *Les adieux, l'absence et le retour*) or his 135 string quartet, with its famous 'Muß es sein? ... es muß sein', have programmes. Schumann's works would provide similar examples of 'poetic ideas' which permeate the music and give it its general shape and meaning without limiting the freedom of the composer as a musical craftsman. So what we are to expect in Strauss is not a musical retelling of Lenau's plot, but a portrait of the main character in his flower and his decline. Waltershausen, in his study of 1921, goes yet further and denies that *Don Juan* is a musical representation of Lenau's Spanish grandee at all, preferring to see the tone-poem as an expression of erotic passion in a quite abstract sense ('der erotische Affekt als solcher', p. 51). We may suspect that he had been reading Kierkegaard! But even if it would be incorrect to generalize the content of Strauss's tone-poem to quite that degree, it is clear that the composer's conception of 'poetic content' is a broad one which enabled him to dispense with overliteral pictorialism and thus to avoid any unduly episodic structure, building up his work on the statement and development of a limited number of highly characteristic and easily recognizable themes. This has led many critics to liken the work formally to a freely constructed sonata-movement, the course of which is dictated both by the 'poetic idea' and by musical logic.[4] Or, to view things from the composer's point of departure, the poetic idea – suggested in the first place by extra-musical considerations – must translate itself into music and must be capable of developing according to musical criteria and principles; it must have a musical structure inherent within itself (Strauss: 'die poetische Idee muß formbildende Kräfte enthalten').[5]

Was Strauss right to insist on the need for a proper awareness of his poetic idea or can the work be fully understood without this knowledge? It is true that anyone with the least notion of Don Juan as a human type would respond without difficulty to those parts of the music which express the hero's mercurial and erotic disposition and the way in which excitement is followed by disillusionment, fulfilment by restlessness – but the muted close would be puzzling to those familiar only with the traditional 'il dissoluto punito' type of ending. This tradition would lead the uninformed listener to expect a violent and dramatic finish, a late Romantic equivalent to Gluck's Dance of the Furies or Mozart's awe-inspiring music for the Statue. But Strauss's closing bars are so much a commentary on the third of his chosen passages from Lenau that the music cannot be divorced from the poetry and still be fully understood.[6]

Don Juan is in essence a musical theme, declared Kierkegaard, that is, fully realizable only through music. He was thinking of Mozart's opera, of course, but it might be interesting to take the works of the four[7] great composers who have concerned themselves in their different ways with Don Juan and try to see these works as expressing different stages in the development of the legend. Purcell's music to *The Libertine* certainly enhances the effect of the play: the justly famous 'Nymphs and Shepherds come away' underlines the shocking contrast between untroubled rustic happiness and the fate which will shortly befall three of the revellers, while the music for the Devils in Act 5 adds drama to what could have seemed mere pantomime stuff and an ill preparation for Don John's final expression of defiance. But the music cannot affect or contribute to our *understanding* of the character of Don John or of the moral issues involved; these are fully conveyed in and through the dialogue and the dramatic action. Gluck provided an elegant and, in parts, highly dramatic musical clothing for a fundamentally trivial entertainment at a time when the legend was being kept alive in forms that did nothing to deepen understanding of Don Juan and his fate. The importance of Gluck's work in the development of ballet towards more dramatic, less 'decorative' modes is beyond question. However, as a stage in Don Juan's history, it is of less consequence. Of necessity, it concerns itself only with the superficial and sensational aspects of the story.

By contrast, Mozart's opera is clearly a watershed. He and his librettist may have thought that they were depicting an uncomplicated, swashbuckling hedonist who, in the end, received his just punishment. But Hoffmann, as we have seen, argued so persuasively for a hidden meaning, contained in and conveyed by the music, that it became very difficult from that moment onwards to regard Don Juan in the old unproblematical way. The new conception of him arguably found its most eloquent expression in Lenau's dramatic poem, and it was this notion of an heroic passion which nevertheless carries the seeds of despair and self-destruction within itself which set Strauss's imagination working. That is: a Romantic conception of Don Juan was taken up by a composer at a time when the expressive richness of the late Romantic musical vocabulary, especially as regards harmony and orchestration, made it possible for that composer to realize the poet's (or the hero's) emotional extremes very exactly in his music. So there is a clear causal link between *Don Giovanni* and Strauss's tone-poem, for all that Mozart and Strauss inhabit widely different musical worlds.

Thus the four most familiar musical treatments of Don Juan mirror a clear transition: from a popular and sensational reading of character and events through to a highly romanticized and idealized interpretation, with Mozart unwittingly providing the link and Hoffmann acting as catalyst. I cannot think of another case where a musical realization of a character or legend led, directly or indirectly, to such a radical re-interpretation and had such a far-reaching impact on both literature and music.

# 12
# Conclusion

The reasons for the perennial fascination of Don Juan are complex. Early audiences must have derived a good deal of vicarious pleasure from seeing someone break the rules of sexual morality and cock a snook at authority. Where this feeling was mixed with envy or pious indignation, there was no doubt some satisfaction in seeing the wrongdoer punished. In addition, the adventurous and, in the final scenes, awe-inspiring events ensured a theatrical success to rival that of Faust. In their twin appeal (their didactic purpose as terrible warnings and their dramatic effectiveness as theatrical entertainment), the two legends resemble and rival one another on the popular stage.

Later, for Hoffmann and other romantic spirits in Germany and France, Don Juan became the great rebel, consumed with divine discontent and roaming the world in a hopeless quest for an ideal. For Kierkegaard and many others, he stood for rebellious sensuality. The point is made tersely by Edmond Haraucourt, who sees him as personifying man's animal nature in its revolt against the subjugation of the flesh demanded by Christianity: 'La bête crie: "Je veux vivre!" Et cette révolte s'appelle don Juan' (1898, Preface, p. xvi). Hayem sees the essence of Don Juan's appeal as lying in the struggle between love and morality, while Ben Levy has talked of the romantic fascination exercised by this 'heroic' bad man, the freeman among slaves. Similar is Shaw's point when he classes Don Juan as the type of man who is delivered from conscience and who delights those who are in thrall to it.[1]

Whether Don Juan is indeed 'delivered from conscience' or tries unsuccessfully to arm himself against its reproaches will vary from work to work, but the general point made by Levy and Shaw is a vital one. Most people for most of their lives have to submit and conform. Hence they delight in stories, theatrical shows and myths which demonstrate various forms of refusal so to do – from the clown who parodies the pompous and self-important to Prometheus and Faust who, in their different ways, rise up in revolt against the gods themselves. Don Juan would indeed fit into this category. It is not simply a question of his defiant sensuality – although, in ages when the Church and society were obsessed with discouraging sexual licence, this must have been the overriding factor. But he is also a rebel in more general terms: scornful of convention, authority and ready-made rules, a man who is determined to be himself. As we have seen, his passionate vitality will often be made to seem somewhat more acceptable through the contrast with social attitudes and institutions which conspire to tame eroticism and make it respectable. In addition he has usually been represented as charming and resourceful, witty, handsome and dashing, proud, ironic and fearless. He probably combines within himself more of the qualities which we would secretly like to possess – and takes more of the liberties that we do not dare to take – than Faust. Certainly it is easier for most men to imagine themselves possessing Don Juan's superabundance of animal spirits than Faust's superabundance of intellectual energy and transcendental curiosity.

The point is well illustrated in Anouilh's *Ornifle*, where the hero is accused by the half-adoring, half-outraged Mlle Supo of being the most wicked man she has ever known. Ornifle defends himself by saying that he is no more wicked than all the others: he simply does what they can only desire ('Il m'arrive seulement de faire ce dont les autres se contentent d'avoir envie', p. 291). The same point is made in the closing scene of Frisch's *Don Juan* by a bishop, no less. Examples could be multiplied.

Some writers have reinforced the argument by putting forward pseudo-biological reasons. Here is Schopenhauer on the subject:

> By nature, man is inclined to inconstancy in love, woman to constancy. A man's love weakens noticeably from that moment in which it has been satisfied. Almost every other woman attracts him more than the one whom he already possesses.[2]

Levy too thinks that most 'normal men' (his phrase) have something in common with the Don Juan type. (Many readers will have encountered barrack-room Don Juans who prided themselves on the number of their conquests and the stratagems employed.) But there are also dramatic reasons for Don Juan's lasting popularity: we enjoy witnessing the ingenuity with which he stage-manages his escapades and his seemingly infinite resourcefulness. And, last but not least, the music which has become associated with him hugely intensifies his appeal.

Yet there is seemingly a point beyond which we cannot stomach Don Juan. In Molière, that point is probably reached in Dom Juan's encounters with his father and in the scene with the mendicant, despite Don Juan's claim to love humanity. In other versions, it is the plight of those whom Don Juan has seduced and abandoned which kills what attraction he might still have possessed.[3] The problem is less acute in Mozart's opera, where the music makes any such moral revulsion less probable. As we have seen, Leporello's catalogue aria has the irresistible comedy of the patter-song, while Donna Elvira, a pitiable character if viewed objectively, is to some extent made into a figure of fun through the deliberate introduction of stylistic parody (exaggerated *coloratura*, mock-Handelian heroics) into the music written for her. But in stage-plays, especially of the more realistic kind, the audience will be much more inclined to take the plight of Don Juan's victims seriously and thus to turn against him. And when he achieves his ends by callous trickery or even takes advantage of a woman while she is lying unconscious (Tolstoi), our abhorrence is complete. Moreover, Levy's 'normal man', even if he secretly envies Don Juan, may well also resent him, especially when, as often happens, the claim to untrammelled freedom is accompanied by open contempt for 'slavish' conformity. Thus it was that so many writers, being out of humour both with this wicked character and with those who hero-worshipped him, took their revenge by punishing or humiliating him, or by showing him a prey to remorse or ennui, or simply overtaken by old age.

Is Don Juan played out as a type and a literary theme? Many twentieth-century writers have thought so, pointing out that early versions depended on a social and religious consensus, according to which the family and marriage were as sacrosanct as God's law, with the result that the libertine simultaneously offended against society and sinned against Heaven. In many traditional versions, the force of this conviction is almost tangible: the women feel dishonoured and defiled[4] while secular and ecclesiastical authorities form an alliance to denounce and pursue Don Juan. To the degree that these conventional beliefs gradually become weaker, so too does Don Juan's power to shock. This is the main theme of Ronald Duncan's comedy, *The Death of Satan* (1955), in which Don Juan returns to earth to find that women are prepared to yield to him casually and husbands are comparatively unmoved by their wives' infidelity. To turn the knife in the wound, a woman journalist lectures him on his quest for the ideal woman and explains it away in terms of psychological complexes. 'What the moral indignation of three centuries could not achieve, our own age has done,' writes H.A. Grunwald in an article of 1962 entitled 'The Disappearance of Don Juan'; 'the Don is dead, not because we are too puritanical for him, but because we are too licentious.'[5]

Shaw, in *Man and Superman*, goes still further, for he clearly believes that the legend is so out of date in its incidents and basic assumptions that it needs to be turned on its head if it is to make acceptable sense ever again. Not only would it be absurd, he says in the 'Epistle Dedicatory', to introduce Stone Guests into a modern Don Juan play; the idea of 'womanly women' is also ridiculous and outmoded. And so Woman must now be cast as the pursuer, responding instinctively to the promptings of the Life Force. If we today still feel that the legend has outrun its course, the reasons are likely to be less biological than Shaw's, a good deal more contingent on contemporary factors and phenomena. It is not only that sexual promiscuity no longer seems so shocking that divine vengeance must be called down on the libertine; where he offends, our purely moral indignation is probably now compounded by medical considerations. In 1915, in the Preface to *Androcles and the Lion*, Shaw wrote that 'unless we gratify our [sexual] desire, the race is lost: unless we restrain it we destroy ourselves.'[6] He was no doubt thinking of the sort of unbridled and destructive sexuality traditionally personified by Don Juan, but the abrupt and alarming spread of a sexually transmitted disease has given those words a literal meaning unforeseeable in 1915 and has arguably made it impossible to set up Don Juan either as hero or as warning example any more. A new work that seriously set out to romanticize him or present him as a Nietzschean Superman would simply be tasteless. If popular culture (detective and spy thrillers, films) is any sort of reliable barometer, there are some signs of growing reluctance to glamorize sexual virility. So perhaps we need to revise Grunwald's judgement from the 'permissive' sixties: the Don is dead because of

CONCLUSION

a new, scare-induced Puritanism. But at the same time – since heterosexual promiscuity is only one of a number of factors contributing to our present predicament – it would hardly be sensible or fair to pick out Don Juan as a stern moral warning for our times.

There is another potential threat to Don Juan: the feeling on the part of half the reading or theatre-going public that the legend, for all its surface vindication of the moral *status quo* and its insistence that the arch-despoiler of women be ultimately punished, must have owed much of its vogue to male chauvinism. There are certainly clear traces of this resentment in George Sand's strictures (see above, p. 64), but I have not come across any further such references. Perhaps the emancipated woman of the past simply ignored works devoted to this despicable character. But late twentieth-century feminism would certainly regard the traditional form of the legend *and* Shaw's restatement of it in *Man and Superman* as equally objectionable; there is little to be said for being a plaything, whether of a seducer vile or of the Life Force. (The superficial impression left by Shaw's play – that Ann is in charge – will not, as we have seen, stand up to scrutiny.)

To my knowledge, there has never been any serious and effective attempt to create a female counterpart to Don Juan; a woman who competed with him in the number of sexual couplings would have to be either a nymphomaniac or a prostitute.[7] Since the theme of Don Juan, as transmitted through the centuries, casts woman as the victim (and often a very gullible or emotionally unstable victim), Don Juan as a character would probably fill most women with revulsion, unless he were shown as overtaken by retribution of some kind, or 'redeemed' through Mozart's music, or represented as overcoming his philandering instincts and sublimating his energies. Certainly the romantically idealized Don Juan of the nineteenth century, displeasing enough to some men, would grate on female susceptibilities. It would seem barely possible for a woman to tolerate a work which showed any given member of her sex as an object to be tested against an impossible ideal of perfection and rejected as soon as found wanting. I cannot easily think of another major theme in European literature that has 'Men only!' written above it more conspicuously. This aspect, present from the beginning, undoubtedly became more acute, the more Don Juan was glorified.

Yet it is not difficult to see why his story has proved so attractive to authors over the centuries. He is a perennial type who is almost bound to provoke strong feelings for or against him and who invites constant re-interpretation as moral views and social circumstances change. No doubt, second- and third-rate minds will have been drawn to him for the wrong reasons, seeing in this universally familiar character an easy option which seemed to reduce the need for original invention but which at the same time – since his story can be so readily transplanted to other ages and countries and adapted at will – did not place constrictions on the writer in the way that historical events and characters may. Hence the undeniable triviality of many Don Juan plays and novels. Moreover, the very proliferation of Don Juan works and the existence of well-established trends of interpretation encouraged derivative treatment. But more exacting and fastidious writers were drawn to this well-worn theme for precisely the opposite reason: because it challenged them to perceive and reveal fresh meaning in it. So there is nothing intrinsically incongruous about the flood of Don Juan works at a time when individuality and 'originality' in literature were being prized as never before. The Don Juan legend is something like a popular tune on which countless composers have written variations – and it would hardly occur to us to accuse Beethoven of flagging originality because he did not always trouble himself to invent original themes. But the process of variation will continue only as long as authors manage to find new potential meaning for themselves and their age in Don Juan and his legend. If they cease to do so, there will be no more Don Juan works – or such as continue to be written will sink to the level of five-finger exercises.

Will further versions appear, then? We may still see plays or stories which ironically debunk the legend and its hero or show woman taking her revenge on the philanderer. But such works would not be new in concept; they would simply demonstrate the authors' unawareness of the many existing plays and stories which have taken those lines. Similarly, we may see more attempts at psychological analysis of Don Juan as a type, possibly casting him as hunter and contender for sexual dominance among his male peers. A recent television programme on Don Juan (BBC2, 7-1-1989) made much of this point. But I find it difficult to imagine that anything both new and plausible could emerge; Don Juan has lain on the psychoanalyst's couch often enough.

Weinstein[8] thinks that Camus' interpretation may turn out to be decisive as far as further treatments are concerned, but one hopes that he may be proved wrong. For all the astuteness of Camus' remarks, a Don Juan work based on such a reading of the type would, in most cases, probably lead to triviality. As we have seen, something resembling Camus' conception seems to underlie Anouilh's treatment of the theme. In *Ornifle*, however, it is effective because of the author's highly ingenious working out of his theme, the witty dialogue and the psychological insight with which he reveals Ornifle's awareness that his way of life is doomed. But a succession of broadly similar treatments would be dreary, for we would be left with a meaningless hedonism (or, rather, a hedonism meaningful only inasmuch as its meaninglessness reflects the meaninglessness of life itself). This seems a tepid notion when compared with the old 'Libertine destroyed' theme, or with the Romantic idealization of the type or, come to that, with the motivation of offended moralists who wished to visit retribution on a Don Juan perversely transformed into a visionary quester. If Don Juan is to be a hedonist, I suspect that most people would prefer the cheerful and unreflecting character conceived by da Ponte and realized so gloriously in music by Mozart to Camus' picture of a man turned womanizer out of a philosophical conviction that life is absurd. Or, to take the argument a stage further, if Don Juan is to be thought of as having a philosophical or speculative cast of mind, many readers would probably find it more acceptable if this turned him *against* philandering, whether to assist the Life Force in its development of higher forms (Shaw), out of an abstract passion for truth (Frisch), or to serve humanity (Creizenach).

# Original Versions of Passages Quoted in Translation

p. 3
Sevilla a voces me llama
*el Burlador*, y el mayor
gusto que en mí puede haber
es burlar una mujer
y dejalla sin honor.

p. 5
*Statua*  D. Gio. dammi la mano.
*D.G.*  Eccola, ma o Dio, che stringo! . . .
*Stat.*  Pentiti, D. Gio.
*D.G.*  Lasciamo dico; oimè.
*Stat.*  Pentiti, D. Gio.
*D.G.*  Oimè, io moro, aiuto.
*Stat.*  Pentiti, D. Gio.
  Qui precipita D. Gio. e si serra.

p. 9
Je me ris de l'espoir d'un langoureux amant,
Et trouve mon plaisir parmy le changement.

p. 9
Il m'a donné l'esprit, l'ame, la connoissance,
La force, la raison, le coeur, l'intelligence,
Et tout cela pour vaincre, et braver les destins
Et non pour affliger l'ouvrage de ses mains.

p. 10
J'ay veu ce qu'on peut voir Briguelle, sur la terre,
Les Esprits fors, les Grands, les Sçavans, et la Guerre,
Il ne me reste plus dans mes pensers divers,
Qu'à voir si je pouvois les Cieux, et les Enfers,
Celuy que je vais voir n'est plus dans ces matieres
Qui souvent font obstacle aux plus belles lumieres,
C'est un esprit tout pur. . . .

Allons donc sans tarder. . . .
L'homme est lasche qui vit dans la stupidité;
On doit porter par tout sa curiosité.

p. 10  Monsieur, je n'entens point vostre Philosophie,
Mais, je crains les esprits.

p. 11  Enfans, qui maudissez souvent et Père et Mère,
Regardez ce que c'est de bien vivre et bien faire;
N'imitez pas Dom Juan, nous vous en prions tous,
Car voicy, sans mentir, un beau miroir pour vous.

p. 12  Je ne sais que dire; car vous tournez les choses d'une manière, qu'il semble que vous ayez raison; et cependant il est vrai que vous ne l'avez pas. J'avais les plus belles pensées du monde, et vos discours m'ont brouillé tout cela.

p. 12  Pour moi, Monsieur, je n'ai point étudié comme vous, Dieu merci, et personne ne se saurait vanter de m'avoir jamais rien appris; mais avec mon petit sens et mon petit jugement je vois les choses mieux que tous vos livres.

p. 16  Nous souffrons des tourmens divers;
Mesme peine est deue à tes crimes,
Et ta fin doit servir d'exemple à l'univers.

p. 16  Je me reservai la liberté d'adoucir certaines expressions qui avaient blessé les scrupuleux.

p. 16  Il est englouti! je cours me rendre ermite.
L'exemple est étonnant pour les scelerats:
Malheur à qui le voit, et n'en profite pas!

p. 25  *D.G.*  Lasciar le donne? Sai ch'elle per me son necessarie più del pan che mangio, più dell' aria che spiro?
*Lep.*  E avete core dingannarle poi tutte?
*D.G.*  E tutto amore. Chi a una è fedele, verso l'altre è crudele; io che in me sento siesteso sentimento, vo' bene a tutte quante.

p. 27  Ein Bonvivant, der Wein und Mädchen über die Maßen liebt, der mutwilligerweise den steinernen Mann ... zu einer lustigen Tafel bittet – wahrlich, hierin liegt nicht viel Poetisches, und ehrlich gestanden, ist ein solcher Mensch es wohl nicht wert, daß die unterirdischen Mächte ihn als ein ganz besonderes Kabinettsstück der Hölle auszeichnen.

p. 29   So steht er da, der rasende Verbrecher,
Obwohl verflucht, doch groß in seinen Sünden –
So fährt er hin in ew'ge Flammenqualen.
Dieß Bild, zu trüb', zu fürchterlich dem Sprecher,
Darf nur Musik geheimnißvoll verkünden,
Darf Mozart nur, der Herr der Töne, malen.

p. 29   Mozart hat sie [diese Tragödie] in unsterblichen Tönen geschaffen, aber der Dichter ... ist noch nicht gekommen.

p. 30   In Don Juans Gemüt kam durch des Erbfeindes List der Gedanke, daß durch die Liebe, durch den Genuß des Weibes, schon auf Erden das erfüllt werden könne, was bloß als himmlische Verheißung in unserer Brust wohnt und eben jene unendliche Sehnsucht ist, die uns mit dem Überirdischen in unmittelbaren Rapport setzt.

p. 30   Immer ... sich betrogen glaubend, ... mußte doch Juan zuletzt alles irdische Leben matt und flach finden, und indem er überhaupt den Menschen verachtete, lehnte er sich auf gegen die Erscheinung, die, ihm als das Höchste im Leben geltend, so bitter ihn getäuscht hatte.

p. 31   Troppo mi spiace allontarnarti un ben che lungamente la nostr'alma desia. ma il mondo ...

p. 45   Faust und Don Juan sind die Gipfel der modernen christlich poetischen Mythologie.

p. 46   'Das Unermeßliche fass' ich, 's ist mein!'
Ruft er; – 'Das All durchwühlen
Muß ich, Wonn' auf Wonne fühlen,
In jedem Wesen mich als Gott empfinden,
Im Höchsten, im Tiefsten, dies Ich, das göttliche, finden.'

p. 46   Als bei süßen Weisen der Schwelger schmaus't/... der Boden dröhnt/Unter'm Tritt des Gast's, die Stimme tönt/ Wie Posaunenklang des jüngsten Gerichts.

p. 47   Wir sind im Leben, um es zu genießen,

Und seine einz'ge Wahrheit ist – Genuß!

p. 48  Die Sage vom Don Juan ist groß, größer als die des Faust, die in ihrer ursprünglichen Gestalt nichts gar Besonderes hat. ... Ich habe auch die Idee, Don Juan zu bearbeiten, und ich würde ihm eine ganz neue Seite abgewinnen.

p. 48  Mein Don Juan darf kein Weibern ewig nachjagender heißblütiger Mensch sein. Es ist die Sehnsucht in ihm, ein Weib zu finden, welches ihm das incarnirte Weibthum ist. ... Weil er dieses, taumelnd von der Einen zur Anderen, nicht findet, so ergreift ihn endlich der Ekel, und der ist der Teufel, der ihn holt.

p. 49  Doch ist sie auch so hoch und himmlisch rein,
Daß ich – lach nicht! – unschuldig möchte sein.

p. 49  Mein Totfeind ist in meine Faust gegeben;
Doch dies auch langweilt, wie das ganze Leben.

p. 52  Unglücklich bin ich, andre nennen's sündlich!

p. 52  Nicht lieblich ist dein Ruhm in ird'schen Landen,
Der Schwarm leert gern ob dir des Zornes Schaale,
Weil treulos du entflohst gar manche Male,
Die selbst du knüpftest, holden Liebesbanden.
Doch glaub': es hat der Dichter dich verstanden,
Fürwahr, du warst berauscht vom Ideale.

p. 52  Zum ersten Mal bei diesem Weibe
Ist in der Liebe mir zu Mut,
Als sollte meine heiße Glut
Auslöschen nie in ihrem Götterleibe.

p. 55  Si Faust et Manfred ont offert ... le type de la perfection humaine, don Juan n'est plus que celui de la démoralisation ... Combien Faust surpasse ... les amours vulgaires de don Juan.

p. 55  N'en était-il pas une, ou plus noble, ou plus belle,
Parmis tant de beautés, qui, de loin ou de près,
De son vague idéal eût du moins quelques traits? ...
Toutes lui ressemblaient, – ce n'était jamais elle,
Toutes lui ressemblaient, don Juan, et tu marchais!

## ORIGINAL VERSIONS

p. 56     Femme comme jamais sculpteur n'en a pétrie,
Type réunissant Cléopâtre et Marie.

p. 56     N'écoutez pas l'Amour, car c'est un mauvais maître;
Aimer, c'est ignorer, et vivre, c'est connaître.
Apprenez, apprenez . . .

p. 56     Don Juan . . . représente . . . l'aspiration à l'idéal. Ce n'est pas une débauche vulgaire qui le pousse; il cherche le rêve de son coeur avec l'opiniâtreté d'un titan qui ne redoute ni les éclairs ni la foudre.

p. 57     Le bonheur? Je n'en ai jamais trouvé que l'ombre; tous les fruits que j'ai touchés se sont réduits en cendre et m'ont rempli la bouche d'amertume; toutes les femmes que j'ai aimées ont trahi mes espérances. Je ne crois à rien, ni à Dieu, ni au diable . . . Ah! si j'avais été aimé: si j'avais trouvé un coeur de femme qui répondit au mien, je raisonnerais autrement.

p. 58     Eh bien, ce sentiment qui tourmente sans trêve,
Cet idéal maudit, cet inconnu, ce rêve
Devant qui les humains succombent tour à tour,
Cet espoir, que les uns cherchent dans la science,
Les autres dans la foi, d'autres dans la puissance,
Moi, je l'ai cherché dans l'amour.

p. 59     Les uns sont monogames, les autres bigames ou polygames: et cela de *nature*.

p. 59     Chacun a la destinée de son sang. . . . Chacun a la moralité de son tempérament.

p. 59     Je me marierais s'il existait une femme à ma taille. – Cette femme ne l'ai-je pas cherchée toute ma vie, sans la rencontrer?

p. 60     Le plaisir facile n'est pas celui qui me tente. J'ai soif de l'impossible. . . . Je trouve en moi le vertige d'horizons immenses qui reculent à mesure que j'avance. Je vais, insatiable, au néant ou à la lumière infinie!

p. 60     Jamais l'âme humaine n'a eu un sentiment plus profond de l'*insuffisance*, de la *misère*, de l'*irréel* de notre vie présente.

## ORIGINAL VERSIONS

p. 61   ... personnage froid, raissonable et vulgaire, ne parlant sans cesse que de vertu et d'économie ... C'est la future bourgeoisie qui va bientôt remplacer la noblesse tombante.

p. 62   Il parle de son ennui mortel ... Il avoue que quelquefois il lui arrive d'envier le bonheur naïf des êtres inférieurs à lui. Ces bourgeois, qui passent avec des femmes aussi bêtes et aussi vulgaires qu'eux, ont des passions par lesquelles ils souffrent ou sont heureux.

p. 64   Fat insolent! où donc avais-tu pris les droits insensés auxquels tu as dévoué ta vie? A quelle heure, en quel lieu Dieu t'avait-il dit: – Voici la terre, elle est à toi, tu seras le seigneur et le roi de toutes les familles; toutes les femmes que tu auras préferées sont destinées à ta couche.

p. 67   ... j'ai cherché!/J'étais celui qui croit qu'un trésor est caché,/Qu'une fleure bleue existe au haut d'une montagne.

p. 67   Ce que c'est que d'avoir passé par l'Allemagne!

p. 68   ... l'abondante littérature qui a voulu faire de Don Juan un personnage complexe: un être démoniaque ... un 'mythe' ... J'ai débarrassé mon héros de ce qu'avait fait de lui le xix$^e$ siècle. Don Juan, dans ma pièce, est un personnage simple.

p. 68   Chaque fois que je fais tomber une femme, c'est comme ci c'était la première fois. Et j'ai besoin de faire ça tous les jours: pour moi, c'est du pain.

p. 71   Sein Ruhm als Verführer ... ist ein Mißverständnis seitens der Damen. Don Juan ist ein Intellektueller. ... Was ihn unwiderstehlich macht ... ist durchaus seine Geistigkeit ..., die ein Affront ist, indem sie ganz andere Ziele kennt als die Frau.

p. 72   ... Unwille gegen die Schöpfung, die uns gespalten hat in Mann und Weib. ... Welche Ungeheuerlichkeit, daß der Mensch allein nicht das Ganze ist! Und je größer seine Sehnsucht ist, ein Ganzes zu sein, um so verfluchter steht er da, bis zum Verbluten ausgesetzt dem andern Geschlecht.

ORIGINAL VERSIONS

p. 76   Der Genussucht des Don Juan ... steht im Faust ... die Einsamkeit des Wissensdranges ... entgegen.

p. 76   Don Juan und Faust ... sind ... gar keine zwei Personen, denn jeder Don Juan endet als Faust und jeder Faust als Don Juan.

p. 76   Don Juan ist der musikalische Faust, ein Stoff, der an den Schranken der Menschheit, der Endlichkeit rüttelt.

p. 76   Gewissermaßen setzt sich jeder Mensch aus Faust und Don Juan zusammen.

p. 76   In ihrer geheimnißvollen Schauerlichkeit stimmen beide Sagen überein, in ihrer ursprünglichen Veranlassung sind sie Seiten- oder Gegenstücke.

p. 77   Wir haben es hier mit einem der tiefsinnigsten christlichen Stoffe zu tun, welchem, wie dem Faust, das Ethisch-Transcendentale als Hauptlebenselement innewohnt.

p. 77   Alle drei [Sagen] schildern die Unruhe, den Unfrieden, die Unersättlichkeit des menschlichen Herzens, das an keinem irdischen, himmlischen oder geistigen Genuß sich ersättigen kann.

p. 78   Krabbe (*sic!*) hat auch diesem Taugenichts [Don Juan] dichterische Aufmerksamkeit geschenkt und ihn Faust zugesellt, was vielleicht Excellenz von Goethe verblüffen dürfte.

p. 78   *Don Juan* ... – *Wozu übermenschlich,*
*Wenn du ein Mensch bleibst?*
*Faust*                         *Wozu Mensch,*
*Wenn du nach Übermenschlichem nicht strebst?*

p. 78   ... Weg mit dem Ziel –
*Nenn* es mir nicht, ob ich auch darnach *ringe* –
... Wohl dem, der ewig strebt, ja Heil,
Heil ihm, der ewig hungern könnte!

p. 78   *Faust*   Ce qui me fait souffrir, c'est que, savant, j'ignore
...
*Don Juan*   Où vais-je? Comment doit se terminer ceci?
Je l'ignore. – Après tout, qu'importe?

p. 80　'Hier ist der Kontrakt. Ich habe erfüllt, was ich dir versprach. In Deinen Lüsten hast Du hingelebt, wie Du gewollt. Die Weiber waren Dein; an Gelde hat Dir's nie gefehlt. Nun bist Du mein. Die Zeit ist verflossen.'
　　　　'Die Zeit ist *nicht* verflossen, – schrie Juan. *Drei Tage* habe ich noch' –
　　　　'Du hast sie nicht!'
　　　　'Ich habe sie!'
　　　　'Du hast sie nicht. – Verrechnet hast Du Dich um die Schalttage.'

p. 82　Seht Ihr, dort, ... dort liegt mein Kind in seinem kleinen Grabe – ja, er ist todt – Kaum ward es geboren, kaum habe ich es küssen können – und schon ist es todt! ... Herr, ... habe ich Euch gesagt, daß mein Kind todt ist?
　　　　– Ja! murmelte Don Juan.
　　　　– Glaubt es nicht ...! Mein Kind lebt – hört Ihr, es schreiet nach der Mutter! ... Ich will mich zur Ruhe legen und von ihm träumen. Er war ein schöner Mann ... – aber er hat mich verlassen, weil ich sein Kind unter meinem Herzen trug. ... Ihr seht wohl, daß das Kind nicht todt sein kann, denn ich muß es ihm ja bringen ...

p. 82　Er ist ... neugierig wie Faust ...; er hat die Liebe zu dem Wunderbaren, die Leidenschaft nach dem Unbekannten, den Durst nach dem Unendlichen.

p. 83　Das Bedauern, nicht noch höher steigen und mehr sehen zu können.

p. 83　Wahrhaftig, ganz Faust's Gretchen!

p. 85　Ist nicht der Strom aus seinem Bett gestiegen,
　　　　Dem er in neuer Bahn gebot zu brausen,
　　　　Daß nun an seinem Ufer Städte liegen,
　　　　An seinem Sturz beglückte Männer hausen?

p. 88　*Hürte*: Sein unzüchtig Wesen wider Gott und alle Ordnung ...

p. 88　*Faustbook*: Doctor Faustus lebt also im Epicurischen Leben Tag und Nacht, glaubet nit daß ein GOTT, Hell oder Teuffel were ... sein Teuffelisches Gottloses wesen ... ein Säwisch vnnd Epicurisch leben ...

## ORIGINAL VERSIONS

p. 88    *Hürte*: Wie ein Scheusal lag der Missethäter in seinem Blute am Boden; die Augen stier aus dem Kopfe herausgetreten, die Zunge zwischen den Zähnen hervorgequollen, das ganze Gesicht blitzblau ...

p. 88    *Faustbook*: Das Hirn klebte an der Wandt, weil jn der Teuffel von einer Wandt zur andern geschlagen hatte. Es lagen auch seine Augen vnd etliche Zäen allda, ein greulich vnd erschrecklich Spectackel.

p. 88    ... denn dem gottlosen Frevler folget immer die gerechte Strafe.

p. 92    Je me suis appliqué à ne conter de don Juan de Maraña, mon héros, que des aventures qui n'appartinssent pas par droit de prescription à don Juan Tenorio, si connu parmi nous par les chefs-d'oeuvre de Molière et de Mozart.

p. 97    Dazu bin ich nicht Don Juan Tenorio geworden, daß ich den Vernichter meiner Träume mit Harfen preise ... Ich will mich nicht retten lassen, ich bin noch nicht schwach genug, um gerettet zu werden!

p. 100    Mein Ich – das *Minus* ist's in der Mathematik,
Die umgekehrte Gottheit nennt's der Denker,
Kurz, ich bin nur ein Nichts, Ihr wißt es schon,
Ich bin des Daseins stete Negation.

p. 100    Ich bin der Geist, der stets verneint,
Und das mit Recht, denn alles, was entsteht,
Ist wert, daß es zugrunde geht ...

p. 101    Ich bin der Arzt der Menschheit, der sie hier
Galvanisirt, daß sich die Spannkraft hebe,
Und wenn es in der Welt nicht einen Teufel gäbe,
So gäb' es keinen Heiligen in ihr!

p. 101    Des Menschen Tätigkeit kann allzuleicht erschlaffen,
Er liebt sich bald die unbedingte Ruh';
Drum geb ich gern ihm den Gesellen zu,
Der reizt und wirkt und muß als Teufel schaffen.

p. 101    Zu hohen Thaten führt ihn seine Bahn,
Von seinem Ruhme wird die Welt erschallen!

Ihm halten Engel Wacht, ihm bleibst du [Satan] fern!
Ihn greifst du nicht. Such' eine Beute weiter!

p. 102   Zurück! du blinde Macht!
Hinweg! laß ab von dem, der glaubt und liebet!

p. 105   Das Wagen reizt mich mehr als das Gewinnen, der Kampf mehr als die Beute.

p. 106   Mich reizt Verbotnes, Unerlaubtes,
Mich lockt Gefahr, Zorn, Eifersucht,
Verstohlen oder dreist Geraubtes –
Nicht in den Schoß gefallne Frucht!

p. 106   Ich gehe aufs Meer, weil ich Freude an Sturm und Gefahr habe, nicht weil ich aus einem Hafen in den anderen segeln will.

p. 106   Liebe ist ihm nur mehr die Betätigung seiner geistigen Potenz in der Kunst der Verführung ... Nicht mehr der physische Besitz ist ihm Genuß, sondern das geistige Erringen. Er pflückt die Frucht nicht.

p. 106   Ihn reizt die Schwierigkeit der Besitzergreifung, die damit verbundene Gefahr, erst in zweiter Linie der Gegenstand.

p. 106   C'est la résistance qui donne du piquant au plaisir.

p. 108   Pour être cruel, il ne faut pas souffrir du mal qu'on fait ... S'il n'était pas cruel, Don Juan serait bientôt esclave.

p. 108   Kein Wort der Reue komme über meinen Mund –
Ich war und will bis in den Tod sein *Don Juan*!
Ich trotze dir, der Hölle und dem ewigen Gott!!!

p. 108   Und doch würgte es ihn, eine Frau, die er einst liebte, so leiden zu sehen. Es ist ein Manko der Schöpfung, dachte er, daß Frauenliebe meist so viel länger dauert als Männerliebe. ... Ihr [Frauen] erfüllt euer Schicksal, indem ihr euch härmt und an der Liebe leidet, und ich erfülle meines, indem ich vom Dämon getrieben wider meinen Willen euch Leid bereite. Diesem grausam tragischen Liebeskampf zwischen Mann und Weib sieht der Weltschöpfer ebenso erhaben gefühllos zu, wie all dem andern millionenfachen Schmerzgestöhn auf Erden! Ich will nach

Gottähnlichkeit streben und ebenso gefühllos werden wie Er!

p. 108 Ich fühle Mitleid mit den Verlassenen, nur überschreitet meine Lebensgier schnell dieses Mitleid. Auch meine Vernunft wehrt sich dagegen. Die sagt sich: Herzeleid gehört nun mal zum normalen Frauenleben; ihr seid von Natur dazu eingerichtet.

p. 109 Pour être heureux dans le crime, il faudrait . . . n'avoir pas de remords. Je ne sais si un tel être peut exister.

p. 109 In meinem Busen ließ kein Grauen/Das oft durch mich gemordete Vertrauen.

p. 109 Am Herzen nagt der Reue gift'ger Wurm.

p. 109 Glücklich! Pah! das Glück ist ein großes Ding und hat in solchen Seelchen nicht Platz.

p. 109 Was ist das Siegel der erreichten Freiheit? – Sich nicht mehr vor sich selber schämen.

p. 109 Frei wähnte ich zu sein . . . aller Gewissensangst, aller knechtischen Torheit dieser Menschen [= less bold and free spirits] auf ewig entrückt! Und nun nistet's in mir – da irgendwo in der Seele nistet's und frißt an mir!

p. 110 Ich bin noch Mensch und bleib' es ohne Zweifel./Mich ficht ganz ordinäre Reue an.

p. 110 Elender! kitzelt dich es zu bereuen?/Dann hättest Du den Teufel sollen scheuen.

p. 110     . . . Ich lebe wie ich muß!
Es ist ein Trieb, ein Wille der Natur,
Süß und unselig auch – es ist ein Drängen,
Dem ich gehorche wie das Kind der Amme.

p. 111 Gut? . . . bös? . . . ich habe mich für diesen Gegensatz nie sonderlich interessiert. Ich tat eben, was ich nicht lassen konnte.

p. 111 Darum sind die Gesetzesverächter, . . . die Disharmonieschaffer, die großen Sünder für das Heil der Welt geradeso notwendig wie die Pflichteiferer und die Sittenstrengen.

## ORIGINAL VERSIONS

p. 112   Nun aber liegt der Natur nichts so sehr am Herzen, wie die Erhaltung der Spezies und ihres echten Typus; wozu wohlbeschaffene, tüchtige, kräftige Individuen das Mittel sind: nur solche will sie. Ja, sie betrachtet und behandelt ... im Grunde die Individuen nur als Mittel.

p. 112   So wurde ich hin- und hergeworfen zwischen Gier – Ekel – und wiederum Gier – ein ewiger Spielball der Leidenschaft.

p. 128   Tout le monde connôit cette mauvaise Piece espagnole, que les Italiens appellent *il Convitato di Pietra* et les François *le Festin de Pierre*.

p. 128   *D.G.*   Giuro al nume che al cielo e al mondo impera,
Voi sarete mia sposa.
*E.*                           E se mancata?
*D.G.*   Cada un fulmin dal cielo, a l'alma infida
Precipiti agli abissi.

p. 128   Commendator, che fai? Perché non vieni
A vendicar il sangue tuo? Quel marmo
Perché non scende a precipizio, e seco
Me non porta sotterra? ...
Deità menzognere, il vostro braccio
Sfido a vendetta. Se fia ver che in cielo
Sovra l'uomo mortal vi sia potere,
Se giustizia è lassù, fulmine scenda,
Mi colpisca, mi uccida e mi profondi
Nell' inferno per sempre.

p. 130   C'était l'heure du terrible souper avec le froid Commandeur de marbre blanc, après lequel il n'y a plus que l'enfer, – l'enfer de la vieillesse.

p. 136   *Baron*   Und sie war auch Braut. ... Ich war als Annas Bräutigam verkleidet. ... Nachher im Garten stieß ich mit ihrem Vater, dem Komthur Don Gonzalo zusammen ...
*Professor* (erschreckt)   Du, was sind das für verrückte Possen!?
*Baron.* .. Und den habe ich leider erschlagen.

p. 146   Der Mann [ist] von Natur zur Unbeständigkeit in der

Liebe, das Weib zur Beständigkeit geneigt. Die Liebe des Mannes sinkt merklich, von dem Augenblick an, wo sie Befriedigung erhalten hat; fast jedes andere Weib reizt ihn mehr als das, welches er schon besitzt.

# NOTES

## 1 THE BEGINNINGS

1 The inconclusive debate concerning the likely sources of *El Burlador* in drama, romance and folklore need not concern us here. For discussion of the relationship of Tirso's play to a (postulated) earlier drama, see Daniel Rogers, *Tirso de Molina, El Burlador de Sevilla* (Tisbury, 1977) (= *Critical Studies to Spanish Texts*, xix), pp. 11–17. For more detailed descriptions of the plot than the compass of this study will allow, see John Austen, *The Story of Don Juan* (London, 1939), pp. 5–19, or L. Weinstein, *The Metamorphoses of Don Juan* (Stanford, 1959), pp. 14–18.
2 See Esther van Loo, *Le vrai Don Juan* (Paris, 1950), pp. 33–5. As one might expect, the (very scrappy) evidence which might argue for a real-life model has been sifted and resifted. For a brief but judicious statement, see Irene Bogner, *'El Burlador de Sevilla' von Tirso de Molina als Kunstwerk* (Würzburg, 1969), pp. 95 f.
3 ii, 269–73. Pages 240 f. in Antonio Prieto's edition: see Bibliography.
4 There are many references to Catalinón's fear, and many manifestations of it. But, at the critical point, his fear of the Statue is less absurd than his master's scoffing.
5 'Fearful Symmetry: the ending of *El Burlador de Sevilla*', in *The Bulletin of Hispanic Studies* (July 1964), 141–59. Anyone interested in the pros and cons of this question will find a detailed discussion here.
6 Cf. Austen, p. 147; Th. Schröder, *Die dramatischen Bearbeitungen der Don Juan-Sage* . . . (Halle, 1912), pp. 114 f.
7 Act 1 Scene 11: here shown by Passarino to the fisher-girl, Rosalba.
8 These two versions are given in G. Oreglia, *The Commedia dell'arte*, trans. L.F. Edwards (London, 1968), pp. 43–55, and G. de Bévotte, *Le Festin de Pierre avant Molière* (Paris, 1907), pp. 335–53. Giovanni Macchia's 1966 essay on Don Juan and the *commedia* (given in *Don Juan. Darstellung und Deutung*, ed. Brigitte Wittmann (Darmstadt, 1976), pp. 258–63) is informative, but perhaps takes the *commedia* versions rather more seriously than they deserve.
9 Villiers, one of the French dramatists who produced a Don Juan play,

## NOTES

owes a debt to an unidentified Italian piece, which is widely assumed to be Giliberto's.

10  *Histoire de la littérature française au xvii$^e$ siècle* (Paris, 1952), iii, 328–30. See too Weinstein, p. 30, and Hans Mayer, *Doktor Faust und Don Juan* (Frankfurt/Main, 1979), p. 117.

11  This argument is put forward, for instance, by W. G. Moore, *Molière, a new Criticism* (Oxford, 1949), pp. 93–7.

12  See H. Carrington Lancaster, *A History of French Dramatic Literature in the Seventeenth Century* (Baltimore, 1936), Part 3, II, pp. 640 f. and 644.

13  See W.D. Howarth's edition (*Blackwell's French Texts*) for an account of this pamphlet and of the troubles with the censors (Introduction, pp. xxxiii ff.).

14  Hence I think that Hans Heckel misses the point when he dismisses Rosimond's play as mere plundering of Molière (see *Das Don Juan-Problem* . . . (Stuttgart, 1915), p. 17).

15  pp. 55 f. As we have seen, this fatalism was already present in Dorimon's play, but as little more than a brief hint.

16  *Mozart's Operas. A Critical Study*, 2nd edn (Oxford: Oxford University Press, 1947), p. 123. Purcell's music can be found in the *Works* (Novello, 1916): *Dramatic Music*, Part II, 45 ff. Purcell composed this music for the 1692 revival of Shadwell's play.

17  The murder of the father occurs in Shadwell, of course, but *The Libertine* is aside from the tradition that leads from France to the popular pieces in German.

18  The 'Laufen' Don Juan play stands alone in that it seeks, if clumsily, to show Don Juan's violence as stemming from outbursts of ungovernable rage (see Bibliography, section 3).

19  For similar usage on the part of Goldoni, see p. 128.

20  Gluck's ballet music is in his *Sämtliche Werke*, ed. R. Engländer (Bärenreiter, 1966), 2. Abt., vol. 1. Angiolini's 1761 Preface, plus the scenario, is given there, together with much other valuable source-material. Gluck's ballet was televised in an elegant performance from Denmark in December 1987, although the scenario did not follow Angiolini exactly.

## 2  DON GIOVANNI: THE OPERA BY DA PONTE AND MOZART AND E.T.A. HOFFMANN'S INTERPRETATION OF IT

1  For details of da Ponte's debts to his predecessors, see F. Chrysander, 'Die Oper Don Giovanni von Gazzaniga und von Mozart', in *Vierteljahrsschrift für Musikwissenschaft*, 4 (Leipzig, 1888), 351–435, or Dent, chapter 8.

2  Act 1 Scene 1. The remark occurs in both Paris editions of 1682, but is absent from the Amsterdam edition of the following year. For Brecht, see his notes on Molière's *Dom Juan: Schriften zum Theater* (Frankfurt/Main, 1964), 6, pp. 342 ff. The notes relate to a performance by the *Berliner Ensemble* in 1953; Brecht had a hand in the translation.

3  *Doktor Faust und Don Juan*, p. 140. Masetto's words come near the

## NOTES

beginning of the Second Act, when he thinks he is talking to Leporello, but is in fact addressing Don Giovanni disguised as his servant.

4 Wolfgang Hildesheimer makes the point that abstract reflection is foreign to Don Giovanni's nature: *Mozart* (Frankfurt/Main, 1977), p. 232.

5 In *Salmagundi. A Quarterly of the Humanities and Social Sciences*, nos. 74–5 (1987), p. 44.

6 Page 82. Shaw, too, dismisses the libretto of *Don Giovanni* as 'coarse and trivial': see the chapter 'The Nineteenth Century' in *The Perfect Wagnerite*, 1898.

7 Quoted by G.N. Nissen, *Biographie W.A. Mozart's* (Leipzig, 1828), Appendix, p. 184.

8 See the beginning of his essay 'Beethovens Instrumentalmusik'.

9 See the booklet, *Il Dissoluto Punito*, produced by the *Württembergische Staatsoper* to accompany their 1987 production, pp. 5 f.

10 See K. Engel, *Die Don Juan-Sage auf der Bühne*, 2nd edn (Dresden and Leipzig, 1887), pp. 188–204, also his *Deutsche Puppenkomödien* (Oldenburg, 1874–9), 3, p. 18; further R. von Freisauff, *Mozarts Don Juan 1787–1887* (Salzburg, 1887), and *Don Juan. Ein Singspiel in zwey Aufzügen. Aus dem Italienischen*, 2nd edn (n.p., n.d.) (= Vienna, end of eighteenth century: copy in the National Library in Vienna).

11 Tirso's Don Juan, by the way, claims shortly before his death (when he must be presumed to be speaking the truth) that he did not seduce Ana.

12 C. Dédéyan, *Le thème de Faust dans la littérature européenne* (Paris, 1954–61), 2, p. 203.

13 See chapter 6.

### 3 BYRON

1 A selection of these popular English pieces is contained in section 3 of the Bibliography. See too Bévotte, *La légende de Don Juan. Son évolution dans la littérature des origines au romanticisme* (first published in 1906, photoreprint, Geneva, 1970), pp. 351–5, and Montague Summers' introduction to his edition of *The Libertine*, in Shadwell, *Complete Works* (London, 1927), III, pp. 12–17.

2 See i, 138 ff.

3 See iv, 94 f., and v, 111 ff.

4 See xii, 81; xv, 12; xv, 30.

5 This takes place in Spain, but it is easy to detect implied criticism of English prudery.

6 i, 17 and 15.

7 See Steffan and Pratt's edition, iv, 293 ff., also S.C. Chew, *Byron in England* (London, 1924), chapters 4–5, and Andrew Rutherford (ed.), *Byron. The Critical Heritage* (London, 1970), pp. 253 ff.

8 ii, 1; vi, 4; xiv, 68. For McGann, see *Don Juan in Context* (London, 1976), chapter 5. See too J.D. Jump, *Byron* (London and Boston, 1972), p. 111.

NOTES

9  i, 84, ii, 216; v, 77. Examples could be multiplied.
10 See *A Journal of English Literary History*, 11 (1944), 135–53.
11 See Bibliography, section 6.
12 See Goethe, *Sämtliche Werke (Jubiläums-Ausgabe)* (Stuttgart and Berlin, n.d.), 37, p. 189; Platen, *Sämtliche Werke in 12 Bänden* (Leipzig, 1909), 4, p. 193; Hebbel, *Werke (Meyers Klassiker-Ausgaben)* (Leipzig, n.d.), 6, p. 236.

## 4 HOFFMANN'S INFLUENCE

1  *Luna, ein Taschenbuch* (Leipzig, 1805), p. 322.
2  Unless one counts the Don Juan of Grabbe's play, *Don Juan und Faust* (1829): see chapter 6.
3  Quoted by Castle in his edition of Lenau: *Sämtliche Werke und Briefe in 6 Bänden* (Leipzig, 1910 ff.), 6, p. 588. *Don Juan* is in vol. 2 of this edition.
4  For a table showing details of Lenau's indebtedness to his sources, see *ed. cit.*, 6, pp. 588 f.
5  Quoted in L.A. Frankl, *Zur Biographie Nikolaus Lenau's*, 2nd edn (Vienna, Budapest and Leipzig, 1885), p. 87. Cf. Stendhal, 'Le malheur de l'inconstance, c'est l'ennui': *De l'amour*, chapter 49 (p. 221 in the edition published by Calmann-Lévi, Paris, n.d.).
6  *Histoire de l'art dramatique en France*, 6 vols. (Paris, 1858–9), 4, p. 36.
7  See M. Breuillac, 'Hoffmann en France', in *Revue d'Histoire de la France*, 13 (1906–7), 427 ff. and 14, 74 ff.; E. Teichmann, *La Fortune d'Hoffmann en France* (Paris, 1961), pp. 133 ff.
8  *Ed. cit.*, 4, p. 36.
9  See *Oeuvres complètes: Oeuvres posthumes*, 1 (Paris, 1939), pp. 79–81.
10 Verlaine, *Oeuvres posthumes* (Paris, 1903), p. 143.
11 'Le Souper chez le Commandeur', in *Poésies Complètes* (Paris, 1842), p. 45.

## 5 REACTIONS AGAINST THE ROMANTICIZED DON JUAN

1  The chapter entitled 'Don Juan' forms chapter 11 in the second volume of the 1833 edition and chapter 62 in the 1839 edition. For the edition used, see Bibliography, section 8.
2  For more on the poetic justice visited on Don Juan by writers who rebelled against the idealized figure created by Hoffmann and his followers, see Bévotte, *La Légende de Don Juan*, 2 vols. (Paris, 1911), 2, chapter 2, and Weinstein, chapter 12. Claude-André Puget wittily shows Don Juan 'check-mated' by a woman in his play *Echec à Don Juan* (1941).
3  For R. Trousson on Montherlant and the Don Juan legend, see *Don Juan. Darstellung und Deutung*, ed. Wittmann, pp. 214–23.
4  This view is also expressed in Shaw's short story of 1887, 'Don Giovanni explains', and there are traces of it in *The Philanderer* (1898) and others of his plays.

NOTES

5   *The Bodley Head Bernard Shaw* (London, 1971), 2, p. 659.
6   *Don Juan und Faust* (1829), Act 1 Scene 1 and Act 3 Scene 1. See too the account of Montherlant.

## 6   LINKS WITH FAUST

1   'Die drei großen Sagen vom Don Juan, vom ewigen Juden und von Dr. Faust', in *Altes und Neues*, 5 (1873), p. 325.
2   For Frisch, see 'Nachträgliches zu Don Juan', in *Stücke* (Frankfurt/Main, 1962), 2, p. 313; for Nettl, *Casanova und seine Zeit* (Esslingen, 1949), p. 133.
3   For more detail on this subject, see my *Faust in Literature* (Oxford: Oxford University Press, 1975) (photoreprint, Greenwood Press, 1987), pp. 168 f. and 172 ff.
4   p. 348. This interesting, if flawed, work is discussed by neither Bévotte, Heckel nor Weinstein.
5   Scene 6. Expression of a deepseated German prejudice! Goethe's Mephisto, at a point where Faust is at his most cynical with regard to women, accuses him of speaking like a Frenchman.
6   p. 58. Free translation of Creizenach's rather woolly German.
7   Heckel and Weinstein are less than fair to this uneven but interesting work. For other links with the Faust tradition, see the accounts of Dumas, Zorrilla and Tolstoi in chapter 7.
8   Hürte, p. 14; *Historia von D. Johann Fausten*, ed. Hans Henning (Halle, 1963), pp. 27, 110, 119.
9   Hürte, p. 58; *Historia*, p. 134.
10  See *Faust in Literature*, pp. 187 ff. for a more detailed discussion of this point.

## 7   THE MAÑARA STORY; ZORILLA; TWO CONTRASTING RUSSIAN DON JUANS

1   See *Le vrai Don Juan*, pp. 40 f. and 53. According to Weinstein, Mañara's biographers contributed much to the ensuing confusion of fact and fiction. Weinstein, chapter 10, gives a good account of this 'rival' Don Juan.
2   Bévotte (1911, 2, pp. 28–32) devotes some attention to Mérimée's possible printed sources. A.W. Raitt, *Prosper Mérimée* (London, 1970), p. 177 thinks that Mérimée may have based his story on hearsay picked up during a visit to Seville in 1830. But the exact route by which Mérimée came by his material is likely to remain uncertain.
3   p. 27. Franz Zeise sees Don Juan in similar terms as 'der letzte Ritter Spaniens' (*Don Juan Tenorio*, 1941, p. 126).
4   The libertine's vision of his own funeral occurs in José de Espronceda's *El Estudiante de Salamanca* (1840). This may be due to the influence of either Mérimée or Dumas or both: see Margaret A. Rees, *Espronceda, El Estudiante de Salamanca* (Tisbury, 1979), pp. 62–4.
5   p. 123. Zorrilla's play became known in Germany through translations

by G.H. Wilde (1850) and J. Fastenrath (1898). For Walter Owen's English translation, see Bibliography, section 5 and for a summary of the plot, Weinstein, pp. 120–2.

6   For Ortega, see *Don Juan. Darstellung und Deutung*, p. 14; for the critical 'balance-sheets', see Weinstein, pp. 119 f. and Walter Owen's Introduction to his translation.

7   Alexander Pushkin, *Selected Works* (Moscow: Progress, 1974) (*Russian Classics Series*), 1, p. 207.

8   For a general account of the Hoffmann vogue in Russia, see C.E. Passage, *The Russian Hoffmannists* (The Hague, 1963). Charles Corbet ('L'originalité du "Convive de Pierre" de Pouchkine' in *Revue de Littérature comparée*, 29 (1955), 48–71) does not think that Pushkin was influenced by Hoffmann. While it seems clear that Pushkin arrived at his view of Don Juan without Hoffmann's help, it would be a strange coincidence if this were also true of his interpretation of Anna. Something similar – Hoffmann's Anna without Hoffmann's Juan – can be found in Frank Thiess (1950).

9   p. 73. The Russian edition has a Dedication to Hoffmann and Mozart in Russian and a quotation in the original from Hoffmann's Don Juan tale.

10  Heckel, p. 74. Tolstoi calls his hero Don Juan Maraña.

## 8   THE 'SPORTING' DON JUAN

1   *Tirso de Molina* (Boston, 1977), p. 109.
2   'L'originalité du "Convive de Pierre" . . .', p. 62.
3   *Casanova und andere Gestalten* (Munich and Leipzig, 1918), p. 22. Written in 1905. There is a similarity to that peculiarly English fictional character, the gentlemanly crook, who advertises his coups in advance and takes unnecessary risks.
4   Walter Mönch, 'Don Juan. Ein Drama der europäischen Bühne . . .', in *Revue de Littérature comparée*, xxxv (1961), 619.
5   For other works which bear on the question of overcoming remorse, see Schmitz's comedy *Don Juanita* (1908) and his *Ein deutscher Don Juan* of the following year, also Albert Lepage's play *Faust et Don Juan* of 1960.
6   *De l'Amour*, chapter 49. Page 215 in the edition already cited.
7   A. Lenburg, *Faust. Ein Gedicht* (Berlin, 1860), p. 75.
8   For another 'Nietzschean' Don Juan, see the account of Bonsels, p. 86.
9   p. 90. A similar claim is made by the hero of Beyerlein's novella of 1938.
10  *Zürcher Ausgabe*, Zürich, 1977, iv, 661.
11  Since the first part of *Die Welt als Wille und Vorstellung* appeared in 1818, the coupling may seem odd. But Schopenhauer only began to exert his grip over the German imagination much later in the century.
12  David Constantine, 'Don Giovanni: Six Sonnets', no. 2, in *Madder* (London: Bloodaxe Books, 1987), p. 22.

13 Kästner (1930), p. 257; Warner (1938), p. 194. See too the account of Hayem, p. 58.
14 Conversely, Molière's Dom Juan, who callously sets out to break up a profoundly loving relationship, seems more than usually repellent.
15 The colon is missing in the Bodley Head edition, but is clearly demanded by the sense.
16 Hebbel's verse-epigram 'Don Juan' (in the collection *Neue Epigramme*) praises Don Juan for his lack of hypocrisy. Perhaps Byron's influence is at work here. Half a century later, when asked whether his love will last, the hero of Schmitz's one-acter *Don Juan und die Kurtisane* (1900) will evade the question: 'Frag' nicht'. (p. 43) But even this degree of honesty is unusual. Molière's Don Juan, of course, rails against hypocrisy as a 'fashionable vice' (Act 5 Scene 2) – but goes on to justify his own hypocrisy as a convenient mask.

## 9 DON JUAN AS A TYPE

1 *De l'Amour*, chapter 49.
2 *Ed. cit.*, pp. 212, 218, 214.
3 Kierkegaard, *Either/Or*, ed. and trans. Howard and Edna Hong, 2 vols. (Princetown, 1987), 1, pp. 85, 92, 107.
4 See the chapter 'Le Don Juanisme', in *Le Mythe de Sisyphe*, first published 1942.
5 *Don Juan et le Donjuanisme*, trans. Lacombe (Paris, 1958), p. 23.
6 See *Don Juan. Une Etude sur le Double*, trans. Lautmann (Paris, 1932) and *Seelenglaube und Psychologie* (Leipzig and Vienna, 1930). A Freudian interpretation is given by Brigid Brophy in her *Black Ship to Hell* (London, 1962).
7 In this he shows little understanding of an ancient convention in drama, according to which a character had only to change clothes in order to carry off a successful impersonation or role-change. Confusions arising from genuine similarity of appearance are in a small minority.
8 That is only a brief summary of Rank's argument, in which he goes on to hive off other parts of Don Giovanni's personality on to other characters in the opera.
9 See *Don Juan . . .*, pp. 251–69: 'La décadence du héros'.
10 *Black Ship to Hell, passim*.
11 In *Don Juan and other psychological Studies*, trans. Perry (London, 1930), p. 21. Lafora was a specialist in nervous disorders. For an interpretation of Don Juan which explains his actions as attempts to overcome an inferiority complex (!), see F.O. Brachfeld (summary in Weinstein, p. 142). A.E. Singer is severe on such dogmatic interpretations: see 'Don Juan among the Psychiatrists', 1948 (reprinted in *Don Juan. Darstellung und Deutung*, pp. 317–28).
12 Ödön von Horvath, in the Preface to his Don Juan play of 1935, makes a similar incautious generalization: all woman surrender to Don Juan, but none really loves him (Elvira?). For Grimsley, see 'The Don Juan

Theme in Molière and Kierkegaard', in *Comparative Literature*, 6 (1954), 316.
13 Wiesbaden (Trautmann, 1856); Hamburg (Engel, 1922); London (Flecker, 1925). The list could be extended.
14 H. Tann-Bergler, *Wiener Guckkastenbilder* (Berlin, n.d. = 1888); A. Ulreich, *Wiener Art aus der Gegenwart* (Vienna, 1925).
15 K.H. Ruppel, in the Preface to his translation (Jean Anouilh, *Dramen* (Munich, 1957), 2, p. 20) talks of a 'paraphrase' of traditional elements.

## 10 THE LEGENDARY FRAMEWORK: AN AID OR A PITFALL?

1 *Opere*, Milan, 1935 ff., 1, pp. 176 and 178.
2 In 'Don Juan oder die Liebe zur Geometrie', in *Die deutsche Komödie vom Mittelalter bis zur Gegenwart*, ed. W. Hinck (Düsseldorf, 1977), p. 309.
3 There is a good discussion by Hiltrud Gnüg of Frisch's attitude towards the legendary tradition in the essay referred to above.
4 The characters also refer to the tradition of which they form part in Friedmann (1881) and in Brigid Brophy's novel *The Snowball* (1964).
5 *Die Chinesische Mauer, eine Farce* (Berlin and Frankfurt/Main, 1955), p. 29.

## 11 RICHARD STRAUSS AND DON JUAN

1 See Fritz Gysi, *Richard Strauss* (Potsdam, 1934), p. 34. Since the works consulted for this account are listed separately in the Bibliography (section 7), subsequent references give only the author's name.
2 The original German can be found on pp. 402 f., 405 and 441 f. of the Lenau edition cited. Since these passages are also given in most orchestral and piano scores of Strauss's tone-poem, I have not quoted them here. 'Dead as stone' in the third extract may come as a surprise to students of Strauss's work. It is a translation of what Lenau actually wrote (*steintot*). Strauss's *scheintot* ('seemingly dead') goes back to a mis-transcription in the first (posthumous) edition of 1851 and survived until Castle corrected it in 1911.
3 See Strauss's letters to Bülow of 24 August 1888 and to his parents of 2 February 1890. The sketchbook referred to is in the possession of the Richard-Strauss-Archive in Garmisch. I am much indebted to Dr Stephan Kohler of the Richard-Strauss-Institute in Munich for drawing my attention to this and for confirming my views on Strauss's attitude towards 'programmatic' interpretations of his work. Later, of course, in *Till Eulenspiegel* and *Don Quixote* for instance, Strauss was to go further in the direction of a detailed (narrative and pictorial) programme.
4 Del Mar, 1, p. 69; Krause, p. 241; Muschler, p. 263; Steinitzer, p. 90.
5 Strauss orally to Willi Schuh: quoted in the latter's article on Strauss in *Musik in Geschichte und Gegenwart*, 12, p. 1487.

## NOTES

6   Strauss also projected an opera on the Don Juan theme, but the plan was never carried out, for reasons that can only be guessed at. Perhaps the huge and daunting shadow of Mozart's and da Ponte's masterpiece deterred him. For the surviving plan, see Schuh, pp. 262–5.
7   Five, if one counts Mahler's settings of songs from *El Burlador*. But these, representing as they do the composer's reaction to a German version of Tirso's play two and a half centuries after the original was written, cannot be seen as standing for an important stage in the development of the legend or contributing to our understanding of the central figure, beautiful though they are as songs. Variations and fantasias on tunes from *Don Giovanni* (Chopin, Liszt) are omitted too, since they belong to the realm of virtuoso piano-music and do not amount to a musical interpretation of the character or the legend.

## 12 CONCLUSION

1   See Hayem, *Le Don Juanisme*, p. 94; Levy, 1937, Foreword, p. 10; Shaw, *The Perfect Wagnerite*, chapter entitled 'Siegfried as Protestant'.
2   *Ed. cit.*, 4, p. 634.
3   This is brought out strongly in Dutouquet's dramatic poem of 1864.
4   Ana in *El Burlador* and Kathrine in *Der schwarze Hans* illustrate this clearly.
5   *Horizon. A Magazine for the Arts*, 4, no. 3 (New York, January 1962), p. 56.
6   Paragraph headed 'Inconsistency of the Sex Instinct'.
7   Weinstein thinks that a study of the 'female Don Juan' might be profitable (p. 170), but he cites only one example. In the fringe section of the 1987 Salzburg Festival, a Mexican group produced a variant on Mozart's *Don Giovanni: Donna Giovanni* (mentioned in *Der Spiegel*, 13 July 1987, p. 133). Extracts were shown in the BBC2 programme on Don Juan of 7 January 1989. All parts in the opera are played by women, who take it in turns to act the hero's role. This is, then, a feminist version which obliquely makes the point that women have as much right to sexual pleasure as men.
8   p. 158. He goes on to show Camus's influence at work in a few cases – but far too few to justify his virtual equation of Camus and Hoffmann in terms of actual/potential influence. I am not aware that examples have proliferated in the thirty years since Weinstein wrote his book.

# SELECT BIBLIOGRAPHY

### SECTION 1  BIBLIOGRAPHY OF THE DON JUAN THEME

Singer, A.E. (1954) *A Bibliography of the Don Juan Theme. Versions and Criticism*, in *West Virginia University Bulletin*, Series 54, nos. 10–11, April.

### SECTION 2  COLLECTIONS OF SOURCE-MATERIAL

Bévotte, G. de (1907) *Le Festin der Pierre avant Molière*, Paris.
Dietrich, Margret (1967) *Theater der Jahrhunderte: Don Juan*, Munich and Vienna. All pieces in German translation.
Mandel, O. (1963) *The Theatre of Don Juan*, University of Nebraska Press, Lincoln.
Rousset, Jean (1978) *Le Mythe de Don Juan*, Paris. Half survey, half anthology. Extracts from the various Don Juan works, where not originally in French, are given in French translation.
Scheible, J. (1845–9) *Das Kloster. Weltlich und geistlich. Meist aus der älteren deutschen Volks-, Wunder-, Curiositäten-, und vorzugsweise komischen Literatur*, 12 vols. Stuttgart and Leipzig. Volume 3 has much material on Don Juan.

### SECTION 3  POPULAR STAGE PLAYS, PANTOMIMES, ETC

Mid-seventeenth century onwards: versions given by the *commedia dell'arte* in Italy and France. See chapter 1, note 8 for the main sources.
1700: *Histrio Gallicus, comico-satyricus, sine exemplo: Oder Die Weltberühmten Lust-Comödien Des . . . Herrn von Molière . . . in das Teutsche übersetzt*, Nuremberg, 1700, 1, pp. 12–110: 'Des Don Pedro Gastmahl – a reasonably faithful version of Molière.
Early or mid-eighteenth century: *Das steinerne Gastmahl, oder die redende Statua* (n.p., n.d.). Scenario of 24 pp. Not from Molière, but from other French and/or Italian sources.
1752: '*Das steinerne Todten-Gastmahl oder Die im Grabe noch lebende Rache*', theatre-bill from Dresden, 11 January 1752. Given by Engel, *Die Don Juan-Sage auf der Bühne*, pp. 187 f.

## SELECT BIBLIOGRAPHY

1757: 'Le Festin de Pierre, Des D. Pedro Todten Gastmahl', theatre-bill of 16 February 1757, in *Theaterzettel der Schuchischen Gesellschaft aus Regensburg* (1756–7): collection in Göttingen University Library.

1761: *Don Juan*. Ballet by Gasparo Angiolini, music by C.W. Gluck. Music, scenario and detailed critical apparatus in Gluck, *Sämtliche Werke*, Part II, 1, ed. R. Engländer (1966), Bärenreiter. This supersedes the earlier edition by Robert Haas (1960), Graz.

3rd quarter of eighteenth century: *Der Laufner Don Juan*, ed. R.M. Werner (1891), Hamburg and Leipzig. Referred to as the 'Laufen' Don Juan play.

1782: *An Historical Account of the Tragi-comic Pantomime intituled Don Juan, or the Libertine Destroyed*. As it is performed at Drury-Lane Theatre, London, 1782. The scenario, with brief (anonymous) Introduction.

1783: Marinelli (1936) *'Dom Juan, oder Der steinerne Gast. Lustspiel in vier Aufzügen nach Molieren, und dem Spanischen des Tirso de Molina'*, in *Deutsche Literatur in Entwicklungsreihen, Reihe Barock: Barocktradition im öst.-bayerischen Volkstheater*, 2, pp. 53–96.

1787: *Don Juan; or, The Libertine Destroy'd: a tragic pantomimical Entertainment . . . as performed at the Royalty Theatre*, 3rd edn, London, n.d. (= 1787). Detailed scenario, different in many particulars from the 1782 version. Much of the action derives from the Angiolini ballet-scenario; Gluck's music was probably used.

*c.* 1810: anon., 'Life of Don Giovanni', Dublin. A trivial retelling of the story as in da Ponte in jocose doggerel.

*c.* 1815: *The History of Don Juan, Or the Libertine Destroyed*, London. Sixpenny chapbook loosely based on Shadwell.

1820: 'W.T. Moncrieff' (pseud. W.T. Thomas) *Giovanni in London; Or, the Libertine Reclaimed: an operatic Extravaganza*. In *The London Stage: a Collection of the most reputed Tragedies, Comedies, Operas*, 4 vols., London, 1824–7, no. 110 (vol. 3).

1869: *Don Juan! or the Libertine destroyed*, comic pantomime. Used as a curtain-raiser at the Bower Theatre in Lambeth. Playbill in M.R. Booth (1965) *English Melodrama*, London, facing p. 81.

### SECTION 4   PUPPET-PLAYS (IN ORDER OF PUBLICATION)

'Don Juan oder der steinerne Gast' (Strasbourg), in Scheible, 3, pp. 725 ff.

'Don Juan. Ein Trauerspiel in 4 Aufzügen' (Ulm), ibid., pp. 760 ff.

'Don Juan und Don Pietro' (Augsburg), in ibid., pp. 699 ff.

'Don Juan oder: Der steinerne Gast', in Engel, K. (1874–9) *Deutsche Puppenkomödien*, Oldenburg, 3, pp. 23 ff.

'Don Juan, der vielfache Mörder oder Das Gastmahl um Mitternacht auf dem Kirchhofe', in Engel, 3, pp. 69 ff. (extracts only).

'Don Juan der Wilde oder Das nächtliche Gericht oder Der steinerne Gast . . .', (lower Austrian), in *Deutsche Puppenspiele*, ed. Kralik and Winter (1885), Vienna, pp. 81 ff.

SELECT BIBLIOGRAPHY

## SECTION 5  LITERARY TREATMENTS OF THE DON JUAN THEME

*c.* 1630: 'Tirso de Molina' (pseud. Gabriel Téllez), *El Burlador de Sevilla y Convidado de Piedra.* Innumerable editions, including that by Antonio Prieto (1974) *Marta la Piadosa. El Burlador de Sevilla*, Madrid, pp. 185–309. Also in the *Obras dramáticas completas* (1946), Madrid, 2, pp. 634–86. I give line references when quoting. The most recent English translation is by Gwynne Edwards, Warminster, 1986.

1640s: Cicognini, J.A., *Il Convitato di Pietra*, in Bévotte, *Le Festin de Pierre avant Molière*, pp. 369–424.

1659: Dorimon, *Le Festin de Pierre ou le fils criminel*, Bévotte, pp. 17–134.

1659: Deschamps, Claude, Sieur de Villiers, *Le Festin de Pierre ou le fils criminel*, Bévotte, pp. 151–275.

1665: Molière, *Dom Juan ou le Festin de Pierre*, first performed 1665, published 1682. I have used W.D. Howarth's edition (1958) in *Blackwell's French Texts*.

1669: Rosimond, *Le nouveau Festin de Pierre ou l'Athée foudroyé*, in Fournal, V. (1875) *Les Contemporains de Molière*, Paris, 3, pp. 313–77.

1675: Shadwell, Thomas, *The Libertine*, in *Complete Works*, ed. Summers, Montague (1927), London, 3, pp. 19–93.

1677: Corneille, Thomas, *Le Festin de Pierre*, in *Oeuvres de Pierre et Thomas Corneille* (1850), Paris, pp. 378–421.

1692: Purcell, Henry, music to Shadwell's *Libertine*, in *Works* (1916), Novello: *Dramatic Music*, part 2, pp. 45 ff.

1736: Goldoni, Carlo, *Don Giovanni Tenorio o sia Il Dissoluto*, in *Opere (I Classici Mondadori)*, Milan, 1935 ff., ix, 209 ff.

1744: Zamora, Antonio de, *No hay deuda que no se pague y convidado de piedra*, printed 1744. Based on *El Burlador* with much additional sensational material. Brief account in Weinstein, p. 50. I have not examined this play.

1787: Mozart, W.A. and da Ponte, L., *Il Dissoluto punito o sia il Don Giovanni.* I have used the vocal score arranged by Ernest Roth and published by Boosey and Hawkes.

1797: Schiller, Friedrich, 'Don Juan' (fragment of a ballad). A reading of Don Juan's character suggested by da Ponte and stressing the quality of arrogance. The fragment was completed by Adalbert Rudolf about 1885; the completed version can be found in Engel, *Don Juan auf der Bühne*, pp. 175–83.

1805: Vulpius, C.A., *Don Juan der Wüstling. Nach dem Spanischen des Tirso de Molina*, Penig, 1805. The title is misleading: *not* based on *El Burlador.*

1813: Hoffmann, E.T.A., 'Don Juan. Eine fabelhafte Begebenheit, die sich mit einem reisenden Enthusiasten zugetragen', in *Poetische Werke* (1957–62), 12 vols., Berlin, 1, pp. 73–88.

1818: Bäuerle, Adolf, *Moderne Wirtschaft und Don Juans Streiche. Posse mit Gesang.* First performed 1818 under the title *Der neue Don Juan.* Edition used: Bäuerle (1823) *Komisches Theater*, Budapest, vol. 5. Shows Don Juan as a thoroughgoing rascal who undergoes an improbable conversion.

# SELECT BIBLIOGRAPHY

1819–24: Byron, *Don Juan*, ed. T.G. Steffan and W.W. Pratt (1957), 4 vols., University of Texas Press. The edition by E.H. Coleridge (1924) (*Works: Poetry*, vol. 6, London), is also useful, although the critical apparatus is much less detailed.

1820: von Schaden, A., *Der deutsche Don Juan*, Berlin.

1829: Grabbe, C.D., *Don Juan und Faust*. Many editions; I give scene references when quoting.

1829: Kahlert, A., 'Donna Elvira', in *Novellen* (1832), Breslau, pp. 75–114. Written 1829. A melodramatic tale, overpraised by some of the critics.

1830: de Balzac, H., 'L'Elixir de longue vie' (in vol. 10 of the *Comédie humaine*). A fantastic short story: in no way a contribution to the interpretation of Don Juan as a character.

1830: de Bury, Blaze, 'Le Souper chez le Commandeur', in *Poésies complètes* (1842), Paris, pp. 1–72.

1830: Pushkin, Alexander, *The Stone Guest*. Edition used: *Selected Works* (1974), Moscow (Russian Classics Series). *The Stone Guest*, trans. Avril Pyman, 1, pp. 127–60.

1832: de Musset, A., 'Namouna. Conte oriental'. Edition used: *Poésies complètes*, ed. Allem (1957), Paris, pp. 239–70.

1834: von Holtei, C., *Don Juan. Dramatische Phantasie*. First appeared as 'von einem deutschen Theaterdichter', Paris (!= Leipzig). I have used this edition. There is also a more modern edition (1923), Berlin. An arrogant and wicked Don Juan.

1834: Mérimée, P., 'Les Ames du Purgatoire', in *Colomba, La Vénus d'Illes, Les Ames du Purgatoire* (n.d.), Paris, pp. 295–399.

*c.* 1835: Duller, E., 'Juan', in *Gedichte* (1845), Berlin, pp. 151–5.

1836: Dumas, Alexandre (Dumas père), *Don Juan de Marana* (sic!). Edition used: *Théâtre complet* (1899), Paris, 5, pp. 1–100.

1836: Robin, Eugène, *Livia. Poème dramatique*, Paris.

1836–7: Creizenach, Th., 'Don Juan', in *Dichtungen* (1839), Mannheim, pp. 1–60.

1838: Gautier, T., 'La Comédie de la Mort'. Edition used: *Poésies complètes* (1924), Paris, 2, pp. 3–49.

1840: Espronceda, *El Estudiante de Salamanca*. Many editions. There is a French translation by R. Foulché-Delbose (1893), Paris. This Don Juan is a reckless sceptic who is damned.

1840: Wiese, S., *Don Juan. Trauerspiel in fünf Acten*, Leipzig.

1842: von Braunthal, Braun, *Don Juan. Drama in fünf Abtheilungen*, Leipzig.

1844: de Gobineau, A., *Les Adieux de Don Juan. Poëme dramatique*, Paris.

1844: Lenau, N., 'Don Juan: dramatische Szenen'. Edition used: *Sämtliche Werke*, ed. E. Castle, Leipzig, pp. 1910 ff., 2, pp. 402 ff. First published in Cotta's *Morgenblatt* (1851), then in *Nikolaus Lenau's dramatischer Nachlaß*, ed. Anastasius Grün (1851), Stuttgart and Tübingen, pp. 1–102. These early editions contain the misreading 'scheintot' which persisted until Castle went back to the manuscript.

1844: Zorrilla y Moral, José, *Don Juan Tenorio*. Many editions. Walter Owen's English translation (1944, Buenos Aires) has an Introduction with a good discussion of the strengths and weaknesses of this work.

## SELECT BIBLIOGRAPHY

1845: Ackermann, E.W., 'Don Juan und Maria. Commedia infernale', in *Aus dem poetischen Nachlasse von E.W.A.* (1848), Leipzig, pp. 129–50.

1847: Mallefille, F., *Les mémoires de Don Juan*. I have used the German translation in 11 volumes (1848–53), Leipzig.

1848: le Vavasseur, G., 'Don Juan Barbon', in *Poésies complètes* (1888–96), Paris, 1, pp. 115–50.

1850: Hörnigk, R., *Don Juan. Tragödie*, Potsdam. One of the less skilful attempts to import material from the Faust tradition into a Don Juan play.

*c.* 1851: Flaubert, G., 'Une Nuit de Don Juan' (brief sketch for a story or novella), in *Oeuvres de Jeunesse inédites* (1910), Paris, 3, pp. 321–5. Too fragmentary for much to be deduced. But, had the work been finished, this would undoubtedly have been a Don Juan of the French Romantic stamp.

1853: Precht, V., 'Don Juan'. Poem in *Düsseldorfer Künstler-Album*, Düsseldorf, pp. 20 f.

*c.* 1853: Baudelaire, C., 'La Fin de Don Juan'. Sketch for a projected Don Juan play, first published posthumously. Edition used: *Oeuvres complètes* (1939), Paris; *Oeuvres posthumes*, 1, pp. 79–81.

1854: Hürte, N., *Wahrhaftige Historie vom ärgerlichen Leben des spanischen Ritters Don Juan and wie ihn zuletzt +++ der Teufel geholt*, Reutlingen.

1855: Mörike, E., *Mozart auf der Reise nach Prag*. Novella, first published in 1855; innumerable subsequent editions. Not a version of a legend, but it contains an eloquent and highly romantic account of the closing moments of Mozart's opera.

1856: Trautmann, P.F., *Don Juan in Wiesbaden. Schwank in einem Akt*, Berlin.

1856: de l'Isle-Adam, Villiers, 'Hermosa. Poème', in *Oeuvres complètes* (1929), Paris, 10, pp. 37–108.

1857: Baudelaire, C., 'Don Juan aux Enfers', in *Les Fleurs du Mal*.

1857: Jourdain, E., *Don Juan. Drame fantastique*, Paris.

*c.* 1857: Spiesser, Fr., *Don Juan, oder: Der steinerne Gast. Seine Thaten und sein furchtbares Lebensende* (n.d.), Cassel.

1858: Widmann, A., *Don Juan de Maranna (sic!). Ein romantisches Schauspiel*, in *Dramatische Werke*, Leipzig, 2, pp. 1–176.

1860: Tolstoi, A., *Don Juan*. Edition used: *Don Juan, dramatisches Gedicht*, trans. C. von Pawloff (*c.* 1863), Dresden.

1864: Dutouquet, E., *Une Aventure de Don Juan*, Paris. The first section, entitled 'Faust', contains a discussion of Faust and Don Juan.

1866: Möser, A., 'Don Juan'. First published in *Neue Sonette*, Leipzig, p. 47, then in *Gedichte*, 2nd edn (1869), Leipzig, p. 226.

1866: Verlaine, Paul (?), Sonnet 'A Don Juan'. Usually attributed to Verlaine; originally published under the pseudonym 'Fulvio'. In P.V., *Oeuvres posthumes* (1903), Paris, p. 143.

1867: Meyr, Melchior, *Der schwarze Hans*, first published in 1867, then in *Erzählungen aus dem Ries* (1870), n.s., Hannover, pp. 1–199. This is the edition used.

1869–71: von Königsmark, W., *Ein neuer Don Juan . . . Ein Sittengemälde aus der Neuzeit*, 5 vols. in 2, Berlin.

*c*. 1870: 'Fernando del Castillo', *Don Jouan. Romantisches Lustspiel . . . aus dem Spanischen übersetzt*, Madrid, 1820. Author's name, place of publication and date are all fictitious. Pornography, using characters from Mozart/da Ponte.
1874: d'Aurévilly, J. Barbey, 'Le plus bel Amour de Don Juan', in *Les Diaboliques*; edition used: Paris, 1934, pp. 95–133.
1880: Lipiner, S., *Der neue Don Juan. Tragödie in fünf Akten* (1914), Stuttgart. Written 1880.
1881: Friedmann, A., *Don Juan's letztes Abenteuer. Drama in zwei Akten*, Leipzig.
1881: Hart, Julius, *Don Juan Tenorio. Eine Tragödie in 4 Aufzügen*, Rostock.
1883: Heyse, Paul, *Don Juan's Ende. Trauerspiel in 5 Akten* (*Dramatische Dichtungen*, 13, Berlin).
1884: Verlaine, Paul, 'Don Juan Pipé', published in *Jadis et naguère*. Edition used: *Oeuvres complètes* (1923), Paris, 1, pp. 413–18. Don Juan as rebel and blasphemer.
1886: Hayem, A., *Don Juan d'Armana. Drame en 4 actes*, Paris. See also section 8.
1886: Proelß, J., 'Don Juan's Erlösung'. Ballad in *Trotz alledem! Gedichte*, Frankfurt/Main, pp. 210–18. A late descendant of Hoffmann's Don Juan.
1887: Shaw, G.B., 'Don Giovanni explains' (short story). Edition used: *Short Stories, Scraps and Shavings* (1934), London, pp. 97–118.
1888: 'Ottokar Tann-Bergler' (pseud. H. Bergler, 'Don Juan im Caféhaus', in *Wiener Guckkastenbilder* (n.d.), Berlin, pp. 162–8.
1889: Aicard, J., *Don Juan 89*, Paris.
1891: Mansfield, Richard, *Don Juan, a Play in 4 acts*, New York.
1895: Roujon, H., *Miremonde*, Paris.
1896: Weigand, W., 'Don Juans Ende. Ein Lustspiel in einem Akt', in W.W., *Moderne Dramen* (1900), Munich, ii, 1–38.
1898: Bierbaum, O.J., 'Don Juan Tenorio', in *Kaktus und andere Künstlergeschichten*, Berlin and Leipzig, pp. 123–76.
1898: Haraucourt, E., *Don Juan de Mañara. Drame en cinq actes*, Paris.
1900: Barrière, M., *Le nouveau Don Juan*, 3 vols. Paris. An extravagant *fin de siècle* novel with clear debts to *A Rebours*.
1900: von Hornstein, F., *Don Juans Höllenqualen. Phantastisches Drama*, Stuttgart.
1900: Schmitz, O.A.H., 'Don Juan und die Kurtisane', in *Don Juan und die Kurtisane, fünf Einakter* (1914), Munich, pp. 5–47. See also section 8.
1903: Bernhardi, O.C., *Don Juan*, Berlin.
1903: Shaw, G.B., *Man and Superman*. Edition used: *The Bodley Head Bernard Shaw*, 1971, 2, pp. 489 ff.
1906: von Gottschall, R., 'Don Juans hohes Lied', in *Späte Lieder*, Breslau, pp. 71 f.
1906: Mournet-Sully, J. and Barbier, Pierre, *La Vieillesse de Don Juan. Pièce en trois actes*, Paris. A late descendant of Hoffmann's Don Juan.
*c*. 1906–8: Trakl, Georg, 'Don Juans Tod', fragment of a tragedy. Edition used: *Dichtungen und Briefe, historisch-kritische Ausgabe*, ed. W. Killy and Hans Szklener (1969), Salzburg, 1, pp. 447–53.

## SELECT BIBLIOGRAPHY

1908: de Regnier, H., *Les Scrupules de Sganarelle*, Paris. Reaction against the romanticized Don Juan.

1908: Schmitz, O.A.H., *Don Juanito. Komödie in 4 Aufzügen*, Berlin. Reworked as *Ein deutscher Don Juan*, 1909.

1909: Anthes, O., *Don Juans letztes Abenteuer. Drama*, Berlin. Also as opera libretto: Paul Graener, *Don Juans letztes Abenteuer. Oper in 3 Akten. Dichtung von Otto Anthes. Textbuch* (1914), Vienna and Leipzig. This is the edition I have used.

1909: Rittner, Th., *Unterwegs. Ein Don Juan-Drama in drei Akten*, Berlin.

1909: Sternheim, Carl, *Don Juan. Eine Tragödie*; edition used: Munich, 1921.

1910: Bethge, H., *Don Juan. Tragikomödie* (n.d.), Leipzig.

1910: Blok, Alexander, 'The Commander's Footsteps', in A.B., *Selected Poems*, trans. J. Stallworthy and Peter France (*Penguin Modern European Poets*) (1970), pp. 86 f. An updated version, but still with faint traces of Hoffmann's romanticized hero.

1910: Langen, Martin, *Don Juan. Trauerspiel in fünf Aufzügen*, Munich. Don Juan idealized and ennobled to a degree where it hardly seems appropriate to attach the name to him.

1911: G.A. (= Guillaume Apollinaire), *Les Exploits d'un jeune Don Juan* (n.d.), Paris.

1911: Baring, Maurice, 'Don Juan's Failure', in *Diminutive Dramas*, London, pp. 119–28. A minor example of the Don Juan-humiliated type.

1912: Lembach, A., *Don Juan. Ein Drama in drei Akten*, Berlin.

1913: Bennett, Arnold, *Don Juan de Marana. A Play in Four Acts* (1923), London. Written 1913.

1914: Rostand, E., *La dernière Nuit de Don Juan* (1921), Paris. Written 1914.

1915: Brausewetter, A., *Don Juans Erlösung. Roman*, Brunswick.

1919: Bonsels, W., *Don Juan. Eine epische Dichtung*, Berlin.

1921: Heymann, R., *Don Juan und die Heilige. Roman*, Leipzig.

c. 1921: Leyst, C., *Don Juans Mission. Drama in 3 Akten* (n.d.), Berlin.

1922: Engel, Ludwig, *Der Don Juan vom Jungfernstieg. Ein Hamburger Roman*, Leipzig.

1922: van Vloten, W., *Don Juan empor! Roman*, Basle and Leipzig.

1923: Glass, Max, *Don Juans Puppen*, Potsdam. A Don Juan novel with a contemporary setting.

1923: Kees, Egon, *Don Juan. Ein Epos in fünf Gesängen*, Lemgo. Takes the adulation of Don Juan (constantly referred to as 'der Held') to absurd lengths.

1924: Becker, Franz Karl, *Don Juans Anfang. Ein Stück in 8 Szenen* (1925), Munich.

1924: Ehrenberg, Rudolf, 'Don Juans Duell mit Gott': one-act play in blank verse, in *Zwischen Tod und Leben*, Berlin, pp. 53–75. One of those Don Juans whose overriding need is to assert his own individuality.

1925: Flecker, J.E., *Don Juan. A Play in Three Acts*, London. Loosely based on Molière; an attempt to transplant the events to England and update them.

1925: Ulreich, Alois, 'Lully der Herzensbrecher', in *Wiener Art aus der Gegenwart*, Vienna.

## SELECT BIBLIOGRAPHY

1925: Zweig, Stefan, 'Leporella'. Edition used: *Ausgewählte Novellen* (1946), Stockholm, pp. 491–524. The story of a noble libertine. The link with Don Juan (character and legend) is tenuous.

1928: Grupe-Lörcher, Erica, *Der wiedererstandene Don Juan. Roman*, Reutlingen (*Enßlins Roman- und Novellenschatz*, vol. 333).

1930: Delteil, J., *Don Juan*, Paris. Novel which combines the stories of Mañara and Don Juan Tenorio.

1930: Kästner, Erich, 'Es gibt noch Don Juans'. Short story, revised 1958, in *Gesammelte Schriften in sieben Bänden* (1959), Cologne, 2, pp. 257–61.

1931: Linklater, Eric, *Juan in America*. I have used the edition published in London in 1962.

1932: Schirokauer, A., *Don Juan auf der Flucht. Roman*, Berlin.

1933: Heimerdinger, A., *Don Juan. Balladenzyklus*, Berlin, Leipzig, Munich.

1934: von Hartenstein, S., *Don Juan. Ein Leben Liebe, Laster, Heiligkeit*, Vienna.

1935: von Horvath, Ö., *Don Juan kommt aus dem Krieg. Schauspiel*. Edition used: *Theater der Jahrhunderte. Don Juan* (1967), pp. 331–77. A late example of Don Juan as quester after an ideal woman.

1937: Levy, Benn W., *The Poet's Heart. A Life of Don Juan*, London.

1937: Linklater, Eric, *Juan in China*. Edition used: London, 1961.

1937: Wolfe, Humbert, *Don J. Ewan*, London.

1938: Beyerlein, F.A., 'Don Juans Überwindung', in *Don Juans Überwindung, Ende gut – alles gut. Zwei Novellen*, 2nd edn, Bielefeld and Leipzig, pp. 5–113.

1938: Townsend Warner, Sylvia, *After the Death of Don Juan*, London.

1939: Kratzmann, E., 'Don Juan in Venedig', in *Regina Sebaldi*, Vienna, pp. 51–76.

1941: Brenner, H.G., *Drei Abenteuer Don Juans*, Berlin. Tales dealing with three stages in Don Juan's career. They concentrate on his role-playing and on his relationship to his servant.

1941: Puget, C.-A., *Echec à Don Juan*, in *Théâtre* (1943), Paris, 1, pp. 113–232.

1941: Zeise, Franz, *Don Juan Tenorio. Ein Lebensbild*, Berlin. A 'romantic reconstruction' of Don Juan's life in the form of a novel.

1948: 'Christian Schneller' (pseud. C.A. Mayer), *Der Sturz. Eine Don-Juan-Tragödie*, Munich.

1950: Broch, Hermann, *Die Erzählung der Magd Zerline* (sic!). Edition used: *Bibliothek Suhrkamp* (1987), Frankfurt/Main, no. 204. A novella whose hero (Herr von Juna – sic!) has a remote connection with the idealized Don Juans of the nineteenth century.

1950: Thiess, Frank, *Don Juans letzte Tage. Novelle*, Vienna and Linz.

1952: Frisch, Max, *Don Juan oder Die Liebe zur Geometrie. Komödie in fünf Akten*, in *Stücke* (1962), Frankfurt/Main, 2, pp. 7–85. The notes ('Nachträgliches zu Don Juan') are in the same volume, pp. 313–21.

1952: Zévaco, M., *Don Juan*, Paris. Costume-piece incorporating elements from the Don Juan legend.

1953: Duncan, Ronald, *Don Juan*. First performed 1953, published London, 1954. Free adaptation of Zorrilla.

1954: Duncan, Ronald, *The Death of Satan. A Comedy*, first performed in 1954 and published London, 1955.
1954: Hagelstange, R., *Die Beichte des Don Juan*, Olten.
1955: Anouilh, Jean, *Ornifle ou le courant d'air*. Edition used: *Pièces grinçantes* (1958), Paris, pp. 211–370. See too K.H. Ruppel's Preface to his German translation, J.A., *Dramen* (1957), Munich, 2.
1956: de Montherlant, H., *Don Juan. Pièce en trois actes*, written 1956 and published Paris, 1958. Quotations are from this edition. Revised and reissued under the new title *La Mort qui fait le trottoir* (1972), Paris.
1956: Pritchett, V.S., 'A Story of Don Juan', in *Collected Stories*, London, pp. 171–5. A gruesome trifle, suggesting that Don Juan can kindle erotic fire even in the dead.
1957: Brües, O., *Don Juan und der Abt*, Rothenburg o.d. Tauber.
1958: Thomas, Gwyn, *The Love Man*, London.
1960: Lepage, Albert, *Faust et Don Juan. Pièce en trois actes*, Brussels. First written as a radio play, 1950.
1963: Borrow, Antony, *Don Juan, a Comedy*, Lympne Hythe.
1964: Brophy, Brigid, *The Snowball*, London. The setting of this novel is a fancy-dress ball which two of the characters attend in the guise of Don Giovanni and Donna Anna. See also section 8.
1965: Heath-Stubbs, John, 'The Don Juan Triptych', in *Selected Poems*, Oxford, pp. 2–9, and again in *Collected Poems, 1943–1987* (1988), Manchester, pp. 219–25. The three poems, suggested by the Mozart opera, were first published singly between 1943 and 1954.
1972: Berger, John G. *A Novel*, London. The hero, [G]iovanni, is a remote descendant of Don Juan. His life and death are linked, by a sort of literary *collage*, to historical events from the turn of the century to the time of the First World War. As much a political novel as contribution to the Don Juan legend.
1987: Constantine, David, 'Don Giovanni: Six Sonnets' in *Madder*, Bloodaxe Books, pp. 22–4.
1987: Goldensohn, Barry, 'Last Act: Don Giovanni': poem in *Salmagundi. A Quarterly of the Humanities and Social Sciences*, nos. 74–5, p. 44.
(It is not, of course, claimed that the above list is exhaustive; it has been estimated that there are at least 600 versions.)

## SECTION 6 IMITATIONS, CONTINUATIONS, AND PARODIES OF BYRON'S *DON JUAN*

1819: anon., *Don Juan, Canto the Third*, London. Not further adventures: assorted satirical observations.
1825: anon., *Juan Secundus*, London. Uses the 'Don Juan stanza' as a vehicle for his views on writing and his poetic likes and dislikes. (Praises Byron.)
1825: anon., *Don Juan. Cantos XVII and XVIII*, London, n.d. One of the less skilful 'sequels'.
1828: Buckstone, J.B., *Don Juan. A Romantic Drama in Three Acts*, London (Dicks' Standard Plays, no. 828). A dramatic extravaganza in prose, loosely based on Byron.

## SELECT BIBLIOGRAPHY

1830: anon., *Don Juan in Search of a Wife*, London, n.d. Borrows the form and style of Byron's poem for a lament on the state of the nation in general and on the taxation system in particular.

1838: anon., *Georgian Revel-ations! . . . with twenty suppressed Stanzas of 'DON JUAN'*, Great Totham. Again simply borrows Byron's form and manner for his (fairly good-humoured) satirical observations on the Irish.

1839: Baxter, G.R.W., *Don Juan Junior: a Poem*, London. Absurd and incoherent doggerel.

1840: W.C. (= William Cowley), *Don Juan reclaimed; or, his peregrination continued*, Sheffield. A more serious and a chaster Don Juan turned reformer.

c. 1843: anon. (G.W.M. Reynolds?), *A Sequel to Don Juan*, London, n.d. Five cantos of further adventures in a passable imitation of Byron's style.

1846: Morford, Henry, *The Shade of Byron*, New York. Combines a continuation of *Don Juan* with a defence of Byron against his critics.

1850: Thomas, John W., *An Apology for 'Don Juan'*, London. Three cantos, two of which were first published anonymously in 1825. A review of Byron's poem in the manner of the poem.

1870: anon., *Don Juan. Canto the Seventeenth*, London. A genuine continuation, taking up the situation where Byron left off.

### SECTION 7  RICHARD STRAUSS

Richard Strauss, *Don Juan. Tondichtung (nach Nikolaus Lenau) für großes Orchester*, Opus 20. Composed 1887–9 and published in 1890. It seems pointless to specify an edition, since they are so numerous and easily available. There is, of course, a library of works devoted to Strauss; I cite only those which bear directly on *Don Juan*.

Armstrong, Thomas (1931) *Strauss's Tone-Poems*, Oxford University Press, pp. 5–12.

Baresel, A. (1953) *Richard Strauss. Leben und Werk*, Hamburg, p. 52.

del Mar, Norman (1962–72) *Richard Strauss*, 3 vols., London. See especially i, 65–75.

Gysi, Fritz (1934) *Richard Strauss*, Potsdam, pp. 42–5.

Krause, Ernst (1956) *Richard Strauss. Gestalt und Werk*, 2nd edn, Leipzig, pp. 239–42.

Mauke, Wilhelm (n.d. = 1897) *Richard Strauss. Don Juan (Opus 20)*, Leipzig. No. 114 in the series *Der Musikführer*.

Mueller, E.H. von Asow,: see the section on *Don Juan* in *Richard Strauss. Thematisches Werkverzeichnis* (1959), vol. 1, Vienna, pp. 83–96.

Muschler, R.C. (n.d. = c. 1924) *Richard Strauss*, Hildesheim, pp. 262–9.

Palmer, Peter (1987) 'Some Musical Echoes of Lenau . . .', in *German Life and Letters*, xl: see especially p. 271.

Schuh, Willi (1976) *Richard Strauss. Jugend und frühe Meisterwerke*, Zürich and Freiburg, pp. 151 and 262 ff. There is also useful material in Schuh's article on Strauss in *Musik in Geschichte und Gegenwart*.

Steinitzer, Max (1914) *Richard Strauss*, 5th–8th edn, Berlin and Leipzig, pp. 89–91.

SELECT BIBLIOGRAPHY

Strauss, Richard, *Briefe an die Eltern, 1882–1906*, ed. Willi Schuh (1954), Zürich and Freiburg.
von Waltershausen, H.W. (1921) *Richard Strauss. Ein Versuch*, Munich, pp. 49 ff.

## SECTION 8  GENERAL BIBLIOGRAPHY

Austen, John (1939) *The Story of Don Juan*, London.
Berveiller, Michel (1961) *L'éternel Don Juan*, Paris.
de Bévotte, G. (1911) *La Légende de Don Juan*, 2 vols., Paris.
Bolte, Johannes (1899) 'Über den Ursprung der Don-Juan-Sage', in *Zeitschrift für vergleichende Litteraturgeschichte*, n.s. xiii, 374–98. An early investigation of possible sources in older plays. Deals with legends concerning invitations and challenges issued to the dead.
Boyd, Elisabeth F. (1945) *Byron's Don Juan. A Critical Study*, London.
Breuillac, M. (1906 and 1907) 'Hoffmann en France', in *Revue d'Histoire Littéraire de la France*, xiii, 427–57 and xiv, 74–105.
Brophy, Brigid (1962) *Black Ship to Hell*, London.
Camus, Albert, chapter on 'Le Don Juanisme', in *Le Mythe de Sisyphe*, first published 1942. I have used the 34th edn, Paris, 1942.
Casanova, de Seingalt Jacques (1960–2) *Histoire de ma Vie*, 12 vols. in 6, Wiesbaden and Paris.
Casanova, Giacomo (1946) *His Life and Memoirs*, trans. from the French by Arthur Machen and selected and edited with connecting links by G.D. Gribble, 2 vols. in 1, New York.
Chatfield-Taylor, H.C. (1914) *Goldoni*, London.
Chrysander, F. (1888) 'Die Oper Don Giovanni von Gazzaniga und von Mozart', in *Vierteljahrsschrift für Musikwissenschaft*, iv, 351–435.
Denslow, S. (1941) 'Don Juan and Faust. Their parallel development and association in Germany 1790–1850', unpublished dissertation, Virginia. A shortened version was published in the *Hispanic Review*, x (1942), 215–22.
Dent, E.J. (1947) *Mozart's Operas*, 2nd edn, Oxford University Press.
Dobrée, B. (1933) *Giacomo Casanova, Chevalier de Seingalt*, Edinburgh.
Doolittle, J. (1953) 'The Humanity of Molière's *Dom Juan*', in *PMLA*, lxviii, 509–34.
Einstein, Alfred (1936) *Gluck*, trans. Eric Blom, London and New York. See pp. 58–62 for the Don Juan ballet.
Engel, K. (1887) *Die Don Juan-Sage auf der Bühne*, 2nd edn, Dresden and Leipzig.
von Freisauff, R. (1887), *Mozarts Don Juan 1787–1887. Ein Beitrag zur Geschichte dieser Oper*, Salzburg.
Gautier, Th. (1858–9) *Histoire de l'art dramatique en France*, 6 vols., Paris. The remarks on Don Juan are in vol. 4.
Gnüg, Hiltrud (1974) *Don Juans theatralische Existenz*, Munich.
Gouhier, H. (1957) 'L'inhumain Don Juan', in *La Table Ronde*, Paris, November, 67–73. Deals with Molière's *Dom Juan*.
Hayem, A. (1886) *Le Don Juanisme*, Paris.

## SELECT BIBLIOGRAPHY

Heckel, H. (1915) *Das Don Juan-Problem in der neueren Dichtung*, Stuttgart.
Helbig, F. (1876–7) 'Die Don-Juan-Sage, ihre Entstehung und Fortentwicklung', in *Westermann's Jahrbuch*, Brunswick, xli, 637–50.
Hirsch, E. (1873) 'Die drei großen Sagen vom Don Juan, vom ewigen Juden und von Dr Faust', in *Altes und Neues*, Wiesbaden, v, 324 ff.
Horn, F. (1805) 'Andeutungen für Freunde der Poesie', in *Luna. Ein Taschenbuch auf das Jahr 1805*, Leipzig, pp. 297 ff. Discusses Faust and Don Juan.
Horn, F., *Poesie und Beredsamkeit der Deutschen*, first published 1823. Includes discussion of Faust and Don Juan, with particular reference to the puppet-plays. Reprinted in Scheible (1847), v, 670–92.
Horn, F. (1841) *Psyche. Aus Franz Horn's Nachlaß*, ed. G. Schwab and L. Förster, Leipzig. See 1, pp. 198 f. for discussion of Don Juan.
Kierkegaard, S. (1843) *Either/Or*, ed. and trans. Howard and Edna Hong, 2 vols., Princetown, 1987.
Lafora, G.R. (1930) *Don Juan and other psychological Studies*, trans. Perry, London.
Lert, E. (1921) *Mozart auf dem Theater*, 3rd–4th edn, Berlin.
Lirondelle, A. (1912) *Le Poète Alexis Tolstoï*, Paris.
Mackay, Dorothy E. (1943) *The Double Invitation in the Legend of Don Juan*, Stanford University Press.
Manning, C.A. (1923) 'Russian versions of Don Juan', *PMLA*, xxxviii, 479–93.
Marañon, Gregorio (1958) *Don Juan et le Donjuanisme*, trans. Lacombe, Paris.
Mayer, Hans (1979) *Doktor Faust und Don Juan*, Frankfurt/Main.
Medwin, Thomas (1824) *Journal of the Conversations of Lord Byron*, London.
Meynieux, A. (1957) 'Pouchkine et Don Juan', in *La Table Ronde*, November, 90–107.
Michaut, G. (1925) *Les Luttes de Molière*, Paris. See chapter 4 for *Dom Juan*.
Moore, W.G. (1949) *Molière, a new Criticism*, Oxford.
'*Dom Juan* reconsidered' (1957) in *MLR*, lii, 510–17.
Müller-Gangloff, E. (1948) 'Faust und Don Juan', in *Vorläufer des Antichrist*, Berlin, pp. 26 ff.
Nissen, G.N. (1828) *Biographie W.A. Mozart's*, Leipzig.
*Obliques. Littérature-théâtre*, nos. 4–5: *Don Juan*, Paris, 1978. A collection of articles, reviews, etc. Includes a French translation of Alexander Blok's poem, v, 50.
Palmer, John (1930) *Molière. His Life and Works*, London.
Passage, C.E. (1963) *The Russian Hoffmannists*, The Hague.
Peacock, Noël A. (1988) 'Dom Juan ou le libertin imaginaire', in *Forum for Modern Language Studies*, xxiv, 332–45.
Petzoldt, L. (1965) 'Don Juan und die volkstümliche Überlieferung', in *iv. International Congress for folk-narrative research in Athens, lectures and reports*, Athens, pp. 354–63. Detailed account of older legends featuring invitations to the dead. Finds over 200 variants in Europe!
Rabany, C. (1896) *Carlo Goldoni*, Paris.
Rank, Otto (1930) *Seelenglaube und Psychologie*, Leipzig and Vienna.
Rank, Otto (1932) *Don Juan. Une Etude sur le Double*, trans. S. Lautmann, Paris.

## SELECT BIBLIOGRAPHY

Rees, Margaret A. (1979) *Espronceda, El Estudiante de Salamanca* (*Critical Guides to Spanish Texts*, 25), Tisbury.

Rogers, Daniel (1964) 'Fearful Symmetry: the ending of *El Burlador de Sevilla*', in *Bulletin of Hispanic Studies*, xli, 141–59.

Rogers, Daniel (1977) *Tirso de Molina. El Burlador de Sevilla*, (*Critical Guides to Spanish Texts*, 19), Tisbury.

Rushton, Julian (1981) *W.A. Mozart, Don Giovanni*, Cambridge University Press. In addition to Rushton's contributions, there are chapters on 'Don Juan before da Ponte' by Edward Forman and 'Don Giovanni as an idea' by Bernard Williams. Chapter 8 ('The Literature of *Don Giovanni*') includes a substantial extract from Hoffmann's tale and Berlioz's tribute to Mozart, both in translation.

Sand, George, *Lélia*, ed. Pierre Reboul (1960), Paris. This is the 1833 edition, together with additions and variants from the 1839 edition.

Schemann, L. (1914–20) *Quellen und Untersuchungen zum Leben Gobineaus*, 2 vols., Strasbourg, Berlin and Leipzig.

Schmitz, O.A.H. (1918) *Casanova und andere Gestalten aus der großen Welt*, Munich and Leipzig. Written 1905.

Schopenhauer, A. (1818–44) *Die Welt als Wille und Vorstellung*. Quotations from the 'Zürcher Ausgabe', Zurich, 1977.

Schröder, Th. (1912) *Die dramatischen Bearbeitungen der Don Juan-Sage in Spanien, Italien und Frankreich bis auf Molière einschließlich*, Halle.

*La Table Ronde*, Nov. 1957: Don Juan number, including a good deal of psychological analysis.

Teichmann, Elizabeth (1961) *La Fortune d'Hoffmann en France*, Paris.

Van Loo, Esther (1950) *Le vrai Don Juan. Don Miguel de Mañara*, Paris.

Weinstein, L. (1959) *The Metamorphoses of Don Juan* (= *Stanford Studies in Language and Literature*, 18), Stanford, California.

Wittmann, Brigitte (ed.) (1976) *Don Juan. Darstellung und Deutung*, Darmstadt (= *Wege der Forschung*, vol. 282). A collection of essays, reviews and critical comments on the Don Juan theme; a useful assemblage of familiar and unfamiliar items.

# INDEX

(Some items, although not dealt with in the text, are described briefly in the Bibliography; these are included below and marked with an asterisk.)

Ackermann, E. W. 51
Adam, A. 11
Adelmann, C. 77
Aicard, J. 60, 83
Angiolini, G. 20
Anouilh, J. 123–5, 127, 131, 136–7, 146, 151
Anthes, O. 51
Apollinaire, G. 122

*Balzac, H. de 177
Barbier, Pierre: see Mournet-Sully, J.
*Baring, M. 180
*Barrière, M. 179
Baudelaire, C. 61–2, 118
Bäuerle, A. 176
Becker, F. K. 113
Beethoven, L. van 142, 150
Bennett, Arnold 93–4
*Berger, John 182
Bernhardi, O. C. 51–2, 54, 106, 108, 110
Bertati, G. 22
Berveiller, M. 121
Bethge, H. 51, 110, 132
Bévotte, G. de 8, 55
Beyerlein, F. A. 170
Biancolelli, D. 8
Bierbaum, O. J. 122
*Blok, A. 180
Bonsels, W. 84, 86–7
Borrow, Antony, 74, 95

Brachfeld, F. O. 171
Braunthal, Braun von 47–8, 52, 81, 90, 109
Brausewetter, A. 29, 133
Brecht, B. 24
*Brenner, H. G. 181
*Broch, Hermann 181
Brophy, Brigid 119, 171–2
Brües, O. 130
Buckstone, J. B. 42
Bury, Blaze de 62
Byron, G. G., Lord 18, 35–44, 94, 111

Calderón de la Barca, P. 34
Camus, A. 117, 120–1, 125, 150–1
Casanova, G. 77
Cicognini, J. A. 4–8
Coleridge, S. T. 18, 37, 73
*Commedia dell'arte* 7–8, 10, 20, 34
Corneille, Thomas 8–9, 16
Crébillon *fils* x
Creizenach, T. 84–5, 87, 151

Da Ponte, L. 4, 6, 8, 22, 24–7, 30–4, 37, 47–8, 52–3, 61, 69–70, 77–9, 86, 88, 90, 93, 98, 107, 113–14, 118–20, 128, 151
d'Aureville, B. 130
Dédéyan, C. 32
Del Castillo, F. 122
De l'Isle Adam, V. 58
Delteil, J. 94

# INDEX

Dent, Edward, 18, 22
*Donna Giovanni* 173
Dorimon, N. 9–11, 19, 25, 80, 96
Duller, E. 45–7
Dumas, A. ('Dumas père') 93
Duncan, Ronald 148, 181*
Dutouquet, E. 173

*Ehrenberg, R. 180
Engel, Karl 30, 77
Engel, Ludwig 122–3, 127, 172
Espronceda, J. de 169, 177*

Faust, 12, 29, 32, 34, 45, 48, 56, 62, 75–90, 93, 95–6, 100, 109, 117, 127, 129–32, 135, 145–6
*Flaubert, G. 178
Flecker, J. E. 123–4, 127
Freud, Freudian, 117
Friedmann, A. 51, 53, 132, 172
Frisch, Max 67, 69, 71, 73–4, 77, 113, 123, 130, 133, 136–7, 146, 151

Gasset, J. O. y 96
Gautier, T. 53, 56–9, 61
Gazzaniga, G. 22
Giliberto, 7–8
Glass, M. 106, 111
Gluck, C. W. von 20–1, 143
Gnüg, H. 130
Gobineau, A. de 132
Goethe, J. W. von 34, 43, 45–7, 53–5, 61, 75–8, 81–6, 90, 100–3, 110, 127; *Werther* 116, 120
Goldensohn, B. 27
Goldoni, C. 22, 128–9, 131
Gottschall, R. von 51, 54
Grabbe, C. D. 70, 78–9
Graener, P.: see Anthes, O.
Grimsley, R. 121
Grunwald, H. A. 148
Grupe–Lörcher, E. 65

Hagelstange, R. von 51
Haraucourt, E. 95, 130, 145
Hart, Julius, 51
Hartenstein, S. von 95
Hayem, A. 58–60, 106, 108, 132, 145
Heath–Stubbs, A. 119
Hebbel, F. 43, 76
Heckel, H. 102–3
Heimerdinger, A. 133
Helbig, F. 76

Heller, J. 74
Hesse, Hermann, 111
Heymann, R. 51
Heyse, P. 52, 105, 129
Hildesheimer, W. 167
Hirsch, E. 77
*Historia von D. Johann Fausten* 87–9
Hobhouse, J. C. 36
*Hörnigk, R. 178
Hoffmann, E. T. A. 26–33, 43–9, 51–60, 62–3, 67, 69–70, 72, 75–6, 79, 85–6, 94–5, 98, 102–3, 120, 143–5
*Holtei, C. von 177
Horn, Franz, 45–6, 76
Hornstein, F. von 65–6, 73
Horvath, Ö. von 171
Hürte, N. 87–9
Hunt, Leigh 39

Ibsen, H. (*Peer Gynt*) 13

Järvefelt, G. 29
Jelusich, M. 94, 112
Johnson, E. D. H. 41
Jourdain, E. 57, 132

*Kahlert, A. 177
Kästner, Erich, 113
*Kees, E. 180
Keller, G. 123
Kierkegaard, S. 76, 116, 120–1, 142–3, 145
Königsmark, W. von 83
Kratzmann, E. 51

Laclos, P. A. F. C. de x
Lafora, G. R. 119–21
*Langen, M. 180
'Laufen' Don Juan play 19, 166
Lembach, A. 54
Lenau, N. 48–52, 54, 57, 67, 100, 129–30, 138–43, 172
Lenburg, A. 110
Lepage, A. 170
Lert, E. 77
Lessing, G. E. 34
Le Vavasseur, G. 64
Levy, Ben W. 123–4, 131, 145–7
Leyst, C. 110
Linklater, E. 42
Lipiner, S. 109–10, 129
Liszt, F. 78
Loo, E. van: see Van Loo

188

# INDEX

McGann, J. J. 40
Machiavelli, N. 107
Mahler, Gustav, 173
Mallefille, F. 82–3, 90
Mañara, Miguel, 91–5
Mansfield, Richard 132
Marañon, G. 117, 119
Marinelli, 19
Marlowe, Christopher 20, 110
Mauke, W. 141
Mayer, Hans 24
Mérimée, P. 92, 95, 102–3
Meyr, M. 123–5, 127, 129
Mönch, W. 107
*Mörike, E. 178
Möser, A. 51–2
Molière, 9–16, 19, 21–2, 24, 26, 29, 61, 80, 92–4, 113, 118, 120, 135–6, 147, 171
Montherlant, H. de 66–9, 71, 73, 117, 131, 133
Moore, Thomas 40
*Mournet-Sully, J. and Barbier, Pierre 179
Mozart, W. A. 6, 21–4, 26–9, 33–6, 45–7, 68–9, 77–8, 90, 92–3, 107, 113–14, 116–17, 119–21, 132, 136, 143–4, 147, 149, 151
Murray, John 39–40
Musset, A. de 55, 57–9, 72

Nerval, G. de 55–7
Nettl, P. 77
Nietzsche, F. 11, 14, 41, 62, 71, 86, 94, 107, 109–12, 148
Novalis 67

Palmer, John 13
Pantomimes (on Don Juan theme) 34–5, 37
Passante, Antonio 8
Platen, A. von 43
Pope, Alexander 40
Precht, V. 53
*Pritchett, V. S. 182
*Proelß, J. 179
Prometheus 146
Puget, C.-A. 168
Puppet-plays 7, 19–21, 26, 29–30, 81
Purcell, Henry 18, 143
Pushkin, A. 68, 97–9, 103, 105–7, 114, 170
Pyman, A. 98

Rank, Otto 117–21
Regnier, H. de 119
Richardson, Samuel x
Rilke, R. M. 54–5, 135
Rittner, T. 51–2, 135
Robin, Eugène 79
Rogers, Daniel 4, 121
Rosenkranz, C. 76
Rosimond, C. la Rose de 9, 16–17, 19, 26
Rostand, E. 66–9, 71, 73, 133
Roujon, H. 65–6, 73, 130

Sand, George 64–5, 118, 149
Schaden, A. von 122
*Schiller, F. 176
Schirokauer, A. 133
Schmitz, O. A. H. 77–8, 106, 129, 170
Schneller, C. 97
Schopenhauer, A. 111–12, 146
Schumann, Robert 142
Shadwell, Thomas (*The Libertine*) 17–18, 25–6, 34, 37, 47, 61, 78, 87, 105, 143
Shakespeare, W., *Hamlet* 29; *King Lear* 13; *Merry Wives of Windsor* 36
Shaw, G. B. 13, 44, 67–71, 73–4, 114, 120–1, 123, 125, 130, 133–4, 137, 145, 148–9, 151, 168
Shelley, P. B. 39
Spießer, F. 88–9
Stendhal 109, 116, 120–1
Sternheim, C. 53
Strauss, D. F. 76
Strauss, Richard 51, 138–44, 172–3
Strauss, Rudolf 122

Tann-Bergler, O. 172
Téllez, Gabriel: *see* Tirso de Molina
Thiess, F. 106, 170
Thomas, Gwyn 115, 125, 130
Tirso de Molina (*El Burlador de Sevilla*) 1–7, 10, 19, 24, 34, 48, 55, 61, 69, 79, 81, 91, 94–5, 105, 118, 120–1, 130, 136
Tolstoi, Alexis 97, 100–3, 147
Townsend Warner, S. 113, 135
Trakl, G. 118
Trautmann, P. F. 172

Ulreich, A. 172

Van Loo, E. 91
Verlaine, P. 62

# INDEX

Villiers, Claude Deschamps, Sieur de 9, 11, 19
Vloten, W. van 108–11, 113, 133
Vulpius, C. A. 80, 90

Waltershausen, H. W. von 142
Wandering Jew 77
Weigand, W. 122
Weinstein, L. 44, 60, 86, 95–6, 150
Widmann, A. 95

Wiese, S. 83–4, 87, 107, 114
Wilson, Margaret 105
Wolfe, Humbert 42

Zamora, A. de 95
Zeise, F. 94
*Zévaco, M. 181
Zorrilla, J. 95–7
'Zur Ouvertüre von Mozart's Don Juan' (anonymous poem) 29
*Zweig, Stefan 180